# Christian Thought

## from Erasmus to Berdyaev

MATTHEW SPINKA

# Christian Thought

## from Erasmus to Berdyaev

**GREENWOOD PRESS, PUBLISHERS**
WESTPORT, CONNECTICUT

**Library of Congress Cataloging in Publication Data**

Spinka, Matthew, 1890-1972.
    Christian thought from Erasmus to Berdyaev.

    Reprint of the ed. published by Prentice-Hall,
Englewood Cliffs, N.J.
    Bibliography:  p.
    Includes index.
    1.  Religious thought--Modern period, 1500-
2.  Religious thought--Europe.  I.  Title.
[BR290.S8  1979]          190          78-11967
ISBN 0-313-21122-1

Reprinted in 1979 by Greenwood Press, Inc.,
51 Riverside Avenue, Westport, CT 06880

Printed in the United States of America

10 9 8 7 6 5 4 3 2 1

# Preface

This book is based on the lectures that, in simpler form, I have delivered for fifteen years to my students in the Hartford Theological Seminary. To the ultimate benefit of this work, many points became clarified in lively discussions with my students, and I am grateful for whatever contribution they made to my thinking.

Paul wrote that he was "debtor to both Greeks and to barbarians." So am I. Even to try to mention all the thinkers who have influenced my own views would be an impossible task. As any man professionally involved in the theological developments of the last fifty years, I have been confronted with many a difficult choice among the warring opinions. Having been trained in what at the time was known as "evangelical liberalism," I at first reacted decisively against the original Barthian repudiation of it. I am glad that Barth himself saw fit to break away from the radicalism of his "crisis" theology to that of his *Church Dogmatics*. But liberalism has also developed some unacceptable interpretations, such as theological humanism and naturalism; furthermore, it has proved inadequate in facing the postwar situation generally.

Caught in this conflict, I found help in the thought of Nicolas Berdyaev, with whose views I became acquainted in the early twenties. Discerning readers may easily find that his influence, although increasingly critically evaluated and by no means exclusive, has remained abiding. This is particularly true of his stress on personalism—human and divine. If this makes me a personalist of sorts, so be it!

While serving as a member of the faculties of the Chicago Theological Seminary and of the Divinity School of the University of Chicago, I was assigned, as my special responsibility, the studies in Eastern Orthodoxy. My interest in this Christian tradition may be seen in the inclusion of such outstanding Russian religious thinkers as Vladimir Solovev, Feodor Dostoevsky, and of course Nicolas Berdyaev. This is perhaps among the first attempts to integrate Eastern Orthodox thinking with Western theological thought and thus, to some degree, to present a more inclusive treatment than has been generally done before. Such treatments too frequently have been in essence parochially Western. To manifest the ecumenical spirit of which many currently boast, we must appreciate the Christian tradition as a whole. The inclusion of the subchapter on Comenius, whose theological views have hitherto been totally ignored, bears witness to my interest in Czech religious history.

My special thanks are due Professor John B. Cobb, Jr., of the Southern California School of Theology, with whom I discussed each chapter at the time of writing and by whose suggestions I have profited, even though the responsibility for the final version is wholly mine. In this connection I wish to mention Professor G. W. Bromiley of the Fuller Theological Seminary of Pasadena, who most kindly read the chapter on Karl Barth which, however, despite his encouragement, I finally decided to omit. I am also grateful to Miss Gladys F. Boggess for her excellent typing of the final text.

*Matthew Spinka*

*Claremont, California, July 6, 1961,*
in memory of the death of *John Hus*

# Contents

# 1

# The Era Is Dying: Let It Die!

## A Survey of the Age of Humanism

We are standing on the threshold of a new, as yet un-
named, era. The old humanist era which has lasted some
six centuries—having had its beginning in the Renaissance
—is visibly dying. The signs of its passing are plainly
discernible. The new age dawned, as far as physical
sciences and technics are concerned, early in the present
century, when Einstein discovered the tremendous energy locked in the atom. This energy was then unleashed
by the ingenious efforts of a team of scientists, who succeeded in splitting the nucleus of the atom by means of
chain reaction. The next problem confronting them was
utilizing its tremendous power in a controlled, usable
form; this was accomplished on July 16, 1945, when the
first atomic bomb was successfully exploded over the
white sands of Alamogordo, New Mexico. After an
agonizing decision was reached to employ this fearful instrument in an effort to put a quick end to the war with
Japan, two bombs were exploded, one over Hiroshima on
August 6 and the other over Nagasaki three days later.
Ever since, the world has stood in paralyzing fear that an
atomic war, with the use of the immensely more powerful
hydrogen bomb, may plunge it into the almost total

1

destruction of its human inhabitants, their civilization, and the physical means whereby they sustain their existence.

Another tremendous scientific achievement signifying the end of the old era and the dawn of a new one has been the successful surmounting of the experimental stage in space exploration. The Russian *sputnik* hurled into space for the first time in human history on October 4, 1957, inaugurated this "conquest of space." It was succeeded by a fairly large number of similar achievements, both Russian and American. The world resounds with boastful and even fantastic predictions —particularly since the Russian global space flight and the American space penetration—of the colonization of the moon and the planets, of "space platforms" and their military uses, and of other previously unimaginable feats of technical ingenuity. Some of this boasting sounds like irresponsible nonsense. But there is a solid residuum of fact in it; man-made machines can now actually enable us to sail interplanetary space. We are no longer earthbound—at least not in the physical sense of the word. In view of all this, it surely seems reasonable to assert that, with a few significant exceptions, we have left the old era behind us, and are facing—fearfully as well as hopefully—a future of technological marvels that stagger the imagination. *Le roi est mort; vive le roi!*

But the signs of a cultural decay of humanism have been in evidence even longer. They have been plainly discernible, particularly during the last one hundred years. It was in this period that humanism became thoroughly secularized and earthbound. It now resembles that queer New Zealand bird, the kiwi, which has lost the use of its wings because it has long ceased to use them. Modern man no longer "lifts up his eyes unto the hills" because he expects no help thence. One is reminded of the deathbed remark of Henry David Thoreau made to the minister who exhorted him to think of eternity: "One world at a time, brother; one world at a time!" Jean Paul Sartre and other atheistic existentialists tell us to make the best of this world, since there is no other. Thus the age has turned upon itself in repudiating its own past. The distinguishing characteristic of that past is that it made man the measure of all things. Now man has ceased to be the highest value: his place is taken by technics. Marx has subordinated him to the well-being of society and thus deprived him of his spiritual nature. Man has become a tender of machines. Nietzsche went even further: he not only proclaimed that "God is dead," for by denying God he inevitably denied the spiritual worth of man as well; and he followed his own logic by advocating the extermination of the "herd man" in favor of an imagined, non-existent "Superman." His disciples today, although denying the spiritual meaning of man and his universe, inconsistently exhort men to create for themselves a tolerably meaningful existence out of the intolerable meaninglessness of the cosmos.

One of the most significant aspects of this humanist-secularist debacle is its religious indifference, or practical atheism. To those of us to whom God and our relation to Him are indispensable, this is the most important aspect of the situation. Our age has long ago outgrown its era of "religious wars." Religion is not important enough to go to war over any more. The causes of modern wars are economic and political. Martin Buber, in a recent small book, has many pertinent things to say about this radical form of irreligion. He sums the present situation by writing: "Eclipse of the light of heaven, eclipse of God—such indeed is the character of the historic hour through which the world is passing." [1] It is indeed true that among the avowed aims of communist leaders has from the beginning been the "liquidation" of all religion, and particularly of Christianity, as superstition. Nevertheless, modern mass men are not irreligious from any deep-seated conviction; rather, they are indifferent, or as the former dean of the Harvard Divinity School, Willard L. Sperry, used to say, they are "imperfectly irreligious." Very few are really atheistic, for that is quite an intellectual feat, reserved for the philosophically-minded few, or for the not so philosophically-minded militant communists. Accordingly, the predominant mood among the majority of secularists is not so much a formulated conviction as an almost unconscious lack of interest in, and an utter indifference to, all religious concerns. As a rule they aim solely at the goal of physical well-being, a high standard of living. This is true not only of the masses in the communist-dominated countries, where it is consciously elevated into an officially inspired aim; but of America and Western Europe, and in fact increasingly of almost the entire world— where it also is the dominant drive. The western liberal democracies have long been under the sway of these predominant economic motives. Our repudiation of the Marxist philosophy conceals from us the fact that we too regard economic well-being as the pre-eminent force in society. The difference is only in the manner of its implementation: in the totalitarian countries the drive for economic well-being is forcibly imposed and rigidly enforced, while in the democracies it is left to the individual's self-interest. Aside from this, the economic virus is in our blood as well.

These then are some symptoms of the passing of what has been fondly called "the humanist age," and its latest phase—secularism. But

---

[1] Martin Buber, *Eclipse of God* (New York: Harper & Brothers, 1952), p. 34. By permission.

this does not mean that all elements of humanism have suddenly disappeared from our culture or will be wholly absent from that of the future. It is only the dominant emphasis, the central characteristic, that has changed. Humanism is no longer the growing point of our civilization. Nor do I mean to convey the idea that religion has already succumbed to the attacks made upon it during the last two centuries and particularly today. As early as the first half of the eighteenth century Anglican Bishop Butler reported that it had come to be taken for granted that Christianity had at last been discovered to be fictitious. But the good bishop did not think that it was "so clear a case." I agree with Butler and am far from conceding that Christianity is either fictitious or that God is dead. But since I am intent upon demonstrating that a shift of cultural emphasis has indeed taken place, I must necessarily isolate such elements of our total culture as are indicative of it. This undoubtedly results in oversimplification; but all analytic efforts must ignore the phases and aspects that are not germane to the subject under investigation and concentrate exclusively upon the latter. One must pay the price of some exaggeration for proceeding in this manner; but no other method is possible. To paraphase Chesterton: No generalization is ever quite true, including this one.

How has this change come about? How has an era characterized by the humanist spirit and Christian faith become dehumanized, secularized, and to a degree de-Christianized? Why has officially espoused and militantly propagated atheism made its appearance for the first time in our era? These and similar questions will constitute the principal theme of the present study, although its scope must be limited largely to the interrelation of philosophy and theology. Our aim then shall be to present in a selective fashion the outstanding humanist and secularist thinkers, principally philosophers, who represent the development of the humanist thesis and its subversion into secularism during the last phase of its history. The selection is guided by our estimate of the impact of their thought—whether positive or negative—on the religious or theological movements of their own or subsequent time. Nor are we concerned with presenting their entire system of thought, but only such aspects of it as have more or less direct bearing on Christian doctrine. And in the second place, we aim at presenting, likewise in a selective fashion, the thought of such Christian thinkers as have reacted, either by accepting elements of the philosophical impact upon them or actively repudiating them. Nor is their whole system necessarily to be included in such a delineation of their thought, but principally their reaction to the humanist or secularist elements of the impact. And in the third place, we intend to show how the humanist ethos has finally been subverted, particularly during the last century, into its opposite—the anti-humanist secularism, which terminated the humanist era.

This is admittedly not the whole story, but to undertake a survey of all cultural movements and their development during the course of our era—including the story of the rise and development of modern science (since that has been one of the principal features of it)—would be a task far beyond the scope of this study and of my limited abilities. Moreover, since all these phases, including science, exhibit the same general characteristics, and since the changes in the philosophical thinking of the modern period have not only been fundamental to all other cultural permutations, but have affected Christian thought most of all, we shall restrict ourselves to the tracing of the most important interrelationships of philosophy and theology. For in dealing with this particular interrelationship, we shall in a significant way become aware of all the rest of its implications. In short, we shall keep in mind that we are answering the question: How has our culture become de-humanized and finally secularized during the five or six centuries of our era? With this understanding of the limits of our aim, let us survey briefly the principal characteristics of the era so visibly expiring before our eyes.

Modern history, particularly the history of ideas, has its true beginning in the Renaissance. This was not merely a period of "awakening the dead" of antiquity, of a mere resuscitation of the antique culture, but of the birth of modern man. This modern man has exhibited positive, creative abilities. As Nicolas Berdyaev characterizes it:

> Humanism was not only the reawakening of the spirit of ancient times, not only a new ethical teaching, a new direction of science and art, but also a new conception of life which sprang up at the dawn of modern history and gave it its whole direction; it created a new attitude toward the world.[2]

Much that is noble and of permanent value has been produced during those six centuries. Human liberties, rights of man, liberal constitutions

[2] Nicolas Berdyaev, "The End of the Renaissance," in *The Slavonic Review* (London: The School of Slavonic Studies in the University of London), IV, No. 10, June, 1925, pp. 2-3. By permission.

guaranteeing inalienable rights and freedoms, have been secured during this time.

The new orientation has been humanistic, or as Jacques Maritain speaks of it, "anthropocentric." "The proper study of mankind is man" is the motto of the Renaissance. Man became the measure of all things —man and his place in nature. The two went hand in hand. If medieval man lived an anonymous life, not yet clearly differentiated from the group of which he was part, Renaissance man attained individuality (although not always personality). Medieval man lived much more consciously in relation to God, or rather the Church, which mediated the supernatural life to him through the sacramental system. Modern man has increasingly emancipated himself from all tutelage of the Church—in fact, from all relation to the spiritual. He has consciously striven to become wholly natural or secular. He ceased being "other-worldly" and concerned himself in the end exclusively with this world. This preoccupation with nature resulted in the triumphs of natural science, a feat undreamed of in man's history. Not only were religious concerns sacrificed to preoccupation with nature—including technics for the conquest of natural forces—but along with it, all genuine interest in the spiritual implications of human life was ultimately largely abandoned. In one sentence, all life became humanized and in the end secularized. It was then in the early Renaissance that the spirit of humanism was born, the spirit of self-assertion, of this-worldliness, of scientific study of nature, and of human autonomy.

Hence, the chief interest of the age was humanistic. Berdyaev, repeating Solovev's phrase, speaks of that aspect of the era as the change from the seeking of Godmanhood to that of mangodhood. God was dethroned and finally bowed out of the universe in the Age of Enlightenment or was denied altogether in the succeeding period. Man took the center of the stage. He went through various stages of self-affirmation. Most of these stages, however, ended in failure. The first stage (followed by others in which modern man successively realized different aspects of his self-affirmation), was in the realm of art. The era began in an outburst of artistic creativity such as had not been witnessed since the days of Phidias and Praxiteles. Giotto, Michelangelo, Raphael, and Titian were its principal representatives. This art was naturalistic even though it often dealt with medieval religious themes. Its Madonnas were veritable flesh and blood human beings in whom the contemporary Italian woman is easily recognizable. The baby Jesus of these Madonna pieces is a well-fed, far from ascetic-looking, Italian *bambino*. The background is no longer an impossibly contorted range of mountains such as remind one of the moon craters, or trees like overgrown cauliflowers (such as one sees even in Giotto's "St. Francis Preaching to the Birds"). The painters of the era have not only discovered the laws of perspective, but also the inexhaustible charm of natural beauty. This newly-discovered worship of beauty becomes in the end thoroughly secular. Rubens is the extreme example of this secularized character of modern art. His vast canvasses are a veritable apotheosis of luscious human flesh exceedingly well fed, lusty, and voluptuous. He is the painter of the lust for life, and no one can legitimately accuse him of the least bit of reticence or false modesty. His men and women are superb animals full of *joie de vivre*. Life is a riot of animality without the faintest trace of otherworldliness. These fat Venuses and athletic Adonises are utterly bourgeois. They are perfectly willing to live by bread alone provided some few luxuries are thrown in; they have little use for the Word of God! The next artistic periods are those of the Baroque and Rococo, which clearly show a degeneration of the artistic impulse and taste by their over-ornamentation and artificiality. The Baroque churches are the best example of this declining taste. The chubby little wooden angels peering over the wooden clouds and the doves suspended on a wire from the church ceiling representing the Holy Spirit show this hardening of the arteries of artistic life.

Today we are witnessing a revulsion against the artistic impulse which characterized the dawn of the Renaissance period. Man's artistic self-affirmation, just like many other forms of his self-expression during the modern period, has led to dismal failure. Modern man has reached a stage in which he has repudiated the best art of his own past. He has abandoned the naturalism which had formerly been the inspiration of his earlier artistic creations, and has turned either to the machine for his inspiration or to the untutored efforts of primitive peoples. Modern art expresses its conceptions in squares, triangles, and other mechanical or geometrical designs, and condescendingly invites us to comprehend the incomprehensible. It has not only destroyed the spirit of man, but now is turning to hideous and grotesque distortion even of his physical form. This signifies the end of Renaissance art. It manifests an exhaustion of the original impulse, a repudiation of the original inspiration. If you do not agree, compare the grotesque ugliness of Sir Jacob Epstein's much lauded "sculpture" with the least of Michelangelo's works.

The same story may be told about modern literature. It begins with the classical creations of Dante, Petrarch, Boccaccio, and Chaucer. Boccaccio created modern fiction. Dante, despite his medieval theology —which, however, must be understood symbolically and as such is lifted above its medieval character—is a true modern, for he fashioned the Italian vernacular as the perfect tool for his incomparable verse. Chaucer, and particularly Shakespeare, represent the modern spirit in the early development of English literature. As an example of some dominant characteristics of the Renaissance, we may turn to François Rabelais (1490-1553). His *Gargantua and Pantagruel* is shockingly coarse, malodorous, and obscene; yet it manifests a superabundant exuberance, an utter abandon to sensuality, and at the same time a robust individuality. His appetite for life is truly gigantic, and his only error is in assuming the same boiling-over vitality in his reader. In all that satirical, anti-clerical and anti-scholastic age, no one satirizes the Church and scholasticism with anything approaching his unashamed, flaunting frankness. He is a sort of satirical cannibal who gulps down vast helpings of hypocritical priests, barren professors, and corrupt officials.[3]

If literature is viewed as a reflection of life in an artistic form, then contemporaneous literature shows life as debased, petty, and sordid. But to regard it merely as a mirror of life, a thermometer, so to speak, registering the temperature of life, is an inadequate understanding of its purpose and function; rather it ought to serve as a thermostat which regulates temperature. As such, literature subserves, for weal or woe, a most important social function—as the communist regimes know so well! In our western culture the moral irresponsibility of our outstanding writers results mostly in woe; for the literature they produce denies to men and women all spiritual qualities and treats them as mere biological specimens driven by psychosomatic urges. Revolting indecencies are regarded as mere "local color." The over-concern with sex, with material and social well-being, predominates. Spiritual aims are rarely envisaged, or are treated with insufferable ridicule. Religious motivation is practically absent in the characters of modern novels, or if mentioned at all, reveals the religious infantilism of both the author and the subject depicted by him. Thus, for instance, the recent recipient of the Nobel Prize for Literature, the late Albert Camus, portrays his characters as either altogether devoid of all religious—or even truly human—motivation or pitifully struggling for some modicum of meaning of life and the universe—and usually failing to arrive at any remotely satisfactory solution, since their creator, Camus, himself knows none. Thus in his novel, *The Stranger*, he pictures a French Algerian whose entire response to life is purely external, psychosomatic, for he does not possess any genuinely spiritual quality or a "personality." He

[3] Egon Friedell, *A Cultural History of Modern Age* (New York: Alfred A. Knopf, Inc., 1923), I, p. 275.

lives in sensations, in a "stream of sensory consciousness." In T. S. Eliot's phrase, he is a "hollow man," a "stranger" even to himself, an alienated, dehumanized biological specimen, certainly not quite a *"homo sapiens!"* One could cite similar examples from the writings of most eminent contemporary writers—Hemingway, Steinbeck, Faulkner, D. H. Lawrence, Sartre—not to speak of such lesser lights as Fitzgerald, Mailer, Sagan, or Nabokov, some of whose works are, or border on, pornography. J. B. Priestley concludes his recent survey, *Literature and Western Man,* by writing:

> Religion alone can carry the load, defend us against the de-humanising collectives, restore true personality. And it is doubtful if our society can last much longer without religion, for either it will destroy itself by some final idiot war or, at peace but hurrying in the wrong direction, it will soon largely cease to be composed of persons. . . . But I have no religion, most of my friends have no religion, very few of the major modern writers we have been considering have had any religion; and what is certain is that our society has none. No matter what it professes, it is now not merely irreligious but powerfully anti-religious.[4]

Surely by and large the humanist era is passing away!

Another instance of the gradual implementation of the humanist principle of self-affirmation is to be seen in the Protestant Reformation. And although some of the thought of the Reformers still represents a survival of the old order and belongs more to the Middle Ages than to the modern era, there are many elements in it distinctly recognizable as modern. The movement may certainly be regarded as the revolt of masses of believers, sparked by a few distinguished leaders such as Luther, Calvin, and Knox, against the overweening authority and lamentable degradation of the historic Church; or, in other words, the affirmation of the Christian believer of his right to stand face to face with God without the obligatory intermediation of sacerdotal priesthood. With varying degrees of consistency the Reformers held the tenet of the "priesthood of all believers." The full implications of this position were not immediately clear to them or to the Protestant rulers. But in time its inner logic—the essential democracy within the Church of God—has worked itself out with much greater clearness. The Anabaptists applied the principle of the "priesthood of all believers" far more rigorously than did Luther, Calvin, Knox, or the English Reformers. No one can accuse Luther or Calvin of being unduly "demo-

---

[4] J. B. Priestley, *Literature and Western Man* (New York: Harper & Brothers, 1960), pp. 444-45. By permission.

cratic," although the latter's insistence on separating the functions of Church and state, and the autonomy of the Church within its proper sphere, ultimately exerted an influence in the direction of political democracy. But for more than a century and a half the rule of *cujus regio ejus religio* held sway. Freedom to choose one's religious affiliation was a privilege of rulers, not of their subjects. It was not until 1689 that the newly enthroned English sovereigns, William and Mary, granted their subjects limited personal religious freedom in the Act of Toleration.

Nevertheless, the innate logic of the Protestant position, which, by its emphasis on private conviction based on personal knowledge of the Scriptural bases of faith, eventuated in an intellectual or rationalistic temper. Not that rationalism was foreign to Roman Catholicism: Thomism, with its Aristotelian presuppositions, was likewise under its sway. But in Protestantism it perhaps had a wider dissemination among the lay membership, particularly where Calvinism in general and Puritanism in particular prevailed. Among the Roman Catholics only the educated classes were more generally affected, for the popular form of piety was pre-eminently sacramentarian and amenable to authoritarian control. At any rate, in its historical development it was in Protestantism that religious individualism attained its distinctly humanistic characteristic of self-affirmation.

But let me hasten to say that I regard religion as an exception to the judgment applied to humanism in general—that most of its cultural elements have ended in relative failure. Without implying any exceptionally effective functioning of the Christian Church in society, and admitting its many faults and even failures, it is still true that it has exhibited a relatively more adequate understanding of essential humanism, in contrast to those who never attained it or subverted it. For it is an elementary Christian axiom that the autonomous man is selfish, being motivated solely by what he regards in a narrow sense as his personal advantage or pleasure. In Christian theology this is the sin of sins, the original sin. Unless and until the sinner—for this is what the man driven by egotistic motives and natural passions is—is transformed by the grace of God and surrenders his will to the Divine Will, he does not possess the true humanist values. The failure to understand this, or the refusal to practice it, have been the primary causes of the failure of our humanist-secularist culture. Accordingly, Christianity as the true humanism, to the degree to which it has remained true to its ideal of transformed humanity—Solovev's Godmanhood—has escaped the worst consequences of the perverted notion of humanism.

Furthermore, I agree with Arnold Toynbee's view that in the collapse of any given culture it is religion which normally survives as the "saving remnant" of the subsequent emergent culture. In fact I cannot conceive of any culture worthy of the name which could be built on frankly irreligious or atheistic foundations. Even the "classless society" of which the Marxists talk so glibly—assuming for argument's sake that any such a fatuous concept is realizable, which is more than doubt-ful—could not possibly be established or perpetuated without good men and women—in other words, without religiously motivated and transformed members of that society!

Let it be clearly understood, however, that Toynbee's "saving rem-nant" must be actually "saving." Except for it and other similar religious forces in the world, the future would look almost uniformly dark. If our consideration of the "failures" of the humanist era has hitherto been somberly discouraging, it is because we have concentrated upon the consequences of secularism. But this is not the whole story; Chris-tian gospel is a "gospel," that is, good news, and if taken seriously, is capable of bringing ordered peace out of the chaos.

The self-affirmation of man in the era just passing is naturally most clearly evident in modern philosophy. It is commonly agreed that the definite beginning of this phase is to be seen in the skepticism of Mon-taigne and the rationalism of Descartes in France, and the empiricism of Bacon, Hobbes, and Locke in England. They shared in common the repudiation of the medieval, particularly the Thomistic, philosophical systems, and placed the inductive study of nature and of man at the center of their concern. But it would be redundant to attempt even a brief survey of modern philosophy in this preliminary sketch, since I have chosen to devote the bulk of the work to its elucidation.

Furthermore, the humanistic spirit of self-assertion has shown itself in the political field, particularly in the American and the French Revo-lutions. Its intellectual leaders—Montesquieu, Rousseau, Condorcet, Locke, Jefferson—repudiated the social theories emanating from me-dieval Thomism. For the Thomistic doctrine of the relation of Church and state acknowledged them as coordinate spheres, the former having to do with the eternal concerns of men and the latter with their tem-poral interests. But both were ordained of God: the king and the priest were equally responsible to God. The Reformers—Luther and Calvin —held essentially the same view. Luther was driven by circumstances beyond his control to grant the state virtual control in the temporal aspects of religious life, reserving for the Church only the strictly spiritual concerns. Calvin, however, carefully worked out the coordina-tion between two spheres, so that the Church was not only autonomous within its proper spiritual sphere, but likewise had the duty vis-à-vis the state of expounding to it the will of God in temporal aspects of life, while the state owed the Church care for the latter's temporal needs.

It is noteworthy that the trend toward political democracy has appeared principally in Calvinistic countries, except in France, where it was accompanied by repudiation of Catholicism. As has already been mentioned, this was the result of the principle of the "priesthood of all believers." On the last page of his *Institutes* Calvin mentions, almost as an afterthought, the exception to the normal coordination of the relations of Church and state: should the magistrate order something contrary to the will of God, then "we must obey God rather than men!" [5] And the remarkable thing about it is that Calvinists found themselves repeatedly facing the exceptional situation: the Low Countries resisting the Spanish rule and finally winning their independence; the Czech Protestants forcing Emperor Rudolf in 1609 to grant them a very remarkable degree of religious liberty in the "Letter of Majesty," and when its provisions were violated, revolting against Ferdinand II, although with disastrous results; the Scots rising up against Regent Mary and establishing Protestant rule in the country; and the English Puritans overthrowing the monarchy of Charles I. The leaven may also be easily discerned in the American Revolution, in which fears of "episcopal tyranny" played no inconsiderable part.

Nevertheless, because the medieval theories of the relation between Church and state were repudiated, modern liberal democracies no longer regard themselves as responsible to God as "a nation under God." Their constitutions make the government responsible to the people. In contrast, totalitarian regimes, both fascist and communist, deny the liberal democratic concept in favor of an extreme and militantly secular statism whereby the rulers hold undisputed sway over both Church and state as well as over the souls and bodies of men. Thus the initially humanistic political philosophies, having for their cause the rights of man, have given rise to anti-humanist totalitarianism.

I do not mean to imply, however, that the emergence of totalitarianism necessarily spells defeat for the democratic form of government. Two mighty political concepts are at present locked in a global struggle, spearheaded by the Soviet Union and the United States. I believe that both are here to stay, although undoubtedly in a mutually modified form.

---

[5] John T. McNeill, ed., *Calvin's Institutes*, II, tr. Ford Lewis Battles. © 1960 by W. L. Jenkins. (Philadelphia: The Westminster Press), p. 1521. By permission.

Another, perhaps the last form of man's self-assertion in the humanist era, is modern economics. Modern man at first sought to conquer nature. With the coming of the Industrial Revolution, which inaugurated the reign of the machine, he has succeeded in conquering nature to a degree never before imagined. Even those who today live in relatively modest comfort exceed by far the luxuries of the past. But modern man has paid a high price for these comforts: he has been conquered by the machine. This has resulted in his substituting economic means for the spiritual ends of life. Thus the machine has done much to destroy the highest aspects of human personality; for modern man has become a helpless victim of mass propaganda, his inner strength sapped by his insidious desire for comfort and security, so that he is willing to surrender his spiritual freedom and integrity for these lesser goods. He is selling his birthright for a mess of pottage. As Berdyaev, who spent a lifetime vividly portraying these dangers, once wrote: "We are now passing through the painful agony of an individualism devoid of all spiritual foundation." [6]

Finally, this leads to the consideration of scientism—a view that science does now or will in time provide a complete and final answer to all human problems—as a substitute for both the religious and humanistic world views. This is the conviction of all positivists— whether logical or illogical. The view repudiates all moral and spiritual sovereignty over life and thought. Its arrogant claims, incessantly dinned into the ears of the hapless masses both in the West and under communist domination, are contradicted by scientists themselves. Albert Einstein humbly confessed that science does not know, cannot know, and never will know what matter is; it is concerned solely with the question of how matter behaves. Nevertheless, there will always exist a cultural lag among the lesser luminaries and scientific fellow-travelers, and the non-scientific masses, who continue to proclaim the saving gospel of scientism.

To sum up: humanism has turned against its own past, repudiating its central concept of man as of the highest cultural value, and has become anti-humanist secularism. It has lost its common spiritual center, with the consequent disintegration of its unity and integrity. It acknowledges no law above its own advantage and pleasures. The humanist-secularist age is passing away, as so many civilizations have done before it throughout the life-span of humankind.

[6] Berdyaev, "The End of the Renaissance," p. 14.

## *Two Early Representatives of Humanism: Erasmus and Montaigne*

We are now ready to turn our attention to the representatives of the humanistic movement proper, which differentiated itself more and more from the traditional Christian culture. Among its principal representatives were Desiderius Erasmus (1466?-1536) and Michel de Montaigne (1533-1592). The former has been known as the "prince of the humanists," and represents the movement in its Christian aspects. He had been greatly influenced not only by the Brethren of the Common Life, in whose school at Deventer he had received his early education, but later by such men as John Colet, Thomas More, John Fisher, and Jean Vitrier. He aimed to reform the Church from within; for that reason, although he not only conceded the need of reform but made that need abundantly and effectively plain—particularly in such works of railing sarcasm and ridicule as *The Praise of Folly*—he yet refused to break with the Church. It was this issue that separated him from Luther, and in the end forced him to an open rupture with the latter.

Erasmus' religious views are best stated in his *Enchiridion militis Christiani*.[7] He strives to counteract the prevailing sacramentarian and ritualistic concepts of Christianity, bypassing the medieval theology in the process, by earnest ethical practice of religious duties. The whole treatise is in a way a moralistic commentary on the Apostle Paul's exhortation to Christian warfare by putting on the "whole armor of God." Erasmus has little of the overwhelming consciousness of sin, such as was felt so acutely by Luther. Man is able to overcome his moral weaknesses by waging a manly conflict for self-mastery. He can control his passions by reason and will—although with the help of the grace of God. But on the whole, Erasmus represents Platonism and Stoicism as much as Christianity. No wonder that in the end, under the goading of the pope and others to clear himself of all suspicion of unorthodoxy, he broke with the Protestant Reformation by attacking Luther in 1524!

---

[7] A new translation of this work, by Ford L. Battles, is included in Matthew Spinka, ed., "Advocates of Reform" in *Library of Christian Classics*, XIV (Philadelphia: The Westminster Press, 1953), pp. 295 ff.

Erasmus' humanism is further seen in his Biblical and patristic studies. It is here that his repudiation of the immediate past—the Scholastic period—is plainly manifested. The impeccable classical Christian scholar turned his attention to the origins of Christianity—the New Testament and the Fathers—and thus helped to direct the whole Reform movement to the sources, a direction already followed by Wyclif, Hus, and other earlier "Advocates of Reform." [M. Spinka, ed., *Advocates of Reform: From Wyclif to Erasmus* (Philadelphia: The Westminster Press, 1953).] First of all, his Greek New Testament, published in 1516, exerted a mighty influence upon the recovery of the New Testament writers' original meanings—particularly of Paul—which had been hitherto lost or obscured by too deeply ingrained connotations of the Latin text. Then for thirty years he labored on the editions of the Greek and Latin fathers; from these exhausting labors he produced some thirty folio volumes of critically edited patristic texts, comprising his favorite, Jerome, as well as Cyprian, Augustine, Arnobius, Chrysostom, Irenaeus, Ambrose, Hilary, Basil, and Origen. This was his way not only of laying the foundations of critical scholarship, but also of diverting the Reform movement from the hated Schoolmen.

In all this Erasmus was a typical humanist; but he used his great classical learning in the service of Christianity as he understood it. He would probably not have produced the Reformation, although much of his spirit appeared later in the Catholic Counter-Reformation, even though it was not openly acknowledged by its leaders. His essentially conservative attitude, coupled perhaps with a scholar's fastidiousness and dislike of controversy, aimed at intellectual and ethical reform from within the Church. Restating my estimate of Erasmus expressed on an earlier occasion, I still hold that he made an immensely valuable contribution to the cause of Christianity:

> If his genius fitted him for work which was mainly intellectual, the cause of the Kingdom has need of such services. He labored unremittingly, and despite the sufferings which his frail bodily frame and consequent ill-health caused him, the results of his labors were astonishing in their mere bulk as in the excellence of their performance. For has not our Lord himself bid us, in summing up all law and prophets, to love the Lord God not only with all our heart and soul, but with all our mind as well? Erasmus loved with his mind; that too is the true service of God and His Church.[8]

In this connection it seems fitting to express a poignant regret that the humanist movement, which was and could continue to be of tre-

---

[8] *Ibid.*, pp. 293-94.

mendous benefit to the cause of Christianity, henceforth diverged ever
more markedly into a development essentially contrary and inimical to
the Christian world view. Zwingli and Calvin were still markedly
humanistic, although they utilized classical learning for the benefit of
their vigorously Christian convictions. But such is not the case with
other outstanding representatives of humanism, who turned the movement into channels eventuating in the complete secularism and irreligious scientism of our own day.

This tendency of humanism is well illustrated in the case of Michel
de Montaigne. Formerly, he was regarded almost exclusively as a
skeptic, whose *Essays* were the breviary of the "free-thinkers." Pascal,
who knew his writings thoroughly, certainly held him to be essentially a denier and a doubter. He writes of him:

> He places all things in universal doubt and in such general doubt
> that this doubt is carried away by itself. That is to say, [he doubts]
> whether he doubts, and since he doubts even this last supposition, his
> uncertainty constantly revolves about itself in a perpetual circle. . . .
> It is in this doubt that doubts itself, and in this ignorance which is
> ignorant of itself, and which he calls his sovereign form, that the
> essence of his opinion lies. . . . In other words, he is an out and out
> Pyrrhonist. All his discourses and all his *Essays* center around this
> principle. It is the only thing he pretends to establish although he
> does not always point out his intention. Thereby he imperceptibly
> destroys everything that men regard as most certain, not in order to
> establish the contrary with a certainty to which he is hostile, but
> merely in order to reveal that, appearances being equal on both sides,
> one does not know on what to base one's belief.[9]

Ralph Waldo Emerson, although he did not share Pascal's attitude
toward Montaigne—for he plainly betrays a certain degree of admiration for the latter—yet agreed with Pascal as to Montaigne's essential
skepticism. He chose him, in his *Representative Men*[10] as the example
of generic skepticism. Emerson's brilliant essay is perhaps the most
skillful and effective portrayal of this class of thinkers. But the critical
scholarship of the last forty years has modified both the picture and
the characterization of Montaigne, particularly by unraveling the
gradual development of the latter's opinions as seen in the different

[9] From *The Great Shorter Works of Pascal*, tr. Emile Cailliet and John C.
Blankenagel. Copyright 1948 by W. L. Jenkins. (Philadelphia: The Westminster
Press), p. 124. By permission.
[10] Ralph Waldo Emerson, "Representative Men" in *Emerson's Complete Works,*
IV (Boston: Houghton Mifflin Company, 1896), pp. 143 ff.

editorial changes and additions to his *Essays*.[11] This change proceeds from what is designated as Montaigne's "stoical" phase to the skeptical, and ultimately results in the final epicurean period. The first of these phases of Montaigne's life is truly humanistic; in it he is an enthusiastic admirer of the classics of antiquity, both Greek and Latin, with complete confidence in the rational power of man. This admiration is particularly lavished on Cato the Younger. Montaigne was then all for practicing stoical virtues. During this period he held that to philosophize is to learn to die.[12] The radical change occurred at the time when at the request of his father he translated Raymond Sebold's *Theologia naturalis* and then wrote the "Apology for Raymond Sebold," (about 1576), where he already strongly voiced the conviction that man without divine grace is nothing. "He will rise, if God by exception lends him a hand; he will rise by abandoning and renouncing his own means, and letting himself be raised and uplifted by purely celestial means. It is for our Christian faith, not for his Stoical virtue, to aspire to that divine and miraculous metamorphosis." [13] Sentiments of this sort would lead us to suppose that Montaigne would henceforth devote himself to religious contemplation and practices. But nothing of the sort is evident in the subsequent writings, at least not in any preeminent degree. He remains a good Catholic who feels it incumbent upon him occasionally to make a thrust or a sally, not by any means humorous, against the Protestants. When he visited Rome, he was presented along with his travel companions to Pope Gregory XIII—the pope who had jubilantly celebrated the Massacre of Saint Bartholomew's Day—and devoutly kissed the latter's slipper. The pope admonished "Monsieur de Montaigne to continue in the devotion he had always borne to the Church and the service of the Most Christian King," as Montaigne himself reports in his "Travel Journal." [14] Nevertheless, religion plays no dominant role in the last fourteen years of his life; the period is rather prevailingly devoted to self-study and analysis of his motives and practices and a minute description of them. He had now chosen for his motto: *"Que scay-je?"* What do I know? His essays henceforth are essentially moralistic. He is not sparing of self-blame for

[11] Reprinted from *The Complete Works of Montaigne*, tr. Donald M. Frame with the permission of the publishers, Stanford University Press. © Copyright 1948, 1957, 1958 by the Board of Trustees of Leland Stanford Junior University. Applies to lines from pages 2, 56, 457 and 714.

[12] *Ibid.*, p. 56 ff.

[13] *Ibid.*, p. 457.

[14] *Ibid.*, p. 939.

his fairly numerous foibles and by no means exemplary habits. As he himself writes in the Preface to his delightfully garrulous *Essays,*

> This book was written in good faith, reader. . . . I have had no thought of serving either you or my own glory. . . . I want to be seen here in my simple, natural, ordinary fashion, without straining or artifice; for it is myself that I portray. . . . Thus, reader, I am myself the matter of my book; you would be unreasonable to spend your leisure on so frivolous and vain a subject.[15]

And he lives up to his word; he continually talks about himself, even though as usual he quotes copiously from the ancient classical writers. He tells us in the greatest detail, and not merely once, about all his bodily functions, habits, infirmities—particularly his stone—foibles, virtues, and failings. Emerson's characterization, despite the fact that he did not have the benefit of the findings of modern critical scholarship, is still essentially correct.

> Montaigne talks with shrewdness, knows the world and books and himself, and uses the positive degree; never shrieks, or protests, or prays; no weakness, no convulsion, no superlative: does not wish to jump out of his skin, or play any antics, or annihilate space or time, but is stout and solid; tastes every moment of the day; likes pain because it makes him feel himself and realize things; . . . He keeps the plain; he rarely mounts or sinks; likes to feel solid ground and the stones underneath. His writing has no enthusiasms, no aspiration; contented, self-respecting and keeping the middle of the road.[16]

It is perhaps in his last essay, "Of Experience," [17] written four years before his death, that we may best observe the final stage of Montaigne's thought. It is "Epicurean" in the sense that it deals almost exclusively with the conduct of our physical existence. It goes extensively into a discussion of health and disease—particularly Montaigne's own—and inculcates a moderate and sensible attitude toward life. And by knowing himself as prone to mistakes, he is therefore tolerant of the failings of others. Above all, he wants men to know and accept themselves for what they are, and be satisfied with their condition, whatever it is. Let man "be what he is, and nothing else prefer." To live well is the greatest task that any man may undertake.

> We are great fools. 'He has spent his life in idleness,' we say; 'I have done nothing today.' What, have you not lived? That is not

---

[15] *Ibid.,* p. 2.
[16] Emerson, *op. cit.,* p. 161.
[17] Frame, tr., *Works of Montaigne,* pp. 815 ff.

only the fundamental but the most illustrious of your occupations. 'If I had been placed in a position to manage great affairs, I would have shown what I could do.' Have you been able to think out and manage your own life? You have done the greatest task of all. To show and exploit her resources Nature has no need of fortune; she shows herself equally on all levels and behind a curtain as well as without one. To compose our character is our duty, not to compose books, and to win, not battles and provinces, but order and tranquility in our conduct. Our great and glorious masterpiece is to live appropriately.[18]

And to live appropriately is to live according to Nature:

> There is nothing so beautiful and legitimate as to play the man well and properly, no knowledge so hard to acquire as the knowledge of how to live this life well and naturally; and the most barbarous of our maladies is to despise our being.[19]

Montaigne will have no asceticism, no straining after being an angel before our time. He speaks disparagingly of

> those venerable souls, exalted by ardent piety and religion to constant and conscientious meditation on divine things . . . [who] scorn to give their attention to our beggarly, watery, and ambiguous comforts, and readily resign to the body the concern and enjoyment of sensual and temporal fodder. . . . Between ourselves, these are two things that I have always observed to be in singular accord: supercelestial thoughts and subterranean conduct.[20]

And he concludes not only the book, but also summarizes his mature wisdom by writing: "The most beautiful lives, to my mind, are those that conform to the common human pattern, with order, but without miracle and without eccentricity." He quotes with approval the thoroughly bourgeois sentiments of Horace:

> Grant me but health, Latona's son,
> And to enjoy the wealth I've won,
> And honored age, with mind entire
> And not unsolaced by the lyre.[21]

Montaigne then is a fitting representative of the humanistic revolt against Scholastic thought, as well as of many characteristic tendencies

---

[18] Michel E. de Montaigne, "Of Experience," from *Selected Essays*, Donald M. Frame, tr. (Roslyn, N.Y.: Walter J. Black, Inc., 1943). By permission.
[19] *Ibid.*
[20] *Ibid.*
[21] *Ibid.*

of the modern age. His writings simply swarm with quotations, illustrations, and allusions to classical writers, and his mind is steeped in the culture of Greece and Rome. Despite that, he is thoroughly modern in making himself the center of all his study, concern, and care. It is after all Montaigne himself who is the measure of all things, whether ancient or modern. This is prophetic of that overweening concern, philosophical, psychological, cultural, and economic, which developed in the period subsequent to Montaigne; Descartes and Locke, in their different ways, turned their eyes inward to study themselves. No wonder that psychology, the study of the soul, was born as a science during this period! The political and economic systems also were conceived with the individual at the center. Indeed, Montaigne's preoccupation with himself was prophetic of what was to follow.

His skepticism, the distrust of "common sense," was also indicative of a similar attitude on the part of the creative thinkers of the modern era. It would perhaps be an exaggeration to assert of him that he arrived at the stage of denying all absolute truth, and asserting that all is relative, although Pascal so understood him. But since modern scholarship insists that in his last phase Montaigne stoutly upheld the Socratic admonition, "Know thyself," he must have had confidence at least to a relative degree in such knowledge. We may therefore concede that the stage of absolute skepticism was reached later. But Montaigne was keenly aware of the limitation of knowledge and certainly condemned all dogmatism.

> He who remembers having been mistaken so many, many times in his own judgment, is he not a fool if he does not distrust it forever after? . . . To my weakness, so often recognized, I owe the inclination I have to modesty, obedience to the beliefs that are prescribed me, a constant coolness and moderation in my opinions, and my hatred for that aggressive and quarrelsome arrogance that believes and trusts wholly in itself, a mortal enemy of discipline and truth. Hear them laying down the law: the first stupidities that they advance are in the style in which men establish religions and laws.[22]

Nevertheless, since many outstanding thinkers understood Montaigne to have denied any possibility of knowledge, we must, for argument's sake, recognize the effect his skepticism had on them. If there is no absolute truth, or if we cannot know it, then all is relative. Hence, a wise man suspends judgment. But even that is futile, since knowledge is never attainable. There would be some sense to it only if there were

[22] *Ibid.*

a possibility that at some future time we shall be able to attain secure knowledge. Therefore, the thing to do is to *abandon* judgment, not merely suspend it.

But one must live. And to live is to act on successive judgments. If people waited to get married until they knew positively whether happiness would result, they would never get married. There is no other way of finding out but to act. Thus one cannot suspend, or above all abandon, judgment in order to live; no one knows what the end will bring. All facts will never be in before one's life is ended. The pre-Socratic Sophists suspended judgment—with dire moral consequences. It was this that Socrates and Plato rebelled against. To quote our Lord, "He that doeth the will of my Father, he shall know whether the words I speak are true."

Although he repeatedly professes himself a Roman Catholic, Montaigne's religious views are conventional. His real interest is in the practical conduct of life, in morality, rather than in mystical communion with God or in the typical Protestant piety—the life of a justified sinner saved by grace. In this he anticipates the religious views of the Deists, to which both Descartes and Locke—particularly the latter —contributed so greatly. As Montaigne himself admits in the words previously quoted, and in a true Catholic fashion, he submits himself in "obedience to the beliefs that are prescribed me." This obedience includes not only religious beliefs, but political as well. As Gilson writes about this conservative attitude of Montaigne:

> If religion is there, why should we change it? It cannot be proved; but the next one will not be more proved, and that one at least is there. There is nothing more dangerous than to touch a political order once it has been established. For who knows whether the next one will be better? The world is living by custom and tradition; we should not disturb it on the strength of private opinions which express little more than our own moods and humours, or, at the utmost, the local prejudices of our own country. A well-made mind is never fully convinced of its own opinions, and therefore doubting is the highest mark of wisdom.[23]

And if one wishes to have Montaigne's own words for this passive obedience to the prevailing mores, whether or not one really agrees with its dictates, one may ponder his almost cynical statement apropos of kings: "What I myself adore in kings is the crowd of their adorers. All deference and submission is due to them, except that of our under-

[23] Etienne Gilson, *The Unity of Philosophical Experience* (New York: Charles Scribner's Sons, 1937), pp. 127-28. By permission.

standing. My reason is not trained to bend and bow, it is my knees." [24] But will not this deference to authority finally result in indifference to truth, religious as well as any other, as historically that actually was the result of this skeptical attitude?

And finally, Montaigne's insistence on living according to nature is prophetic of the all-dominating emphasis of the eighteenth-century thinkers upon reason and nature. Their essentially moralistic attitude combative of all "enthusiasm," including vital religion; their absorption in nature, particularly natural sciences; are all in direct line of descent from Montaigne.

From the foregoing it is fairly clear in which direction Montaigne's mature thought tends, despite much that is really sensible and wise: it is restricted primarily to a concern with the individual himself, for he may know only himself, and that with infinite pains and never quite perfectly. All concern with the ultimate questions of man's destiny and of the meaning of life are beyond our reach. "We entangle our thoughts in generalities, and the causes and conduct of the universe, which conduct themselves very well without us, and we leave behind our own affairs and Michel, who concerns us even more closely than man in general." [25] Moreover, this selfish concern deals largely with our physical well-being, since larger meanings are beyond our reach. This comes close to modern repudiation of all meaningfulness of life, which is essentially nihilism. Montaigne is the first great denier; for him, no amount of labor or thought will avail to disclose to us the ultimate purpose of human life. Despite all his professed admiration for Socrates, he could not repeat the latter's judgment that "Life without reflection [i.e., without seeking its ultimate meaning] is not worth living."

In conclusion, the skepticism of such men as Montaigne, and even in a more radical form by later thinkers of his type, presents the modern man with this challenge: has life any ultimate meaning beyond the mere satisfaction of his creaturely wants? If it does, can we know it? And if we do, by what means: faith? experience? reason? feeling? will? intuition? In the future, philosophical systems were evolved that based themselves on each one of these alternatives, or on their denial.

[24] Montaigne, *Selected Essays* (Walter J. Black edition.)
[25] *Ibid.*

# 2

# Cartesianism—Reason Faces Inward

## René Descartes, the Founder of the Rationalist School of Philosophy

Archbishop Temple in his Gifford Lectures, entitled *Nature, Man, and God*, begins his chapter on "The Cartesian Faux-Pas" with an outburst of ill temper: "If I were asked," he writes, "what was the most disastrous moment in the history of Europe I should be strongly tempted to answer that it was that period of leisure when René Descartes, having no claims to meet, remained for a whole day 'shut up alone in a stove.'"[1]

What could have called forth such a severe tirade from the otherwise suave and sweet-mannered archbishop? It was the conviction of the exceedingly important, although in his judgment disastrous, effect which the vanquisher of Aristotelianism and the inaugurator of the "critical" philosophy has exerted on the modern age. Let us then turn our attention to this mighty genius

---

[1] *Nature, Man, and God,* by William Temple, by permission of Mrs. Temple (London: St. Martin's Press, Inc. and Macmillan & Co., Ltd., 1940), p. 57.

whose influence for both weal and woe has been so decisive to our day.

In that charming and urbane little book, *Discourse on the Method*, Descartes tells us that

> And as I was returning from the coronation of the Emperor to join the army [that of Maximilian of Bavaria who participated in the opening battles of the Thirty Years War], the setting in of winter detained me in a quarter where, since I found no society to divert me, while fortunately I had no cares or passions to trouble me, I remained the whole day shut up alone in a stove-heated room, where I had complete leisure to occupy myself with my own thoughts.[2]

This important event occurred on November 10, 1619, probably at Ulm, exactly a year after Descartes had met Dr. Isaac Beeckman, a Dutch physician who was instrumental in awakening in Descartes an enthusiasm for the study of the natural sciences. Accordingly, "as regards all the opinions which up to this time I had embraced, I thought I could do no better than endeavor once and for all to sweep them completely away so that they might later on be replaced either by others which were better, or by the same when I had made them conform to the uniformity of a rational scheme."[3] This then indicates the emergence of a concrete resolve on Descartes' part to rethink the entire cultural heritage of the past—in other words, the Aristotelian world view—and to test everything on the basis of new critical principles, of which he had perhaps caught a glimpse on that fateful November day. He assures us, furthermore, that he contemplated no world-shaking revolution and no conscious attempt to overthrow the entrenched Aristotelian system. "My design has never extended beyond trying to reform my own opinion and to build on a foundation which is entirely my own. . . . The simple resolve to strip oneself of all opinions and beliefs formerly received is not to be regarded as an example that each man should follow . . ."[4]

Nevertheless, the principle of universal doubt became the means of a veritable scientific revolution and the chief characteristic of the modern age. "Modern philosophy, however, starting with Descartes, no longer rests upon faith, but on the contrary is based upon doubt, upon the desperate idea that at the bottom of existence there may be no God,

---

[2] E. S. Haldane and G. R. T. Ross, trs., *The Philosophical Works of Descartes* (New York: Cambridge University Press, 1931), I, p. 87. By permission.

[3] *Ibid.*, p. 89.

[4] *Ibid.*, p. 90.

but rather a wicked genius, the relentless forces of nature or the blind instincts of life by which man is deceived." [5]

But was Descartes' basic principle "*de omnibus dubitandum*" entirely his own? For after all Montaigne had brought forth the thesis that man knows nothing and can know nothing positively in a way which was tremendously impressive; and although Descartes does not publicly admit it, he must have been greatly troubled by Montaigne's conclusions. He agreed with the latter that all the learning of the past rested on mere unverified tradition and hence was worthless as far as critically tested truth was concerned. But was Montaigne right that the truth could never be found? Was radical skepticism the answer? The glimpse of the solution Descartes had caught in that stove-heated room had shown him that a way out could be found. He must fight Montaigne! He must test everything, including Montaigne! He could not live with the conviction that the distinction between the true and the false is impossible of discernment, that man can do nothing but doubt. There is a way of distinguishing between the true and the false—the critical method of verification. "Descartes, flung by doubt into the abyss of desperation, found the Archimedean point in the certainty of his own Ego and in the evidence of his ideas." [6]

The famous *Method* of which Descartes had caught a glimpse in 1619 was elaborated by him first of all in *Rules for the Direction of the Mind*,[7] which he appears to have used for his own guidance. They were published again in a much shortened form in the book issued eighteen years later under the title *Discourse on the Method*.[8] Of the Rules, the second is of utmost importance for distinguishing truth from falsehood. By this invaluable rule "we reject all such merely probable knowledge and make it a rule to trust only what is completely known and incapable of being doubted." [9] Truth then is to be found within, in the thinker's mind, not outside in the "objective" world. It is innate. It is this feature which constitutes the distinctive difference between rationalism and empiricism. Another rule is the common sense methodological direction for dividing the subject into its constituent parts. The third is equally helpful; namely, that of starting from the simple and advancing to the more difficult; and the last is making certain that

[5] Erich Frank, *Philosophical Understanding and Religious Truth* (New York: Oxford University Press, Inc., 1945), p. 36. By permission.

[6] *Ibid.*, p. 6.

[7] Haldane-Ross, *op. cit.*, I, pp. 1-77.

[8] *Ibid.*, pp. 81-130.

[9] *Ibid.*, p. 3.

nothing belonging to the subject under consideration is omitted. These admirable rules must indeed be observed by anyone who wishes to find the truth; but the trouble with the method is that neither Descartes or anyone else has succeeded in applying them with the rigidity which they require. For were he or anyone else really to start with a *radical* doubt, he would have to doubt the truth of the existence of rationality. If reason or truth do not exist, it would be silly to seek them. If the universe is unreasonable, all we do is likewise unreasonable. But once we grant the presupposition that the universe is reasonable, we already admit a truth which is not proved "*a posteriori.*"

Getting started, then, with presumably a clean sweep of all he had learned at the excellent Collège la Flèche under the good Jesuit fathers —as well as since his school days—and having applied his rules to his search for a starting point for critically verified knowledge, Descartes arrived in the course of time at three basic truths, or "simple natures" as he called them: his own existence as a thinking being (but *not* as a body); the existence of God; and the reality of the material world. These were not ideas, but essential, "ontal" substances.

Thus, the first absolute truth which Descartes affirms is that of his own existence. To be sure he had to start with doubting even that; but he could not doubt that he doubted, since he doubted; he, therefore, thought; *ergo,* he existed. *Dubito, cogito, ergo sum.* This conclusion meets all the requirements of his method. It is perfectly clear and distinct and therefore true. He arrives at it by direct intuition rather than deducing it syllogistically from the act of thinking. This then removes the objection commonly made against the first truth of Descartes; namely, that he makes existence dependent upon his thinking. He himself removes all doubt about this matter in his reply to Hobbes who objected that thinking is a mere activity and does not itself prove "the thing that thinks." To this objection Descartes replies that he did not say "that understanding and the thing which understands are one and the same if 'understanding' is taken for a faculty, but only if taken for the thing itself that understands. . . . It is certain that thinking cannot exist without a thing that thinks," [10] *i.e.,* the ego. But this "I" which exists is not to be identified with the body, the existence of which has not yet been proved. Instead, it is to be understood as a mental entity, while the body (as shall be proved later) is material. The basic difference between these two entities is that the former is unextended while the latter is extended.

---

[10] S. V. Keeling, *Descartes* (London: Oxford University Press, 1934), p. 95. By permission.

But to turn to a critical examination of this first truth of Descartes. It cannot be granted that even this starting point is impeccable and because of its hidden "*faux pas*," it has led modern philosophy into a *cul de sac*. In the first place, if Keeling's interpretation of *cogito ergo sum* is correct, then Descartes has formulated the definition wrongly by putting the cart before the horse. He should have inverted the order to read: *sum, ergo cogito;* for no one can think unless he first exists. Later philosophy, misled by the false order of this Cartesian dictum, has placed all the emphasis on epistemology (analysis of how man thinks) rather than on man's existence. In fact, the latter was subsequently lost in various forms of anti-humanist denial of personality. Accordingly, what was so clear to Descartes that it excluded all doubt, has proved quite unclear to other modern philosophers. Thus, for instance, David Hume denied that being conscious of a stream of ideas proved a substantial self behind that experience.

In the second place, one cannot think without thinking *something*. The subject-object relationship is inseparable; but Descartes, and particularly some of the more radical of his hypercritical successors, tended to fix attention predominantly, if not exclusively, upon the "stream of consciousness"—the process of thinking, rather than the subject-object relationships with which thought is occupied. It is as if one could be thinking absolutely nothing. Of course, merely thinking something does not prove the reality or the truth of what one is thinking about. But the sundering of the subject-object relationship has eventuated in the denial of the object of thought. As Archbishop Temple summarizes this mischievous "*faux pas*":

> What Descartes indulged in his stove was purely academic doubt; he was really as sure of the stove as of himself. If it be urged that this academic doubt was not an empirical absence of assurance but an 'ideal supposal' I must reply that this method is permissible enough but that Descartes found the wrong residuum. What he ought to have reached as the irreducible basis of all thought, including doubt, was the subject-object relationship. Then all the subsequent trouble would have been avoided. But academic doubt is in itself only an extension of nursery make-believe-'Let us pretend that we do not know that there is a Sun, or that Napoleon existed, or that selfishness is bad, and see if we can prove any of these things.[11]

And in the third place, Descartes' dictum, *cogito ergo sum*, is faulty in so far as it singles out for exclusive emphasis only one constituent aspect of personality, namely, the intellect. Feeling and will are ignored.

[11] Temple, *op. cit.*, p. 66.

This has led to an overemphasis on reason which was characteristic of the entire eighteenth century—the Age of Reason—and which has called forth by way of reaction the Romantic movement with its own overemphasis on feeling. Later on by way of reaction came the period when the will came into its own. Thus, Descartes is responsible to no mean degree for the excessive rationalism of modern philosophy, even though Western culture had been prone to this excess even during the dominance of the Aristotelian system.

Having proved to his satisfaction that at least he himself exists, Descartes poses the question whether anybody or anything else likewise exists. For to be altogether alone in the universe cannot be too comfortable. And since in the Cartesian system the truth is within, he again sought within himself for whatever other "simple natures" there might exist. As has already been stated, the second basic truth of the Cartesian metaphysics is the existence of God: for Descartes found within himself a clear idea of God. But to have an *idea* of God does not yet prove that God *exists*. In order to prove the latter, Descartes adduces two arguments: the first of these consists in the affirmation that his idea of God "is also very clear and distinct." "By the name of God I understand a substance that is infinite [eternal, immutable], independent, all-knowing, all-powerful, and by which I myself and everything else, if anything else does exist, have been created." [12] And since the idea of an infinite being could not be produced by Descartes, who was only a finite being, he concluded that it was given him by intuition from God Himself. *Ergo*, "we must conclude that God necessarily exists." [13]

The second proof of God's existence which Descartes presents in Chapter 5 of the *Meditations* appears to be almost identical with the Anselmic ontological argument.

> I clearly see that existence can no more be separated from the essence of God than can its having its three angles equal to two right angles be separated from the essence of a [rectilinear] triangle, or the idea of a mountain from the idea of a valley; and so there is not any less repugnance to our conceiving a God (that is, a Being supremely perfect) to whom existence is lacking (that is to say, to whom a certain perfection is lacking), than to conceive of a mountain which has no valley." Accordingly, "it follows that existence is inseparable from Him, and hence that He really exists." [14]

---

[12] *Meditations*, III, in Haldane-Ross, *op. cit.*, I, p. 165.
[13] *Ibid*.
[14] Haldane-Ross, *op. cit.*, I., p. 181.

For although with other ideas, such, for instance, as that of a winged horse, it is possible to separate the notion of existence from that of essence, it is not so with the idea of God. For the nonexistence of a *perfect* Being is unthinkable.

Once established to Descartes' satisfaction, the idea of God is accorded a most prominent place in his system. Not only does the world of physical objects depend upon God for its being, for He created it (as shall be proved later), but the fact of God's veracity guarantees the dependability of all his creation.

> The fact of God's veracity can therefore be used as a general principle to prove that whatever depends on God for its existence or nature cannot be 'deceptive,' unreal, 'ungenuine,' and hence that our clear and distinct ideas are true. So there is no longer any reason to continue our enquiries under the restrictive hypothesis that we may be so constituted intellectually as to be unable to reach certain knowledge.[15]

In other words, once we accept the existence of ourselves and of God as verified knowledge, we are in a position to acquire real knowledge of many other things. It follows, therefore, that one who denies the existence of God places himself in a most precarious position in regards to knowing anything securely!

But, unfortunately, Descartes' "proof" of the existence of God is not conclusive, if we admit no other factors than those allowed by his *Method*. He was undoubtedly sincerely convinced of the truth of his proposition and as such was a genuine believer in a philosophical religion. Nevertheless, a keen thinker like Blaise Pascal clearly understood the far-reaching implications of Descartes' postulates and realized that they were essentially destructive of the very bases of spiritual religion and of faith. He could not forgive Descartes because all the latter needed God for was "to make Him give a fillip to set the world in motion." [16] Such was the considered judgment of that other scientific genius of the seventeenth century, whose religious insight was far superior to that of Descartes.

Pascal's judgment was indeed right; for although superficially it may appear that Descartes was but repeating the argument of the great Christian thinker, Anselm, this appearance is deceptive. The very

---

[15] Keeling, *op. cit.*, p. 108.

[16] From the book, *Pensées* by Blaise Pascal. Translated by W. F. Trotter. Everyman's Library. Reprinted by permission of E. P. Dutton & Co., Inc. Also by permission of J. M. Dent & Sons Ltd., London, 1904, p. 31.

essence of Anselm's view is that faith is primary and reason subsidiary, i.e. secondary. Anselm's faith was "seeking to know." "I do not seek to understand that I may believe, but I believe in order to understand." In his famous *Proslogium,* Anselm seeks to show that as soon as one tries to make the proof of the existence of God depend on his own reasoning, he no longer gets God but only an abstract idea of Him. In other words, Anselm's argument presupposes faith, does not in itself result in faith. It is this aspect of the Anselmic, ontological proof which is subverted by Descartes as well as by all who followed him in seeking to base the proof of the existence of God on reason rather than on faith. "This criticism holds good," writes Erich Frank, "for all the attempts of modern metaphysicians to prove the existence of God through logical arguments alone and without the presupposition of faith; it is unavoidable that at some point reason will discover the illusory character of its purely speculative proofs of God." [17]

That Descartes' proof of God, although absolutely basic to his system, was actually soon discarded by the subsequent thinkers of the critical school is a matter of common knowledge. Of his first proof—namely, that his idea of God was most clear and distinct and that since it was not derived from himself, it must have been implanted in him by God Himself—the subsequent philosophers made short shrift. They simply denied that *they* had any such idea of God in their consciousness and thus exposed the basic weakness of the Cartesian proof, namely, that the existence of God depends upon our having a clear and distinct innate idea of it. Moreover, once Descartes' own view of the physical universe as wholly mechanical became generally accepted, and as men discarded the notion that only God could have given the machine its initial momentum, the need for God disappeared.

In the next place, the ontological argument put forth by Descartes was thoroughly discredited by Kant, who knew it only in the Cartesian, rather than in its original Anselmic, form.[18] Kant held that one cannot argue on the basis of the phenomenal in order to prove the existence of the noumenal. He was followed in this matter by most of the later philosophers. The net result was the virtual abandonment of the attempt to prove God's existence by these means and the consequent conclusion; that since He cannot be proved by intellectual arguments, He does not exist.

Having established the existence of the Creator and the Prime Mover of the universe, Descartes felt no difficulty in asserting, as the third

---

[17] Frank, *op. cit.,* p. 37.
[18] *Ibid.,* p. 51, n. 32.

undoubted verity, the existence of the material world. He defined matter, in distinction from the mental substance, as spacially extended, while mind was not. In fact, for him space and matter were identical. Thus although Cartesianism is often characterized as dualism in the sense that there exist on the one hand the unextended substances of minds and of God, and on the other hand matter as the extended substance possessing immense diversity of modes, one could as well define it as pluralism.

The basic mode of the material world is mechanistic. The universe is one vast, immensely complicated machine, governed wholly by mechanical laws. Accordingly, it can be rationally understood, for there is nothing in it which transcends natural laws of geometry and physics. This, of course, has been essentially the view of the natural sciences down to Planck and Einstein.

But if matter consists wholly of extension, the universe-in-motion as the natural sciences know it has not yet been accounted for. Thus Descartes had to find an explanation of motion. And since besides the material substance there existed only minds and God, and minds could not be the cause of movement in the physical universe, there remained only God to whom the origin of movement and its impartation to inert matter could be ascribed.

In applying this theory to man, it logically follows that he is composed of two entirely disparate substances, namely, mind and body. The latter is a machine wholly subject to mechanical laws. This duality of elements created for Descartes an extraordinary, in fact, insuperable, dilemma. For he could never solve the problem of interaction between them. That interaction existed was a matter of common-sense observation and experience. Yet logically it could not exist; since mind and body are entirely disparate, the mind cannot influence the body, nor the body the mind. Furthermore, since motion is *not* a property of matter, mind cannot move the body, for it would thus *add* to the amount of the existing motion caused by God. This would contradict another of Descartes' axioms: namely, that the amount of both matter and motion in the world is constant. Accordingly, he cannot explain even such a simple action as that of raising an arm, or taking a step, unless he ascribes the action to God, which he does not do. To be sure, he speaks of the state of mind as being the "occasion" of the simultaneous state of the body and vice versa; moreover, he indulges in a fanciful theory that the brain contains a fluid—the *animal spirits*—which is affected by the mind and which in turn acts on the body to the extent of changing the direction, although not the amount, of motion. But all such specious explanations patently contradict his primary assumption that the two elements are totally disparate and therefore cannot be the "occasion" of each other's states, nor can they act on each other under any conceivable circumstances. Indeed, his immediate successors—Malebranche, Geulincx, and Mersenne—found this problem of the greatest difficulty, and the first-named resorted to the heroic conclusion that all movement, both of the body and the mind, is the result of the direct intervention of God—in other words, a miracle. "I deny," [Malebranche says], "that my will produces ideas in me, for I cannot even conceive how it could produce them, since, being unable to act without knowledge, it presupposes ideas, and therefore does not cause them. All causality, then, is divine causality." [19]

The dualism of the Cartesian world view has led to long drawn-out attempts to overcome it, for philosophers are usually, it seems, predisposed to monism. Thus most of the later philosophers are monists, either asserting that reality is basically material or that it is mental. Naturalistic scientists usually favor the former. But both groups hold only partial and inadequate views of reality. Equally unsatisfactory is the attempt of some to combine these two views; thus Bertrand Russell asserts that whatever happens in the physical world occurs in our minds and any distinction between the concepts of mental or physical is illusory.[20]

The Cartesian view of the physical universe, for which its author claimed certainty guaranteed by divine veracity, has thus failed even more dismally than his other supposed verities. For the Cartesian (as well as the Newtonian) mechanistic physics has suffered the same fate at the hands of the present-day physicists as had the Aristotelian at the hands of Descartes and Newton. The "new" physics, derived from the discoveries of Einstein and Planck and other investigators, has supplanted the "mechanistic" explanations of the universe by the theories of relativity and quantum, and has in addition swept away the confident materialism of the nineteenth century. Today the best definition of matter is that which identifies it with the sources of our sensations. What the *nature* of matter is none can say, for we can deal only with its appearance as registered by our precision instruments and as defined by our mathematical equations. There is practically no proposition of the Cartesian physics which is still held. Sir James Jeans sums up his judgment of it in the terse remark: ". . . the system was mostly erroneous." [21]

---

[19] Quoted in Keeling, *op. cit.*, p. 210.
[20] Quoted in Sir James H. Jeans, *Physics and Philosophy* (New York: Cambridge University Press, 1943), p. 199.
[21] *Ibid.*, p. 108.

Thus although most of Descartes' specific achievements in natural sciences have been transcended by the new physics, his basic assumption that all nature may be comprehended by scientific method and reason has remained the guiding principle of the natural sciences. In this respect Descartes has contributed to the revolution in science and is one of the pathfinders of modern philosophy. Not only is the idea of mechanism in nature due to him, but also the application of this idea to man as well. The atheistic materialists of the second half of the eighteenth century—LaMettrie, d'Holbach, and others—could derive their whole concept of man as machine from Descartes. Thus the basic humanistic character of the Renaissance was already undermined by the essential anti-humanism of mechanistic rationalism.

In such a universe there is no room not only for man, but for God as well. For as has already been indicated, the idea of God was actually undermined by the Cartesian metaphysics, although Descartes himself did not foresee such as a result. He remained outwardly a faithful Catholic, yet his actual position could not but repudiate the Church's faith. His aim was to attain knowledge—including that of God—by reason alone. His philosophy has set in motion the natural theology of Deism and ultimately has led to the dispensing with God altogether, when He was thought to be no longer needed. As Etienne Gilson sums up this aspect of the matter:

> . . . such a world [as Descartes pictured] being indefinitely extended in space, its creator had to be infinite; such a world being purely mechanical and devoid of final causes, what was true and good in it had to be such because God had created it by a free decree of his will, and not conversely; the mechanical world of Descartes rested upon the assumption of the conservation of the same quantity of motion in the universe; hence the God of Descartes had to be an immutable God and the laws established by his will could not be allowed to change, unless this world itself be first destroyed. In short, the essence of the Cartesian God was largely determined by his philosophical function, which was to create and to preserve the mechanical world of science as Descartes himself conceived it.[22]

The new philosophy which has eventuated in modern critical thought divided itself into two main streams: the Rationalistic, or Continental, comprising chiefly Spinoza and Leibnitz, and the Empirical, or English, deriving from Francis Bacon but represented chiefly by John Locke, George Berkeley, and David Hume.

---

[22] Etienne Gilson, *God and Philosophy* (New Haven: Yale University Press, 1941), pp. 87-88. By permission.

## *Baruch Spinoza's Deterministic Pantheism*

The greatest of the rationalistic philosophers after Descartes was Baruch (Benedict de) Spinoza (1632?-77). A Sephardic Jew, a member of the Amsterdam Jewish community, he was educated as a prospective rabbi in the system of the medieval Jewish philosophical tradition then current. And although he departed from it to the extent that he was excommunicated from the community, he nevertheless continued to think in the essential terms of that tradition—a position which is stressed strongly by Harry A. Wolfson and Richard McKeon.[23] In fact, Wolfson's erudite work traces practically all of Spinoza's thought as either dependent on, or opposed to, the medieval Aristotelian thinkers who wrote in Hebrew, Latin, and Arabic—men like Avicenna, Averroes, Maimonides, and others. Of course, the paramount influence of Aristotle is presupposed. He claims that it is only when these influences are given their due importance that the system of Descartes is accorded its proper place. Nevertheless, the more common classification of Spinoza as a Cartesian may be accepted in the sense that in working out his own system, he consistently employed the geometrical method of the latter, although he frequently contradicted Descartes even in basic concepts. He lived in almost complete retirement, earning his living by grinding lenses. He took no active part in any movement of the time and watched life as a detached observer.

Spinoza wrote his celebrated, posthumously published *Ethic* in conformity with the dictum that philosophy can demonstrate its propositions with as great a logical cogency and irresistible clarity as the geometrical axioms of Euclid. But if he follows the Cartesian method in this matter, he departs from Descartes in the basic concept of the source of our knowledge; instead of starting with the certainty of his own mind and deriving the concept of God therefrom, Spinoza begins with the certainty of God and derives all the rest from that axiom. To put it in another way, Spinoza denies the fundamental Cartesian dualism—the radical difference between thought and matter—in favor

[23] Harry A. Wolfson, *The Philosophy of Spinoza* (Cambridge, Mass.: Harvard University Press, 1934), 2 vols. Also Richard P. McKeon, *The Philosophy of Spinoza* (New York: Longmans, Green and Co., Inc., 1928), esp. Chapter I.

of radical monism. He postulates as his starting point God as the sole existing substance, of which thought and matter, as well as an infinite number of other modes, are attributes. In this way he indeed escapes the irreconcilable contradictions of Cartesian dualism, in which the two realities, mind and matter, exist side by side but cannot interact. Spinoza's God, then, represents the ultimate essence of all things, and in Him all contradictions are reconciled. "By God," he writes, "I understand Being absolutely infinite, that is to say, substance consisting of infinite attributes, each one of which expresses eternal and infinite essence." [24] This basic presupposition is affirmed as a self-evident axiom of rationality; Spinoza speaks of no necessity of doubting all things before one may attain to a certainty of knowledge. For him it is a rationally necessary assumption that substance exists. He defines substance as that "which is in itself and is conceived through itself"; *i.e.*, its existence is necessarily included in its essence.[25] To deny existence to substance would be to affirm that nothing exists—which is manifestly absurd. Or to put it in another way, just as a triangle must have three sides, the sum of which equals two right angles, and there can be no such thing as a square triangle or a square circle, so the existence of God is necessarily implied in His essence. Moreover, there is only one substance, outside of which nothing can be conceived. Spinoza calls this substance God, although one must not jump to the conclusion that this God is the God of Abraham and Isaac, or the Father of Jesus Christ.

Thus Spinoza has no difficulty in asserting the existence of God, and no need of resorting to any of the traditional proofs for His existence. Nevertheless, he did retain the proof that the idea of God is immediately, intuitively given. Hence, no other proof is needed; so that ". . . while His essence is unknown, the fact of His existence, that He is a real being and not a mere figment of our imagination, is known to us—and it is known by a direct and immediate kind of knowledge which of all the kinds of knowledge is the most valid." [26] Essentially, Spinoza's presupposition being *a priori*, and resting upon the rationality of the cosmos, it is closest to the ontological arguments of Augustine and Anselm; the assumption of a reasonable universe *already contains and presupposes* an admission that Reason exists in the universe. Hence the ontological proof of the existence of Reason or Truth. It only remains to call this Reason or God. Spinoza calls it God.

[24] W. Hale White, *Ethic of Benedict de Spinoza* (Oxford: The Clarendon Press, 1943, 4th ed.), I, def. vi. By permission.
[25] *Ibid.*, def. iii.
[26] Harry A. Wolfson, *op. cit.*, II, p. 353.

Having established the *a priori* starting point, Spinoza proceeds to dispose of the medieval concepts of God's non-materiality as well as of Cartesian dualism by designating mind and matter (or as he called the latter, extension) attributes of the divine substance. To be sure, God is not limited to these two attributes: since He is infinite, His attributes are likewise infinite. But these two—thought and matter—are the only ones apprehended by our knowledge. To us human beings only these two are accessible. "Thought is an attribute of God, or God is a thinking thing." [27] But likewise, "Extension is an attribute of God, or God is an extended thing." [28] It follows therefore that God is both thought and matter, both mind and body. The ascription of materiality (although not corporeality) to God is the daring *new* aspect of Spinoza's thought. The finite manifestation of God's attributes are called modes, of which man is one. God then is the immanent cause of all existent things; they depend on Him not only for the beginning of their existence, but for its continuation as well. Moreover, all things are determined by God, so that nothing in nature is contingent. There is no such thing as free cause. In fact, God Himself is determined by His own nature, and should not be thought of as possessing "free will." "Hence it follows . . . that God does not act from freedom of the will." [29] All that exists, therefore, exists necessarily and cannot exist otherwise than it does.

This concept of God clearly reveals the pantheistic nature of Spinoza's thought. God is Nature—*Deus sive Natura*. God is identified with the universe, for He is its immanent cause, and does not transcend it: "God is the immanent and not the transitive cause of things." [30] He is not the Creator producing the world *ex nihilo*, or in the sense that He willed to create the sort of universe as He pleased. Spinoza's chief argument against the notion of God as creator is that since He *is* material, He does not need to create matter. Furthermore, since God is eternal, the universe is likewise being produced eternally by His inner necessity. Natural laws therefore necessarily are what they are and from all eternity cannot be otherwise. "All things have been predetermined by Him, not indeed from freedom of will or from absolute good pleasure, but from His absolute nature or infinite power." [31] This then is determinism with a vengeance: the universe governed by

[27] White, *op. cit.*, II, prop. 1.
[28] *Ibid.*, II, prop. 2.
[29] *Ibid.*, I, prop. xxxii, cor. 1.
[30] *Ibid.*, I, prop. xviii.
[31] *Ibid.*, I, appendix, p. 38.

inexorable, unchangeable laws from which no deviation is possible. "Since I have thus shown, with greater clearness than that of noonday light, that in things there is absolutely nothing by virtue of which they can be called contingent . . . their fixed character has been proved." [32] Accordingly, all notion of free will, whether in God or man, must be rejected. Spinoza thus ". . . explains the orderly and seemingly purposive actions of man as determined by an eternal law of necessity. . . . It is this eternal necessity, and not will and its free exercise, that makes man's actions . . . assume a tendency toward a certain end as if guided by an intellect and carried out by a will." [33]

Moreover, there is no teleology in Spinoza's system, no "far-off divine event to which all creation tends." ". . . nature does nothing for the sake of an end, for that eternal and infinite Being whom we call God or Nature acts by the same necessity by which He exists; . . . Since, therefore, He exists for no end, He acts for no end." [34] It is we, human beings, who delude ourselves into thinking that we aim at an end. We interpret—although mistakenly—all things from the point of view of our advantage, and regard natural objects, yea, even God, as means toward an end. "This is the reason why each man has devised for himself, out of his own brain, a different mode of worshipping God, so that God might love him above others, and direct all nature to the service of his blind cupidity and insatiable avarice." [35] But a man of reason—man informed by science—knows better. Or does he?

However, if all things are necessarily what they are, how is it possible for man to pursue a purpose in a purposeless universe? Does not this imply freedom which Spinoza so strenuously denies? And furthermore, if man acts toward an end, does he not regard this end as good? But how can there be a distinction between good and evil in a universe governed by necessity? Spinoza lamely affirms that these terms indicate no positive quality in things themselves, but are mere modes of thinking which men form from comparing one thing with another. Nevertheless, he retains the terms, although he redefines them: by "good" he means things that are useful to us, and by "evil" the opposite.[36] And yet, he is genuinely interested in providing an ethic whereby a reasonable man could conduct himself to the greatest advantage. The amazing thing about the whole undertaking is that Spinoza proceeds as if man *could*

[32] *Ibid.*, I, prop. xxxiii, schol. 1.
[33] Wolfson, *op. cit.*, II, pp. 338-39.
[34] White, *op. cit.*, IV, preface, pp. 177-78.
[35] *Ibid.*, I, appendix, p. 40.
[36] *Ibid.*, IV, def. I and II.

choose one way or another, that is to say, as if he possessed ethical freedom, a postulate which he vigorously denies. Thus, for instance, in *A Political Treatise* written shortly before his death he writes:

> . . . I have looked upon passions, such as love, hatred, anger, envy, ambition, pity, and the other perturbations of the mind, not in the light of vices of human nature, but as properties, just as pertinent to it, as are heat, cold, storm, thunder, and the like to the nature of the atmosphere, which phenomena, though inconvenient, are yet necessary, and have fixed causes, by means of which we endeavour to understand their nature, and the mind has just as much pleasure in viewing them aright, as in knowing such things as flatter the senses.[37]

In view of statements like these—and after all that has been said of the necessity under which God and man act; after what has been said of man as a mode of divine attributes of mind and matter—it seems almost incredible that Spinoza should still undertake to construct an ethical system which must basically rest on the assumption of moral freedom. This appears to me as a fundamental and insurmountable contradiction which vitiates his whole system.

Nevertheless, Spinoza proceeds to elaborate his ethics, which is "natural" rather than hedonistic or eudaemonian. His discussion of "passions" in the fourth part of his *Ethic* often reveals an acute observation and keen knowledge of human nature. "Passions" are defined as "inadequate ideas," whatever that means. He distinguishes the various kinds of ethical conduct and concludes that "we do not know that anything is certainly good or evil excepting that which actually conduces to understanding, or which can prevent us from understanding." [38] And the *summum bonum* of life? Spinoza professes that "the highest good of the mind is the knowledge of God [understand, Nature], and the highest virtue of the mind is to know God." [39] And since God is free from passions and unaffected by either pain or pleasure, and therefore neither loves nor hates, the highest human emotion in respect of Him is the "*amor Dei intellectualis.*" [40] "He who loves God cannot strive that God should love him in return." It is not for hope of reward or for fear of punishment that men should love God, but simply because He is the supreme reality worthy of love and devotion.

---

[37] A Political Treatise, in R. H. M. Elwes, tr., *The Chief Works of Benedict de Spinoza* (London: G. Bell & Sons, Ltd., 1917-19), I, pp. 288-89. By permission.

[38] White, *op. cit.*, IV, prop. xxvii.

[39] *Ibid.*, IV, prop. xxviii.

[40] *Ibid.*, V, prop. xix.

In summing up Spinoza's views, let us first of all note that all the essentials of modern naturalism and philosophical determinism are already present in them. From that point of view, he is one of the most important of modern thinkers who has contributed mightily to the present-day secularism. His system is essentially Stoic morality, but without its presuppositions, for it is predicated on rationalistic pantheism. Despite that, it is incomprehensible how Bertrand Russell could say of Spinoza that "ethically he is supreme." [41] In further stages of secularization of Western culture, the term "God" has dropped out altogether and the alternative term "Nature" has been adopted exclusively. In this sense, Goethe, the greatest of Spinoza's disciples, concluded that he is no longer a Christian. [42] Spinoza himself certainly was not an atheist, although his religious views were incompatible with any of the historic creeds, even with that of Judaism. Nevertheless, his ecstatic disciples, such as Novalis, conferred upon him the epithet of "the God-intoxicated man." Yet the sober judgment of Etienne Gilson, with the exception of the ascription of atheism, is justified: "A religious atheist, Spinoza was truly inebriated with his philosophical God." [43]

[41] Bertrand Russell, *A History of Western Philosophy*. Copyright 1945 by Bertrand Russell. (New York: Simon and Schuster, Inc.), p. 369. By permission.
[42] Goethe in his letter to J. K. Lavater, quoted in Erich Frank, *op. cit.*, p. 20, note 10.
[43] Gilson, *op. cit.*, p. 102.

# 3

# Lockean Empiricism—Reason Faces Outward

## Introduction: Thomas Hobbes

English empiricism derives principally from Sir Francis Bacon. He repudiated the Aristotelian deductive method in favor of the inductive, which in the end became the scientific, method. Among his most influential pupils no one attained to greater influence and notoriety than Thomas Hobbes (1588-1679) who converted Baconian empiricism into a thoroughgoing materialism. By way of introduction to English empiricism we may take a brief look at Hobbes.

For him, nothing exists but matter-in-motion: all reality

is corporeal, that is to say, body; and hath the dimensions of magnitude, namely, length, breadth, and depth; also every part of body, is likewise body, and hath the like dimensions; and consequently every part of the universe, is body, and that which is not body, is no part of the universe: and because the universe is all, that which is no part of it, is *nothing*.[1]

[1] Sir William Molesworth, ed., *The English Works of Thomas Hobbes of Malmsbury* (London: J. Bohn, 1839-45), III, p. 672.

Accordingly, man is wholly material, and his behavior is mechanical. There can be no intelligible talk of any spiritual part of him, and hence no free will. His conduct is strictly determined.

Nevertheless, human nature is dynamic, driven everlastingly by desires. Men are possessed of an "insatiate self-assertion, a restless desire of power after power." Basically, therefore, man is wholly selfish. Hobbes rejects the Aristotelian idea that man is by nature a social animal. Being selfish, men are naturally at war with each other. Thus war is man's natural condition: men are either wolves toward each other, or lambs and wolves. The strong dominate the weak. Dog eats dog. The law of the jungle, the survival of the fittest, as Darwin expressed it later, is the natural condition of humankind. Men go to war for self-defense, self-glory, or prey.

Such being the natural state of society, security, peace, and civilization have no chance of establishing themselves permanently. Periods of peace are only truces between wars, during which both sides are nursing their resources for future conflicts. Consequently, industry languishes because no one can be certain of security. All live in fear and dread.

The only way man's anarchy and rapacity may be curbed is by the establishment of the supreme power of the state. This is the familiar counsel of Machiavelli. It can be accomplished only by a voluntary surrender by each man of his original anarchic freedom; accordingly, Hobbes propounds the theory which later goes under the name of "the social contract."

> Anarchical aggressive freedom must be utterly surrendered before the security—within limits—can be attained. So it is that men come together, cancel their insecurity by mutually renouncing their anarchical strivings after power, and vest all their wills in one supreme authority, Leviathan, constituting him their lawgiver, sovereign, and plenipotentiary irrevocable.[2]

The social contract once adopted, the Leviathan becomes absolute in his power, in no wise accountable to his subjects. This is *statism*. The sovereign may be an individual—a king—or an oligarchy, or democracy. In any case, he possesses absolute power of legislation and administration. Such being the case, private judgment, political, moral, or religious autonomy is the chief cause of sedition. The state must possess total power over the bodies and minds of its subjects. The

[2] Radoslav A. Tsanoff, *The Moral Ideals of Our Civilization* (New York: E. P. Dutton & Co., Inc., 1942), p. 157. By permission.

latter, on the other hand, must render absolute obedience to the commands of the state. The Church, too, is merely a servant of the state, and is in duty bound to perform the state's bidding. Its chief task is to keep its members in subjection to the state, as if the latter's commands were of divine authority. It is therefore for the state to decide what sort of organization and even the doctrine the Church is to have and teach.

## John Locke, the Founder of English Empiricism

John Locke (1632-1704) was born in a Puritan home, his father, an attorney, having joined the Parliamentary party during the Civil War. He was sent to the Westminster School, where his studies were confined to the classics. When he wrote on education later in life he criticized the preponderance of language studies during his schooling. In 1652 he was elected to junior studentship at Christ College and for the next thirty years lived at Oxford. This college was then headed by John Owen, an Independent divine and an adherent of Oliver Cromwell, but it was tolerant in its attitude. Locke took his M.A. there. When the Restoration came in 1660, he welcomed it along with most other Englishmen. He secured the position of a tutor, but the post was not lucrative enough to enable him to marry. He turned to medical studies, but he never practiced as a professional physician. Instead, his medical studies introduced him to natural sciences, which he pursued henceforth. He became a friend of Sir Robert Boyle and Isaac Newton. In philosophy, he was influenced by Descartes, although he likewise adhered to the Gassendists and to their modification of Cartesianism.

In 1666 Locke met Lord Ashley, afterwards the Earl of Shaftesbury, and became his personal physician and his adviser in political and cultural affairs. Under these circumstances, he moved to London. Since Lord Ashley was one of the founders and promoters of the colony of Carolina, Locke had a hand in the preparation of the Constitution for this colonization project. He was elected fellow of the Royal Society in 1668. When in 1672 Ashley was raised to earldom and later appointed to the office of the Lord High Chancellor, Locke was likewise advanced. But when his noble patron joined the opposition to the Court, Locke went to Holland where he met Philip van Limborch, a leader of the Arminian Remonstrants and therefore theologically a liberal. He was greatly influenced by him. When James II came to the throne (1685), Locke was listed among the traitors and consequently went into hiding.

In 1686 Locke's *Epistola de tolerantia* was published in Latin, and was translated into English three years later. Since the Dutch William, with his English wife, Mary, had ascended the English throne the year previously, Locke returned home. His views became very influential during the new regime, which granted toleration to dissenters the same year that Locke's theories of religious tolerance were published. He made contacts with the Cambridge Platonists—Ralph Cudworth and others—and accepted many of their ideas.

But his great work, which placed him in the forefront of the new philosophical movement—empiricism—appeared in 1690 under the title *Essay concerning Human Understanding*. He had worked on it for the past nineteen years. He tells us that he conceived the work as the result of a meeting held in his room with five or six friends, at which were discussed principles of morality and revealed religion; but they were completely baffled by "the difficulties that rose on every side." They concluded ". . . that before we set ourselves upon inquiries of that nature, it was necessary to examine our own abilities and see what *objects* our understandings were, or were not, fitted to deal with." [3] In applying himself first of all to this problem, Locke bases all knowledge upon experience (hence empiricism), which in turn is made up of sensations, demonstrations, and intuitions.[4] This is the basic tenet adopted by Locke apparently in opposition to Descartes' concept of innate ideas, although intuitions come close to them. By sensation he means a representational idea of the object we perceive; in other words, "Since the mind, in all its thoughts and reasonings, hath no other immediate object but its own ideas, which it alone does or can contemplate, it is evident that our knowledge is only conversant about them." [5] The mind then is at first a *"tabula rasa"* in the true Aristotelian sense, for the latter also spoke of the mind of infants as "a tablet not yet written on." [6] On this blank tablet sensations are registered in the same passive manner that a projector casts moving pictures on a screen. Accordingly, there is nothing in understanding that was not first in

[3] John Locke, *An Essay concerning Human Understanding* (Oxford: The Clarendon Press, 1894), I, p. 9. By permission.
[4] R. I. Aaron, *John Locke* (New York: Oxford University Press, 1937), p. 85. By permission.
[5] Locke, *An Essay*, II, p. 168.
[6] Aristotle's *De anima*, Kenelin Foster and Silvester Humphies, trs. (New Haven: Yale University Press, 1951), p. 420.

sensation—another Aristotelian principle. The sensory impressions—figure, solidity, mobility—are combined by the mind into ideas: simple ideas are fundamental, but may be combined further into complex ideas by relating one with another. Thus simple ideas are passively received by the mind; the complex are made by it. In asserting the power of the mind to combine ideas, Locke goes beyond mere sensation and adds to it reflection. "These two are the fountains of knowledge, from whence all the ideas we have, or can naturally have, do spring." [7] In the functioning of reflection, Locke includes thinking, reasoning, believing, willing—in short, everything that is not given in sensation.

But if we know only our ideas, i.e., representations of whatever it is that we sense, do we know the external object that causes them and is presumably their source? It would appear that we do not. Nevertheless, Locke shrank from the radical consistency of such of his followers as Berkeley and Hume and refused to deny the reality of knowledge of external objects. In fact, he taught that knowledge consists "of a conformity between our ideas and the reality of things." But is this not begging the question? Since we know nothing aside from the sensations in our minds, how can we know "the reality of things"? He merely asserts that we suppose their existence, but do not know their substance.[8] He furthermore distinguishes between "primary qualities" —extension, figure, solidity, number, and mobility—which all objects must possess and retain no matter what changes they otherwise undergo; and "secondary qualities"—color, sound, temperature, odor, and taste which are products of our own minds. This on reflection proves quite confusing; if the primary qualities are necessarily possessed by the object, why not the secondary? Or if the secondary qualities are produced by our minds, why not the primary? How can an object really have a shape but not color? It appears to us as possessing both.

But even so we are not yet quite clear what constitutes the act of knowing. For since it is affirmed that mind compounds simple ideas into complex, it is inaccurate to say that the *mind* does anything unless one means that there exists a personal self, an *ego*, which uses the mind as an instrument. Locke fully admitted this obvious implication. In fact, he followed Descartes in asserting that besides the sensations and reflection, we possess an intuition of our own existence which needs no further proof. "I think, I reason, I feel pleasure and pain: can any of these be more evident to me than my own existence?" [9] But although

---

[7] Locke, *An Essay*, I, p. 122.
[8] *Ibid.*, I, p. 230.
[9] *Ibid.*, II, p. 305.

in this way he sometimes admits the existence of a "substance" that is not a material object—hence something *not* perceived by our senses —and therefore he calls it "intuition"; at other times he denies it, and calls it only a "supposition" of something of which we do not know the actual ground.[10] Thus he is at best inconsistent or self-contradictory as to the existence of a personal self capable of using the mind, for on another occasion he asserts that thought is the function of the mind. If it were so, then the terms "mind" and "personal self" would be, to all intents and purposes, indistinguishable one from the other.

There remains still another reality which is not apprehended in sensation—namely God. Locke was particularly deeply concerned with religious questions toward the end of his life, and wrote several treatises dealing with this subject. Although he ventures the opinion that God's existence may be grasped by reason, just as Thomas Aquinas did, His nature or essence is altogether beyond our rational powers. ". . . We more certainly know that there is a God than that there is anything else without us." [11] In fact, in comparison with the knowledge derived from our senses that "reaches very little farther than our experience," our knowledge of God is much more certain; he calls it "demonstrative" knowledge, and asserts that in comparison with sensory experience it is greatly to be preferred. Thus he makes a sharp distinction between "knowledge based on sensory experience" and "faith" resting on reason and intuition. But although Locke agrees with Descartes in asserting that we know God's existence by intuition or faith, he does not follow the latter in basing his proof on the ontological argument. Instead, he relies on the cosmological proof: since we ourselves exist and the world of objects exists, these facts must have been produced by an intelligent Being. Along with Paul he holds that "the invisible things of him from the creation of the world are clearly seen, being perceived through the things that are made, even his eternal power and divinity." [12] But since the lesser—the human mind—cannot comprehend or contain the greater—the Divine Being—Locke stoutly defends the orthodox doctrine of revelation, although he limits the defense to reasonable proofs. "The bare testimony of divine revelation is the highest certainty . . . whether the things proposed agree or disagree with common experience, and the ordinary course of things . . ." Faith, then, is "an assent to revelation." *"Only we must be sure that it be a divine revelation, and that we understand it right."* [13] "Whatever

[10] *Ibid.*, I, pp. 391, 396.
[11] *Ibid.*, II, pp. 310 ff.
[12] Romans 1:20.
[13] Locke, *An Essay*, II, p. 383.

God hath revealed is certainly true: no doubt can be made of it. This is the proper object of faith; but whether it be a *divine* revelation or no, reason must judge; . . . . *Nothing that is contrary to, and inconsistent with the clear and self-evident dictates of reason, has a right to be urged or assented to as a matter of faith, wherein reason hath nothing to do.*" [14] We are, consequently, back at natural reason that vouches for the truth of divine revelation. When the latter contradicts what we know by reason, we must reject it. In other words, revelation must be reasonable.

In 1695 Locke published anonymously his treatise on *The Reasonableness of Christianity as delivered in the Scriptures*, in which he enlarges on his idea of the essence of Christianity. One immediately senses his affinity to the Deistic assumption that historic Christianity has accumulated many nonessential doctrines and therefore must be purged of these accretions. But Locke is still sufficiently unemancipated from the textproof method of the authoritarian orthodoxy to resort to it in proving his own position. He reduces the Christian gospel to rather meager proportions: in the first place, "The law of faith, then, in short, is for every one to believe what God requires him to believe . . . [i.e.,] that believing on the Son, is the believing that Jesus was the Messiah; giving credit to the miracles he did, and the profession he made of himself." [15] This includes also the miracle of His rising from the dead. Our Lord's messiahship is proved then by His miracles, by the prophecies concerning Him, and by His direct claims. But Locke does not define his connotation of either of the terms "Christ" or "Messiah." Moreover, since he omits the doctrine of the Trinity from his own enumeration of the reasonable Christian tenets, and attacks it in his denial of the Athanasian Creed, it must be assumed that he did not accept as basic the Incarnation of the divine Christ in the human Jesus. He employs the term "son of God" in connection with Jesus Christ, but in the same way as he use it about Adam. He finds no reason for asserting Christ's pre-existence as Logos, or His consubstantiality with the Father. Nor does he hold the doctrine of Atonement in its historic orthodox sense.

This reduced compass of the Christian faith naturally met with denunciation from those for whom the faith included many more *essential* doctrines, and who called his merely an "historical" faith. On

---

[14] *Ibid.*, II, pp. 425-26.
[15] John Locke, *The Reasonableness of Christianity*, I. T. Ramsey, ed. (Stanford, California: Stanford University Press, 1958), p. 32. By permission.

the other hand, the Deists hailed it with gleeful satisfaction. Locke defended himself vigorously against the former by writing:

> If they please to call the believing that which Our Saviour and his apostles preached and proposed alone to be believed, an historical faith, they have their liberty, but they must have a care how they deny it to be a justifying or saving faith, when Our Saviour and his apostles have declared it so to be, and taught no other which men should receive, and whereby they should be made believers unto eternal life; unless they can so far make bold with Our Saviour, for the sake of their beloved systems, as to say, that he forgot what he came into the world for; and that he and his apostles did not instruct people right in the way and mysteries of salvation. . . . And I challenge them to shew, that there was any other doctrine, upon their assent to which, or disbelief of it, men were pronounced believers or unbelievers; and accordingly received into the Church of Christ . . . or else kept out of it.[16]

But as Locke himself states, besides the required belief in the Messiahship of Jesus Christ, a Christian is required to repent and live in accordance with the new ethic revealed by Christ. This ethical teaching is comprised, in the simplest and completest manner, in the Sermon on the Mount. In this sermon Christ teaches the laws of His kingdom, and commands His disciples that "they should be exemplary in good works." [17] Christian life is as simple as that! Let the Christian merely observe the precepts of the Sermon on the Mount and he will be recognized by Locke as a true and genuine member of Christ's Church! One is astounded by the inadequacy of Locke's comprehension of the Sermon, an inadequacy clearly revealed by his remark that in the Sermon our Lord ". . . not only confirmed the moral law; and clearing it from the corrupt glories of the scribes and Pharisees, he enforced it with unspeakable rewards and punishments in another world . . ." [18] Did Locke really expect that any Christian could fully observe the "new moral law," including the precept "Be ye perfect, as your Father in heaven is perfect"?

Locke then summarizes his understanding of the essential and rational Christianity as follows: "These two, faith and repentance, *i.e.*, believing Jesus to be the Messiah, and a good life, are the indispensable conditions of the new covenant, to be performed by all those who would obtain eternal life." [19]

---

[16] *Ibid.*, pp. 43-44.
[17] *Ibid.*, p. 48.
[18] *Ibid.*, pp. 48-49.
[19] *Ibid.*, pp. 44-45.

What, then, was Locke's relation to the Deists? Aaron, in his book, argues that he was not a Deist, although he shared many of their presuppositions, and the Deists delighted in claiming him as their own. He points out, however, that the more advanced and typical of the Deists —Toland, Collins, Tindal, and Wollaston—repudiated divine revelation altogether and consequently rejected "the mysterious and supernatural elements in the Christian religion." [20] Locke, on the other hand, despite his latitudinarianism, rationalism, and moralism, and, toward the end of his life, his intimate friendship with Collins, retained both the revelational character of Christianity and belief in some miracles—including Christ's own miracles.

On the other hand, his most recent biographer, Maurice Cranston, regards Locke's argument as "plainly Unitarian or Socinian": but

> he persisted in saying that he was not. . . . *The Reasonableness of Christianity* is a Unitarian or Socinian book in everything but name, and it is, in a way, odd that Locke, who was so scrupulous about the proper usage of words, should have failed to admit it. He did not want the bad name of Unitarian or Socinian, and so he managed to persuade himself that he was not a Unitarian or Socinian. [21]

This was also the judgment of Locke's contemporary opponents, particularly John Edwards and Bishop Stillingfleet, who branded his views as clearly Socinian. [22] This led to a protracted controversy on Locke's part with both of these writers. Cranston thinks that Stillingfleet "had a sound case to make, but he did not make it well." [23]

Our further concern with Locke has to do with an aspect of his lifework which has exerted a tremendous and most beneficial influence on the future, namely, his advocacy of religious toleration. His earliest treatise on the subject—as has already been mentioned—was a Latin letter to his Dutch friend, van Limborch, published in 1686. Three years later an enlarged English edition was anonymously published under the title, *A Letter concerning Toleration*, and its principles may be clearly discerned in the Act of Toleration issued by William and Mary in the same year. These principles then influenced or practically formulated the church-state relationships in most democratic countries, the earliest among them being the newly created United States of America. An almost incomprehensible feature of this and

---

[20] Aaron, *op. cit.*, p. 302.
[21] Maurice W. Cranston, *John Locke, a Biography* (New York: The Macmillan Co., 1957; London: Longmans, Green & Co., Ltd., 1957), p. 390. By permission.
[22] *Ibid.*, pp. 412 ff., 429 ff.
[23] *Ibid.*, p. 413.

other of Locke's idiosyncracies is his denial of the authorship of this work, in which he stoutly persisted almost to the end of his life. He even denied knowledge of its English translator, a Unitarian by the name of William Popple.[24]

Locke asserts in this treatise, first of all, the principle of separation of church and state. Civil government exists for the purpose of "procuring, preserving and advancing civil interests." These comprise "the just possession of the things belonging to this life." The magistrate is armed with authority, backed by force, for an equitable administration of ordered society where each citizen is assured of his property rights. This is his whole duty. "All civil power, right, and dominion is bounded and confined to the only care of promoting these things; and that it neither can nor ought in any manner to be extended to the salvation of souls." [25] The reasons given for this limitation are as follows: (1) true religion consists of an inward persuasion, and cannot be imposed by force; (2) the magistrate's powers, however, consist only of outward force; (3) furthermore, men must follow in religious matters the light of their own reason, not the dictates of their civil governors. This then is the total rejection, on Locke's part, of the hitherto dominant principle of *"cujus regio, ejus religio."* It is among the earliest philosophical assertions that the individual has the right and duty of deciding his religious belief for himself.

What then is the Church? "A church," Locke writes, "I take to be a voluntary society of men, joining themselves together of their own accord, in order to the public worshipping of God, in such a manner as they judge acceptable to him, and effectual for salvation of their souls." [26] Here is a definition of the Church—although with an important modification—held long before by the Anabaptists and later the Congregationalists, cast in a philosophical terminology by an Anglican! How many "wars of religion" would have been prevented, had it been accepted sooner!

Locke then amplifies his concept by asserting that the Church constitutes a free social group: "Nobody is born a member of any church," and nobody is bound to join any particular church (although Locke does *not* say that a man need not join *any* church, i.e., remain non-confessional). Moreover, a man is free to leave one church and join another, if he so wishes.

---

[24] *Ibid.*, pp. 320–21.
[25] A Letter concerning Toleration, in *The Works of John Locke*, VI (London, 1812), pp. 10 ff.
[26] *Ibid.*, pp. 13 ff.

This does not mean that a member of a given church can do as he pleases: every church has the right to adopt its own rules and regulations, and its members must either submit to them or leave. But he denies that the Church must necessarily comprise some such requirement as the episcopacy. "Let them show me the edict by which Christ has imposed that law upon his church," he challenges.[27] Accordingly, Locke counsels that no more be required by way of ecclesiastical regulations than what "the Holy Spirit in the Holy Scriptures declared, in express words, as necessary to salvation."

On the other hand, if the Church finds it necessary to discipline its members on account of an infraction of its regulations, this must not exceed the maximum penalty of disfellowshipping—i.e., excommunicating—the offender. "This is the last and utmost force of ecclesiastical authority; no other punishment can thereby be inflicted, than that the relation ceasing between the body and the member which is cut off, the person so condemned ceases to be a part of that church."[28] Accordingly, excommunication does not affect the offender's civil status, his goods, or his rights. Moreover, "no private person has any right in any manner to prejudice another person in his civil enjoyments, because he is of another church or religion."[29] "No-body therefore, in fine, neither single persons, nor churches, nay, nor even commonwealths, have any just title to invade the civil rights and worldly goods of each other, upon pretense of religion."[30]

Not only has the magistrate no right to take upon himself the cure of souls, but he has no responsibility for it either. All men are free to seek religious guidance where they please. "Shall it be provided by law," Locke mockingly asks,

> that they must consult none but roman physicians . . . ? What, shall no potion, no broth, be taken, but what is prepared either in the Vatican, suppose, or in a Geneva shop?" "Why am I beaten and ill-used by others, because, perhaps, I wear not buskins; because my hair is not of the right cut; because, perhaps, I have not been dipt in the right fashion; . . . because I avoid to keep company with some travellers that are less grave, and others that are more sour than they ought to be, or in fine, because I follow a guide that either is, or is not, cloathed in white and crowned with a mitre?"[31]

[27] *Ibid.*, p. 14.
[28] *Ibid.*, p. 16.
[29] *Ibid.*, p. 17.
[30] *Ibid.*, p. 20.
[31] *Ibid.*, p. 24.

But are pagans and idolaters to be granted freedom? Indeed, Locke replies. For if the American Indians should be deprived of their rights on account of their paganism, why not a dissenting Christian or Jew in England?

The same rule applies to doctrine: the magistrate has no right to prohibit any religious doctrine that contradicts no civil law.

> If a roman catholic believes that to be really the body of Christ, which another man calls bread, he does no injury thereby to his neighbor. If a jew does not believe in the New Testament to be the Word of God, he does not alter thereby anything in men's civil rights. If a heathen doubt of both Testaments, he is not therefore to be punished as a pernicious citizen. . . . I readily grant, that these opinions are false and absurd. But the business of laws is not to provide for the truth of opinions, but for the safety and security of the commonwealth.[32]

Nevertheless, there are some exceptions to these general principles: no opinion destructive of general good may be tolerated by magistrates. Such opinions as that "faith is not to be kept with heretics"; and that "kings excommunicated forfeit their crowns and kingdom"; or that "those that will not own and teach the duty of tolerating all men in matters of mere religion," [33] none of such can be permitted. Likewise, if membership in a church implies that its members "ipso facto deliver themselves up to the protection and service of another prince," it is not to be tolerated. For it would entail foreign jurisdiction in the country, which is not lawful. And lastly, no one who denies the existence of God is to be tolerated.[34]

Even more important for the Anglo-American culture are Locke's ideas bearing on the political and economic organization of society; for both England and America are still predominantly influenced by them. His treatise, *Concerning Civil Government*, gives the best statement of his views on this subject. He defines civil government as power:

> Political power, then, I take to be a right of making laws with penalties of death, and consequently all less penalties, for the regulating and preserving of property, and of employing the force of the community in the execution of such laws, and in the defense of the commonwealth from foreign injury, and all this only for the public good.[35]

The revolutionary aspect of his thought consists in Locke's recognition of the people as the source of all political power, reminding one of Marsiglio of Padua's *Defensor pacis*. All human governments are therefore derived from, and exist by, the consent of the people. He restates in its essentials the Hobbesian theory of primitive society—which was later presented by Rousseau under the name of the Social Contract—by picturing it as holding all property in common, with the exception of that produced by the individual's own labor. However later, when men produced more than they could consume, they invented the use of money as a medium of exchange. It was in such a wise that some gathered more wealth than others and government then became necessary for the protection of the men of property against the rapacity of their fellows. But by consenting to this new arrangement, each man placed himself in subjection to government.

What then are the chief aims of political societies? Locke defines them as the preservation of the lives, liberties, and possessions of its members:

> For the preservation of property being the end of government, and that for which men enter into society, it necessarily supposes and requires that the people should have property, without which they must be supposed to lose that by entering into society, which was the end for which they entered into it, too gross an absurdity for any man to own.[36]

Whenever a government fails in these ends, it becomes a tyranny, and the people ". . . have a right to resume their original liberty . . ."[37] But who shall judge as to when a government becomes tyrannous? The people, Locke answers. It takes no great insight to recognize in this theory the source of the ideas which inspired both the American and the French Revolutions and created modern democracies.

Accordingly, the influence of the Lockean philosophy, despite its evident weaknesses, has been enormous and it is difficult to over-estimate it. His empiricism has exercised a formative influence on all subsequent development of philosophy, while his religious and political thought has been nothing short of revolutionary.

[36] *Ibid.*, p. 459.
[37] *Ibid.*, p. 494.

## George Berkeley and Immaterialism

George Berkeley (1685-1753), born at Dysert Castle, County of Kilkenny, Ireland, was educated at Trinity College, Dublin. After graduating, he remained there as tutor. Later he traveled, joining in London the circle of Steele, Addison, and Swift. In the course of his career he became Bishop of Cloyne in Ireland (1734-52) and may perhaps be remembered by Americans for his three-year residence in Rhode Island. He was deeply interested in utilizing Lockean empiricism in defense of orthodox Christianity. Along with Bishop Butler, he should be counted among the principal apologists for Christianity against the Deists and skeptics. His chief apologetic work, *Alciphron, or the Minute Philosopher*,[38] was written at Newport, R.I. (in 1731) and published the next year. It is in the form of a dialogue, wherein the author only thinly disguises the names of the skeptics and Deists against whom he polemicizes: Bernard Mandeville, author of the exceedingly popular *The Fable of the Bees, or Private Vices Public Benefit* (1714); Earl of Shaftesbury, whose *Characteristics* (1711) he attacks with more respect, but still with vigor; and particularly Anthony Collins, whose *Discourse on Free Thinking* (1713) he regards as plainly atheistic. But his own philosophical contribution to empiricism was formulated early in his career in his *An Essay toward a New Theory of Vision* (1709),[39] when he was twenty-four years old. Later in life (in 1732), when he republished it, it was attacked by an anonymous writer, and Berkeley thought it worth while to defend the work in his *The Theory of Vision . . . Vindicated and Explained*,[40] where he not only restates, but also expands his argument by incorporating the mature views he had formulated in his *Principles of Human Knowledge* (1710), *Three Dialogues* (1713), and *Alciphron.*

His views of the philosophy of vision lead him to conclude that all we see is our sensation. Corporeal reality is perceived by sight as colors and shapes—distance or third dimension not being included in

[38] *The Works of George Berkeley, Bishop of Cloyne*, A. A. Luce and T. E. Jessop, eds. (Edinburgh: Thomas Nelson and Sons Ltd., 1948 ff.), III, pp. 31-329. By permission.
[39] *Ibid.*, I, pp. 161-239.
[40] *Ibid.*, I, pp. 243-79.

this strictly sensory experience, for these latter are inferred by reason on the basis of experience.[41] Nor do we conclude that the sun is the size of a football, although it may strictly speaking appear so to us; we have learned on the basis of reasoning from experience derived from astronomical considerations that its size must not be judged from visual premises alone. It follows, therefore, that all sensations are mental. Colors, for instance, do not actually exist in the object considered as the mysterious source of sensations, but only in the mind. The object itself is colorless; but by means of light waves of a certain length (I am here following the modern theory, not the Berkeleyan) a corresponding cone or rod in our retina is affected and in turn this organ conveys the stimulus to the visual center in the brain—and lo! we "see red." Helen Keller, for instance, could readily comprehend the notion of "blue" as a number of a wave-length, but that did not help her to comprehend it as color. Thus science, based on sensory data, affords us only an appearance, not the reality itself. It is subjective rather than objective.

In his *Essay* Berkeley restricted his treatment to vision, and even seemed to accept the common notion that so far as touch is concerned, we actually experience the real object we touch. But this was merely a concession to the common prejudice, as he made clear later in his *Vindication*. All our experience is mental; therefore, his basic and distinctive doctrine is that we can perceive only the sensory qualities of objects, not the underlying essential matter independent of the apprehending mind. Nor does he follow Locke in distinguishing between the "primary" and "secondary" qualities of objects. Both are merely an appearance. Thus *esse* is *percipere* and *percipi*—to be is to perceive or be perceived. "The essence of the mind is to perceive, and the essence of the sensible world, which he identifies with the physical or material word, is to be perceived." [42] That being so, what can we possibly mean by a "substance" back of the perceived qualities? And if we do not and cannot perceive it, how can we affirm that it exists? There is no such *substance* as matter; and if there were, we could know nothing about it, since we are equipped with senses capable of apprehending only the sensory qualities. This then is properly designated as the doctrine of immaterialism, although it has often gone under the name of absolute idealism.

Berkeley's doctrine of immaterialism has ever since been the butt

---

of ridicule and derision on the ground that it denies common-sense objective reality. The story is told that when doughty Dr. Samuel Johnson learned of the good bishop's theories, he viciously kicked his toe against the ground, thereby fondly imagining that he proved the substance of the ground. But what he really proved was that he felt a pain in his toe, which Berkeley did not deny. The latter did not assert that the source of our sensations—the object, in common parlance—did not exist, but only that its perception is limited to its sensory qualities. What he denied was the possibility of knowledge of the substance of this object. Nevertheless, the initial "*faux pas*" of Cartesianism is well illustrated by Berkeley's immaterialism, which restricts knowledge to sensation and thus denies the possibility of the object's essential apprehension.

But what has this theory to do with orthodox Christianity and its defense against skeptics and atheists? As for Berkeley, it was basic to such a defense, and he prided himself on the discovery of its apologetic value in proving the existence of God. The full title of his *Theory of Vision . . . Vindicated,* includes the subtitle, *Visual Language shewing the immediate Presence and Providence of a Deity.* But the argument is presented *in extenso* in *Alciphron,* on which we shall draw for its statement. In Dialogue IV (section 6) Berkeley expounds his conception of vision as the "divine language" by which the Author of Nature daily and hourly—yea, every moment of our waking existence—speaks to us by means of sensory signs in essentially the same manner as if He addressed us in oral speech:

> Upon the whole, it seems the proper objects of sight are light and colours, with their several shades and degrees; all of which, being infinitely diversified and combined, form a language wonderfully adapted to suggest and exhibit to us the distances, figures, situations, dimensions, and various qualities of tangible objects; not by similitude, nor yet by inference of necessary connexion, but by the arbitrary imposition of Providence, just as words suggest the things signified by them.[43]

Accordingly, God speaks to the eyes of men continuously; and what is true of the sight, is true of the other senses as well. Therefore, "you have as much reason to think the Universal Agent or God speaks to your eyes as you can have for thinking any particular person speaks to your ears." Moreover, since all objects exist only as they are perceived, and it cannot be supposed that human minds are constantly perceiving

[43] Berkeley, *Works,* III, p. 154.

them, their permanent existence is to be ascribed only to God's mind.[44] Thus, if skeptics deny the existence of God because He cannot be seen or heard, Berkeley replies that visual sensations are the "divine language" to us, and that "God is not far from every one of us; and in Him we live, and move, and have our being." [45]

Berkeley, therefore, regarded his theory as ". . . a new argument of a singular nature in proof of the immediate care and providence of a God, present to our minds, and directing our actions: . . ." [46] Therefore, the visual theory has a religious and doctrinal significance, and its rejection involves also a repudiation of the implied argument for the sensory and immediate proof of the existence of God Who is in constant communication by these means with His creatures.

## David Hume and the Debacle of Lockean Empiricism

President Thomas G. Masaryk of Czechoslovakia, who had formerly been Professor of Philosophy at the Charles University in Prague, used to urge his students to become thoroughly acquainted with Hume. He did so not because he was an admirer of the skeptical philosopher, although he regarded him as the keenest, wittiest, and the most consistent member of the Lockean school, but because the latter's system was such a complete and thoroughgoing *reductio ad absurdum* of Lockean empiricism. Thus, once anyone had observed Hume giving that Humpty Dumpty of empiricism a push from his perch, he could never put him together again. The best exposition and reply to skepticism is a thorough study of Hume, skepticism's principal exponent.

Hume was born in Edinburgh (1711) of landed gentry, although his father was not rich. He was destined by his family for law, but developed an insurmountable aversion for this calling. He studied at the University of Edinburgh, where he busied himself with philosophy and literature. After graduating, he went to France and settled for over two years at La Flèche in Anjou—where Descartes had been educated at the local Jesuit College. Returning to London in 1737, he sought a publisher for his *Treatise of Human Nature*. But first he tried to secure

---

[44] Morris, *op. cit.*, p. 76.
[45] Berkeley, *Works*, III, p. 159.
[46] *Ibid.*, I, p. 255.

Dr. Joseph Butler's recommendation of it. In this he failed, although the two-volume *Treatise* was published in 1738 and the third volume two years later. All were published anonymously, and according to his own somewhat exaggerated statement, "fell dead-born from the press." [47]

The cool, not to say frigid, reception with which his work met naturally hurt and disappointed the young and confessedly ambitious philosopher. It was indeed his greatest production and all his subsequent philosophical writings, with the exception of his three treatises on religion, were no more than a reworking of the *Treatise*. Later he recast the bulky work by modifying its style and omitting some portions, and published it in separate volumes: *An Inquiry concerning the Human Understanding* is essentially Book I of the *Treatise;* other parts likewise appeared as independent works. But since our interest is mainly in *An Inquiry* and the three treatises on religion, we shall turn our attention first of all to *An Inquiry*.

In his epistemology he reduces the mental perceptions to two kinds: impressions and ideas.

> By the term *impression*, then, I mean all our more lively perceptions, when we hear, or see, or feel, or love, or hate, or desire, or will. And impressions are distinguished from ideas, which are the less lively perceptions, of which we are conscious, when we reflect on any of those sensations or movements above mentioned.[48]

The distinction between the two states is that of clearness and intensity. The sensation of cold rain or the enjoyment of a juicy steak are far more vivid and in the latter case more satisfying than a mere recollection of them afterwards. "The most lively thought is still inferior to the dullest sensation."

Thus all our mental states are ultimately derived from sensory impressions or past experience. This is the radical form of his doctrine, although he was not always consistent in applying it. Knowledge then consists of a combination of "the materials afforded us by the senses and experience." That being so, what we really "know" are our mental states, sensations or ideas, not the real entities or "substances" which presumably produce the impressions. "Substance" in this connection would designate some entity back of whatever it is that caused the

---

[47] John Laird, *Hume's Philosophy of Human Nature* (London: Methuen & Co., Ltd., 1932), pp. 7-8.

[48] *The Philosophical Works of David Hume*, IV (Boston: Little, Brown and Co., 1854), p. 16.

sensory image in our minds, whether it be material or spiritual entity. Thence it follows that the notion of "substance" must be rejected. Accordingly, also the notion that truth consists of correspondence or agreement between our impressions or ideas and reality obviously loses all meaning, for we can never know the external cause of our mental states and therefore cannot speak of an agreement or disagreement with it. Hume's doctrine then is strict phenomenalism, an assertion that all we know are our sensations, or at most, appearances of the external world, and never realities or "substances." But since the mind never has anything present to it but its perceptions of objects, it can never experience their connection. The supposition of such a connection is, therefore, unfounded.[49] Thus the Cartesian entities of mind and its ideas, God, and the world of matter, are reduced to nothing more than sensations and ideas. But Berkeley's elaborate and presumably empirical defense of the "spiritual substance" is also summarily denied. Nevertheless, Hume still entertains the notion of God, though inconsistently, when he writes, "The idea of *God*, as meaning an infinitely intelligent, wise, and good Being, arises from reflecting on the operations of our own mind, and augmenting, without limit, those qualities of goodness and wisdom." [50]

But since sensory impressions are the source of all our percepts, the idea of God could not arise in any other way than in a sensory, i.e., material fashion. But God is not material. And if Hume would argue, as he seems to do, that the concept is derived from our ideas—which according to his own definition are only pale recollections of our sensory impression—how could we recollect what we have never experienced? On the basis of Hume's epistemology, the idea of God is obviously impossible.

Continuing the development of his epistemology, Hume writes of the association of ideas. He notes that in experience we find a customary or habitual connection among our ideas, so that common-sense, uncritical individuals regard these associations as necessary and speak of them as laws. He distinguishes three more or less constant interrelationships or associations of ideas: resemblance or contrast, contiguity in time or place, and cause and effect. And although he readily admits that such association of ideas constantly and even regularly occurs, he denies that there exists in it any necessary connection. At any rate, we never perceive any such connection—it does not produce a sensory impression, and therefore does not exist, any more than the "substance"

---

[49] *Ibid.*, IV, pp. 84 ff.
[50] *Ibid.*, IV, pp. 17-18.

can be said to exist. "One event follows another, but we can never observe any tie between them. They seem *conjoined*, but never *connected*." [51] Accordingly, what we call cause and effect is an instance of such regular *conjoining;* but although we *feel* it to be connected, in reality it is not, for then we would have to perceive such a connection, and we do not. This assertion of the association of ideas which excludes their necessary connection is basic to Hume's whole system, even though he is not always consistent in observing it.

Since all our knowledge consists ultimately of sensory impressions, what is it that originates them? Hume's answer, characteristically, is that we do not know and cannot know, since we are aware only of the state of our minds. He does not deny that there might exist an external reality which produces our impressions—as men of common sense assume; he only denies that we can ever know it, although we might believe it. As he does so often, here he again contrasts reason and belief.

All objects of human reason may be divided into relations of ideas and matters of fact. In the first category are geometry, algebra, and arithmetic. The relation of one idea to another in these disciplines is discoverable "without dependence on what is anywhere existent in the universe." But matters of fact are founded upon reasoning from that form of associations of ideas denoted as cause and effect—in other words from our experiences of the effects of custom.

> All inferences from experience, therefore, are effects of custom, not of reasoning. Custom, then, is the great guide of human life. . . . Without the influence of custom, we should be entirely ignorant of every matter of fact, beyond what is immediately present to the memory and senses.[52]

Note well that this is not what we call scientific truth, but only probability. Hence, there can be no certainty in what Hume calls matters of fact, or what we call natural sciences. For the latter rest their conclusions on the assumption that there exists a necessary connection between cause and effect. To illustrate: Hume would not deny that ordinarily the sun rises on each morrow, but he would deny that it does so necessarily. He would not deny that every time temperature drops to 32° Fahrenheit, water freezes. But he would insist that we cannot *sense* the cause; only the fact that water freezes at a certain temperature. Therefore, any *idea* of the *cause* is false because it is not

[51] *Ibid.*, IV, pp. 84 ff.
[52] *Ibid.*, IV, pp. 51-52.

given in sensory experience. In other words, all statements regarding matters of fact—of natural sciences—are descriptive, not explanatory. They give us only a description of what happens, never an explanation of why it happens. This is the familiar postulate in modern science— when the scientist is aware of and remembers that he cannot explain reality, but that he only describes phenomena.

It remains to consider the crucial question as to who or what it is that is assumed to experience sensory impressions or to reproduce them in ideas, associating the ideas in accordance with the three-fold pattern. In other words, what does Hume say about a center of consciousness, of personal identity? It is in this respect that Hume's fidelity to his fundamental empirical principles, even at the cost of manifest absurdity, shows itself with amazing clearness. For since we can never be aware of our identity through sensory impression, Hume is driven to the conclusion that an assertion of it is fictitious. "For my part, when I enter most intimately into what I call *myself* . . . I never can catch *myself* at any time without a perception, and never can observe any thing but the perception." [53] Moreover, "the claim to personal identity would have been a fiction even if we had had an invariable impression of ourselves, unless that impression had been uninterrupted. Identity, he says, is 'nothing but the *invariableness* and *uninterruptedness* of any object.' " [54] Accordingly, belief in human "personality," not to say in the survival of that personality, is meaningless, a fiction. All that we may mean by the term "person" is a flux of transitory sensory data and their transitory associations. Applying Hume's system to modern art, Prof. Northrop says:

> . . . it follows that instead of the immortal, personal selves and material objects being the real things, and the associated, sensuous materials of art being mere appearances, it is the associated sensed aesthetic materials which are the sole reality, and the persisting Protestant persons and the three-dimensional material, external objects which are the meaningless and hence unreal and illusory things.[55]

It is this which makes of Hume's philosophy a *reductio ad absurdum* not only of empiricism, but of all attempts at knowing anything whatever. No wonder that Kant, who inherited this debacle of Lockean

[53] *Ibid.*, I, p. 312.
[54] Quoted in Paul Marhenke, "Hume's View of Identity," in *University of California Publications in Philosophy*, XX (Berkeley, California: 1935), p. 161.
[55] F. S. C. Northrop, *The Meeting of East and West* (New York: The Macmillan Co., 1946), p. 118. By permission.

empirical philosophy, had to make radical changes in its presuppositions before he could proceed with the building of his own system on its foundations! As Archbishop Temple concludes, after Hume finishes with the empirical assumptions of his predecessors, Locke and Berkeley, nothing is left, ". . . except a flux of ideas—caused by nothing and held by nothing, but just happening." [56]

Did Hume himself feel the absurdity of his skeptical conclusions? It is hard to say; but it appears that in his candid moments he understood the consequences of his world view. Was he aware that he had undermined the rational basis of any system of knowledge? That the great Humpty Dumpty of the eighteenth century—Reason—had by his agency a great fall, and that henceforth "all the king's horses and all the king's men cannot put Humpty Dumpty together again?" Once he wrote:

> It seems to me, that the only objects of the abstract sciences, or of demonstration, are quantity and number, and that all attempts to extend this more perfect species of knowledge beyond these bounds are mere sophistry and illusion . . . ; and these may safely, I think, be pronounced the only proper objects of knowledge and demonstration.
> All other inquiries of men regard only matter of fact and existence; and these are evidently incapable of demonstration.[57]

He actually recommends that

> Carelessness and in-attention alone can afford us any remedy. For this reason I rely entirely upon them; and take it for granted, whatever may be the reader's opinion at this present moment, that an hour hence he will be persuaded there is both an external and internal world. . . .[58]

This analysis of his epistemology resulting in utter skepticism as to the possibility of any certain knowledge about anything real might be regarded as a sufficient treatment of Hume's attitude toward religion. And yet, since our interest is chiefly in the religious aspect of philosophical doctrines, let us, for good measure, consider his three works specifically devoted to religion. The first of these is *The Natural History of Religion*,[59] in which Hume has dealt Deism a mortal blow.

[56] Temple, *Nature, Man, and God*, p. 70.
[57] Hume, *Philosophical Works*, IV, pp. 185-86.
[58] *A Treatise of Human Nature*, I, L. A. Selby-Bigge, ed. (Oxford: The Clarendon Press, 1896), p. 218. By permission.
[59] Hume, *Philosophical Works*, IV, pp. 419 ff.

For Deism was grounded on the assumption that religion is wholly reasonable and that originally it comprised nothing but the most rational principles of monotheism (cf. the system of Herbert of Cherbury). Hume, on the other hand, sought to demonstrate by a more historical method that religion originated in polytheism and idolatry, in fear of the mysterious powers of nature, and only gradually developed into monotheism. Historically, polytheism had been characterized by a low moral standard coupled with a tolerant attitude toward the multifarious religious practices, while monotheism had elevated the moral standards but with the accompaniment of intolerance and persecution. Thus, in time, the Deistic movement languished and passed into skepticism (as in Hume's own case) or atheism (as particularly in France). This is probably what Louis de Boland had in mind when he defined a Deist as one who as yet had not had time to become an atheist.

The second of these essays is entitled *Of Miracles*[60] and in it Hume denies the possibility of miracles on the ground that they are contrary to the laws of nature. As Basil Willey has sagely remarked, the man who proved that anything may be the 'cause' of anything, also denied the possibility of miracles, on the ground that they violated the laws of nature. Since there is no such thing as "cause" but only an association of ideas of customary sequence, there can be no "laws" of nature; hence, miracles are said to break what does not exist.

The third essay, entitled *Dialogues concerning Natural Religion* (published posthumously in 1779),[61] is regarded as representing Hume's mature judgment on the subject. He worked at it for some twenty years, but left its publication to his literary executor, Adam Smith. The latter, however, refused to comply with the request, and the work was published finally by Hume's nephew. The argument there presented is so involved and ambivalent that its interpretation is still a lively subject of controversy. Thus, for instance, at a symposium sponsored by the Aristotelian Society and devoted to this work, three professional philosophers of recognized eminence—A. E. Taylor, J. Laird, and T. E. Jessup—found it impossible to come to any common agreement as to Hume's intended meaning.[62] I certainly do not wish to be numbered among those who rush in where angels fear to tread! And although in

---

[60] Hume, *An Inquiry*, pp. 125 ff.

[61] Norman Kemp Smith, ed., *Dialogues concerning Natural Religion* (Edinburgh: Thomas Nelson and Sons, Ltd., 1947, 2nd ed.). By permission.

[62] Aristotelian Society, *Hume and Present Day Problems* (London: Harrison and Son, Ltd., 1939), supplementary vol. XVIII, pp. 179-228.

presenting, in the briefest outline, the arguments of the three friends participating in the discussion which constitutes the essay I shall lean on the interpretation of the editor, Norman Kemp Smith, I do so without prejudice to other interpretations.

The *Dialogue* deals with the proof of the existence of God based on the argument from design, or as we might term it more technically, from teleology. This argument was regarded at the time as an absolutely certain proof for God's existence, and as such was relied on by the orthodox and deistic Christians alike. To attack it, or to assert that it was insufficient or inconclusive, would therefore be tantamount to atheism. Hume then undertook to accomplish just that—to refute this presumably impregnable argument. No wonder that he chose to mask his intention by deliberate ambivalence, or even by an explicit and fervent declaration of his belief in God—a mere protective pretense, as the editor acknowledges it to be.[63] The three friends engaging in the dialogue are Demea, Cleanthes, and Philo. Demea is a none too perceptive defender of the orthodox position who at first regards himself as an ally of Philo against Cleanthes but later avows the Thomistic argument for the ultimate Cause as the original mover of the entire chain of dependent cause and effect series. In the end he discovers that Philo had made sport of him throughout the conversation, and thereupon retires from the contest. The main argument is then carried on between Cleanthes and Philo. The former defends the thesis then currently held, ascribing "the origin of all things to design and intelligence." [64] Philo objects to it on the ground that in all our experience we find that "thought has no influence on matter," [65] so that if we restrict the argument only to empirically known reality, Cleanthes' contention does not hold. Philo goes even further and argues that empirically considered, the world resembles "more an animal or a vegetable" [66] than the works of human contrivance. And since the argument rests on the assumption that the character of the effect proves the nature of the cause, it follows that God would be of an animal or vegetable nature! No wonder that Cleanthes at last discovers that "Philo, from the beginning, has been amusing himself at both our expense," as he tells Demea. That appears to be actually the truth of the matter, so that

---

[63] *Dialogues*, pp. 57-75, particularly p. 70. In fact, the whole Part XII may be understood as an attempt to mask Hume's real opinions; in other words, as a deliberate camouflage.

[64] *Ibid.*, p. 180.

[65] *Ibid.*, p. 186.

[66] *Ibid.*, p. 176.

we, the readers of the *Dialogues,* are left with the task of separating Philo's jest and pretense from genuine conviction. However, we may be fairly certain—or may we?—that in Part XI he avows his actual beliefs: there he affirms that if the world were the work of a good God, evil would not exist; its conduct by general laws would not be productive of so much ill, but would "render the whole world happy"; the imperfections of the physical endowments of animals and men would be eliminated; and the break-down of parts would not cause the destruction of the whole. "On the concurrence, then, of these *four* circumstances does all or the greatest part of natural evil depend." [67] Accordingly, the works of nature, if considered to be the creation of God, do not prove Him either to be good or skilful. Philo concludes that the "first causes of the universe" prove to possess "neither goodness nor malice." The dialogue then concludes with a fulsome profession of Philo's belief in God, which obviously is insincere if his previous arguments are to be regarded as valid. Hume endeavors even to the end to mask his real intention by declaring, through the supposed narrator, "that Philo's principles are more probable than Demea's; but that those of Cleanthes approach still nearer the truth." [68] But there can be no doubt that it is Philo's—*i.e.,* Hume's—arguments that are intended to prevail. And they amount, in the estimate of the age and his own, to a demolition of the argument from design, and therefore, to a repudiation of the proof of the existence of God.

In conclusion, we may return to the far more unequivocal and consistent reasoning of his *Inquiry* and accept his conclusions regarding religion—as well as all metaphysics—as representing his real judgment: religion is a matter of belief, not of knowledge. As belief, Hume perhaps even shared much of its customary assumptions, although he never made this aspect of his thought clear. It is his repudiation of religion as knowledge—a view Kant later held—which confirms our judgment in regard to his attitude toward it. Moreover, he rejected the clericalism of the ecclesiastical system of the time; and yet he never joined Voltaire in the latter's "*écraser l'Infâme!*"

> When we run over our libraries, persuaded of these principles, what havoc must we make? If we take into our hand any volume, of divinity or school metaphysics, for instance; let us ask, *Does it contain any abstract reasoning concerning quantity or number?* No. *Does it contain any experimental reasoning concerning matter of fact or existence?*

[67] *Ibid.,* pp. 205-210.
[68] *Ibid.,* p. 228.

No. Commit it then to the flames: for it can contain nothing but sophistry and illusion.[69]

But do the books dealing with mathematics or natural sciences contain objective truth? According to Hume, no. Why should they not, then, be consigned to the flames as well?

[69] Hume, *An Inquiry*, pp. 187-88.

# 4

# Religion in the Age of Reason

## Blaise Pascal, the Religious Existentialist

In Blaise Pascal (1623-62) we meet the type of scientific thinker—fully a match for Descartes—turned religious thinker as the result of a profound conversion experience. He was born at Clermont in Auvergne, the son of Etienne Pascal, the scientific-minded Second President of the *Cour des Aides*. That old disciplinarian educated his sickly but gifted son from his earliest infancy in classical languages, mathematics, and scientific studies. The precocious youngster, when at the age of barely sixteen he wrote a *Treatise on Conic Sections*, was recognized as a budding genius even by such an outstanding authority of the time as Father Mercenne. According to the latter's judgment, young Pascal's work went beyond anything that had been produced up to that time. Descartes himself felt jealous of the accomplishments of his teen-age rival, and henceforth the paths of the two began to diverge. Three years later, young Blaise invented a calculating machine, a clumsy contraption still in existence, which nevertheless comprises the essential principles of later cash registers. Blaise wished to save his father from the labors of calculating, over which the latter sat up too late at night. Later Blaise turned his attention to the subject of atmospheric pressure, and as a result invented the barometer.

Although he was brought up in a strict piety—his favorite younger sister, Jacqueline, later became a nun of Port Royal, having assumed the name of Euphemia—his religious training consisted of the conventional Catholic catechetical instruction. Nevertheless, under his father's influence it partook of what may be called a liberal attitude. It was, however, his contact with Jansenism, particularly with its stronghold, the convent of Port Royal—then under the direction of Mother Angélique, one of the daughters of Antoine Arnauld, a leader of the Jansenists—that brought about Pascal's "first conversion." It took the form of a zeal for the study of the Scriptures and of St. Augustine by way of Jansen's *Augustinus*. It was this study that prepared him for the struggle with the Jesuits and their Molinist theology, finding its most effective expression in the *Provincial Letters*. However, it was only on November 23, 1654, that his real conversion occurred in a blinding mystical vision, which he described immediately afterwards in the *Memorial* [1] in ecstatic ejaculations: "Certitude. Certitude. Feeling. Joy. Peace. . . . Joy, joy, joy, tears of joy . . . . Renunciation, total and sweet." Henceforth, he devoted himself, despite the increasing ravages of disease, to the all-consuming task of writing his religious *magnum opus*, *An Apology for the Christian Religion*. Unfortunately, his death at the early age of thirty-nine prevented him from completing this work; he left behind a mass of material scribbled on odd pieces of paper, which has since been edited by a number of editors and published under the title of *Pensées*. The arrangement of these jottings necessarily depends upon the reconstruction of the supposed original aim of the author. The only thing the editors have had as a guide is the report of Filleau de la Chaise, the author of *Discours sur les Pensées*, published in 1672, in which he asserts that he had a conversation with Pascal about the arrangement of the latter's projected work. According to him the book was to be divided into two main sections, the first of which aimed at portraying the state of a religiously unawakened man, calculated to arouse him to the perils of his position. Pascal himself entitles this section "Misery of man without God." The second part was then to be devoted to the description of the true way of salvation, or as Pascal phrases it, "Happiness of man with God." [2]

[1] From *The Great Shorter Works of Pascal*, tr. Emile Cailliet and John C. Blankenagel. Copyright 1948 by W. L. Jenkins. (Philadelphia: The Westminster Press). By permission.

[2] From the book *Pensées* by Blaise Pascal, tr. W. F. Trotter. Everyman's Library. Reprinted by permission of E. P. Dutton & Co., Inc. Also by permission of J. M. Dent & Sons, Ltd., London, 1904, p. 19.

With this all too inadequate sketch of Pascal's life, we may focus our attention on his essential contribution to religious thought, most of which is of permanent value. It is of particular interest that we are dealing with a truly scientific mind turned upon the religious meaning of life; as such, Pascal is better able to speak to the condition of our scientific age than others who do not possess this special qualification.

First of all, Pascal begins his study with the consideration of the inadequacies of the views of Montaigne and Descartes. Of the former he writes: "Montaigne's faults are great. . . . One can excuse his rather free and licentious opinions on some relations of life; but one cannot excuse his thoroughly pagan views on death . . . his only conception of death is a cowardly and effeminate one." [3] Of Descartes he writes: "I cannot forgive Descartes. In all his philosophy he would have been quite willing to dispense with God. But he had to make Him give a fillip to set the world in motion; beyond this, he has no further need of God." [4]

In decribing man's place in nature, Pascal writes: Man is

> . . . Nothing in comparison with the Infinite, an All in comparison with the Nothing, a mean between nothing and everything. . . . This is our true state; this is what makes us incapable of certain knowledge and of absolute ignorance. We sail within a vast sphere, ever drifting in uncertainty, driven from end to end. When we think to attach ourselves to any point and to fasten to it, it wavers and leaves us; and if we follow it, it eludes our grasp, slips past us, and vanishes for ever. Nothing stays for us. [5]

> When I see the blindness and wretchedness of man, when I regard the whole silent universe, and man without light, left to himself, and, as it were, lost in this corner of the universe, without knowing who has put him there, what he has come to do, what will become of him at death, and incapable of all knowledge, I become terrified, like a man who should be carried in his sleep to a dreadful desert island, and should awake without knowing where he is, and without means of escape. And thereupon I wonder how people in a condition so wretched do not fall into despair. [6]

> When I consider the short duration of my life, swallowed up in the eternity before and after, the little space which I fill, and even can see, engulfed in the infinite immensity of spaces of which I am ignorant, and which know me not, I am frightened, and am astonished at being here rather than there; for there is no reason why here rather

[3] *Ibid.*, p. 20.
[4] *Ibid.*, p. 31.
[5] *Ibid.*, pp. 23-24, 26.
[6] *Ibid.*, p. 271.

than there, why now rather than then. Who has put me here? . . .
The eternal silence of these infinite spaces frightens me.[7]

In these words one feels the authentic despair of which the modern
Existentialists, whether Christian or atheist, speak. To the latter, a
meaningless universe is indeed a cause of despair; and to the former,
life faced with inescapable death would indeed be meaningless, if God
did not supply the meaning.

Can a man rely on his native endowment—on reason or on the
natural sciences which were just then beginning their triumphal march
through modern history, of which the century was so confident? Indeed not!

> Man is only a subject full of error, natural and ineffaceable without
> grace. Nothing shows him the truth. Everything deceives him. These
> two sources of truth, reason and the senses . . . deceive each other in
> turn. The senses mislead the reason with false appearances, and re-
> ceive from reason in their turn the same trickery which they apply
> to her; reason has her revenge.[8]

Our self-love also stands in the way of finding truth; for we deceive
ourselves, because we do not want to know the truth about ourselves.
"He does not wish any one to tell him the truth; he avoids telling it to
others. . . . I set it down as a fact that if all men knew what each said
of the other, there would not be four friends in the world." [9]

Man's discontent with himself and the world drives him to continual
preoccupation with trivialities, just to escape from himself. This explains in our day the vogue of the moving pictures, the radio, and
television. But if Pascal's age was spared these modern horrors, it had
its own full complement of petty diversions. He writes:

"Hence it comes that play and the society of women, war, and high
posts, are so sought after. Not that there is in fact any happiness in
them, or that men imagine true bliss to consist in money won at play,
or in the hare which they hunt; we would not take these as a gift. . . .
They do not know that it is the chase, and not the quarry, which they
seek." [10] Thus men weary themselves after some imaginary conquest,
only to weary of it as soon as they attain it. And "The last act is tragic,
however happy all the rest of the play is; at the last a little earth is
thrown upon our head, and that is the end for ever." [11]

[7] *Ibid.*, p. 84-85.
[8] *Ibid.*, pp. 37-38.
[9] *Ibid.*, pp. 45.
[10] *Ibid.*, pp. 54, 56.
[11] *Ibid.*, p. 85.

But this very misery of the natural man's condition contains a clue to his greatness. For if he is a reed, he is a thinking reed. Although subject to all manner of nature's forces capable of crushing him and thus at their mercy, he is still more than the universe, for he knows these dangers of which he is the victim, while the universe knows nothing of it all. For he grasps the universe by his thought. Hence,

> All our dignity consists, then, in thought. By it we must elevate ourselves, and not by space and time which we cannot fill. Let us endeavour, then, to think well; this is the principle of morality.[12]

But do men indeed use their reason to lift themselves above the accidents of the physical life? Do they know by the light of reason what is the true end of life, the *summmum bonum?* The most terrible thing about natural man is that he neither knows nor cares. Men are

> indifferent to the loss of their existence, and to the perils of everlasting suffering. . . . Nothing is more indicative of a bad disposition of heart than not to desire the truth of eternal promises. Nothing is more dastardly than to act with bravado before God. . . . Let them recognize that there are two kinds of people one can call reasonable; those who serve God with all their heart because they know Him, and those who seek Him with all their heart because they do not know Him.[13]

But men, even those regarded as the wisest among them, do not seek God. The Stoics thought of finding rest within themselves. Others sought happiness outside themselves. But both groups were wrong. "Happiness is neither within us nor without us. It is in God, both without us and within us." [14]

But how shall one find God? Pascal, who had learned from his father not to seek rational proofs in matters of faith, nor to apply faith to matters of reason, rejected the Thomistic proofs for the existence of God. He knew exceedingly well that men are not converted by arguments—at least not to religion, at most to theology. He, too, had been a rationalist until he experienced the blazing vision of the living God, the mystical ecstacy of joy, that taught him to recognize the deepest levels of religious certainty.

Nevertheless, he still resorts to what is essentially a rational argument for the existence of God, the so-called wager argument. One has a

---

[12] *Ibid.*, p. 133.
[13] *Ibid.*, pp. 78, 80.
[14] *Ibid.*, p. 178.

feeling that it was meant for the intellectuals who neither experienced nor were impressed by Pascal's own existentialist ground of faith. In fact, he admits as much when he deals with the intuitive knowledge of God. He writes that to those who have not attained to this kind of experience we can impart the knowledge of God "only by reasoning, waiting for God to give them spiritual insight, without which faith is only human, and useless for salvation." [15] Even so, it is an unconvincing exhortation to a prudential choice more worthy of a Montaigne than of a Pascal. He points out that many rationally incomprehensible things exist, of which we do not and cannot have a proof. Nothing is certain. It is as incomprehensible that God should exist as that He does not exist. We must therefore choose:

> Let us weigh the gain and the loss in wagering that God is. Let us estimate these two chances. If you gain, you gain all; if you lose, you lose nothing. Wager, then, without hesitation that He is.[16]

Pascal's real ground of certainty of the existence of God rests on much firmer grounds; it is his mystical experience which no amount of argument could shake. Without it, no reasoned proof is adequate; with it, it is unnecessary, even though it may be helpful. In words which have become almost household expressions of deepest Christian conviction, Pascal writes:

> The heart has its reasons, which reason does not know. . . .

> It is the heart which experiences God, and not the reason. This, then, is faith: God felt by the heart, not by the reason.

> We know truth, not only by the reason, but also by the heart, and it is in the last way that we know first principles; . . . And it is as useless and absurd for reason to demand from the heart proofs of her first principles, before admitting them, as it would be for the heart to demand from reason an intuition of all demonstrated propositions before accepting them. . . . Therefore, those to whom God has imparted religion by intuition are very fortunate, and justly convinced.[17]

This insight, this existential experience, the intuition of the heart, places Pascal among the existential religious thinkers, such as Augustine, Anselm, Kierkegaard, and the Russian religious philosophers, Vladimir

---

[15] *Ibid.*, p. 111.
[16] *Ibid.*, p. 93.
[17] *Ibid.*, pp. 109-111.

Solovev and Nicolas Berdyaev. They all understood that faith precedes knowledge, and further that "The knowledge of God is very far from the love of Him," as Pascal wrote.[18] Nevertheless, Pascal did not condemn reason any more than the other existential thinkers did; he only designated its proper function, whereby it performed its important, but not exclusive, service. By the heart, Pascal meant the biblical concept of man's personality and the intuitive appropriation of God by *all* man's powers, not by reason alone.

This then brings us to Pascal's treatment of the historic Christian faith. As has already been mentioned, he was an ardent adherent of the Augustinian theology as interpreted by the outstanding contemporary Jansenist leaders. It brought him into violent conflict with the Jesuits and the Sorbonne, who were chiefly instrumental in securing the repeated papal condemnations of Jansen's *Augustinus* and its French defender, Antoine Arnauld. Although throughout his lifetime Pascal's authorship of the *Provincial Letters* remained a surprisingly well-kept secret, he having assumed the pen-name of Louis de Montalte, the work has since been recognized as indubitably his. It is the most subtle and exceedingly effective attack of its time upon the Jesuit perversions of historic Catholicism as well as of Christianity as a whole. He accuses the Jesuits of fostering and defending immorality by claiming that nothing can be imputed to men as sin *"unless God bestows on us, before committing it, the knowledge of the evil that is in the action, and an inspiration inciting us to avoid it."* [19] Accordingly, it is really God's fault if man sins, for no one can really be cognizant of all the evil involved in a particular action or all its consequences. Temptation to sin would cease to be temptation if one were fully aware of its tragic consequences. The apple which Eve accepted from the serpent and gave to Adam looked extremely good to them—what evil was there in eating it? And if they did not remember the divine prohibition against eating it, it was God's failure of not bestowing on them the remembrance, or the inspiration for not transgressing it!

He furthermore charged the Jesuits with waiving moral requirements, especially in the case of sinners occupying important social or political status, "in order to keep on good terms with all the world," and thus governing the consciences of all. This they did by means of the novel doctrine of "probable opinions." This doctrine, ascribed par-

---

[18] *Ibid.*, p. 110.
[19] Blaise Pascal, *The Provincial Letters*, Thomas M'Crie, tr. (New York: Robert Carter & Brothers, 1856), p. 101.

ticularly to two Jesuit theologians, Escobar and Sanchez, claimed that it is permissible to ignore the plain teaching of the Scriptures and the Fathers of the Church, no matter how clear and well established they might be, provided one could find an opinion even of "a single *very grave doctor*," [20] which would allow the contrary action.

Pascal saw another grave moral perversion in the Jesuit doctrine of mental reservation. This taught that no promises are binding, if made with the mentally formulated intention of not keeping them.[21] One may even swear to a thing while mentally asserting its opposite, whereupon he is held to be blameless of false swearing. A convenient doctrine indeed for sinners! The Jesuits were also charged by Pascal with practicing the doctrine of "*directing the intention*," [22] whereby one was allowed to use means in themselves reprehensible, provided he aimed at some good objective. This comes about as close to the maxim that the end justifies the means as anything can, despite the violent denial on the part of Jesuit defenders that the phrase itself has ever been used!

Although with some reservations as to the accuracy of every aspect of Pascal's attack on the Jesuit casuistry, H. F. Stewart, an authority on Pascal, still affirms that "there can be no question . . . that the effect of his bitter campaign was to raise the moral tone of his time, to fortify the conscience against misuse of casuistry, and set an example of honest debate. In a word, he won a great spiritual and moral victory." [23]

But it must not for a moment be supposed that Pascal's or Jansenists' Augustinianism implied or indicated any favorable attitude or inclination toward Protestantism. Pascal roundly denounced Luther, Calvin, and Vinet, and declared positively, even vehemently: "I have no sort of connection with any community except the Catholic, Apostolic and Roman Church, in the bosom of which I desire to live and die, in communion with the pope, the head of the Church, and beyond the pale of which I am persuaded there is no salvation." [24]

In the light of later theological developments, particularly of existentialism, it is evident that the contributions Pascal made to them were most notable. As such, he deserves to be counted among the outstanding Christian thinkers of the modern age.

[20] *Ibid.*, pp. 118, 127.
[21] *Ibid.*, p. 165.
[22] *Ibid.*, p. 152 ff.
[23] H. F. Stewart, *The Secret of Pascal* (New York: Cambridge University Press, 1941), p. 30.
[24] Pascal, *The Provincial Letters*, p. 343.

## John Amos Comenius and His Pansophic Principles[25]

John Amos Comenius (1592-1670) is best known to the world as the pioneer in modern educational theories and methods. More particularly is he remembered as the author of a series of elementary Latin textbooks for which many generations of schoolboys in the bygone days have called him blessed. But although he has richly deserved the praise he has received for his pedagogical reforms, that contribution by no means exhausts his astonishingly many-sided accomplishments. For he was the author of almost two hundred treatises dealing with scientific, linguistic, pedagogical, philosophical, political, literary, and above all religious and theological subjects. He was likewise a fervent enthusiast for religious and political peace during one of the most disturbed periods of European history—the era of the Thirty Years' War. And above all, he was a convinced believer in pansophy—the principle of the unification of all scientific, philosophical, political, and religious knowledge into one all-embracing, harmonious world view. Thus he endeavored to produce an encyclopedic, unified system of education which would fuse into one whole all knowledge, ethics, and religion, and by having all people educated in this system, aimed ultimately at securing universal peace. His pansophy is, therefore, the dominant principle of almost everything he wrote, pervading it either explicitly or implicitly.

After the outbreak of the Thirty Years' War Comenius was compelled to leave his home and family in Fulnek, Moravia, and to seek refuge on the estates of his powerful noble friend, Karel of Žerotín. Later (1629), he had to leave Bohemia altogether, and settled at Leszno in Poland. In 1631 he published his *Janua linguarum reserata* which made him internationally famous almost overnight. He already had in mind the rudiments of his pansophic principle while he wrote the treatise. He adumbrated it in a private letter to his London friend, Samuel Hartlib (1595-1662), an enthusiastic supporter of all educational reforms and the "master of innumerable curiosities." Hartlib thereupon

[25] Portions of my article, "Comenian Pansophic Principles," in the June, 1953 issue of *Church History*, pp. 155–65. By permission. Also cf. my *John Amos Comenius* (Chicago, University of Chicago Press, 1943), chap. V.

requested Comenius to give him a more precise idea of the intended work, a request with which Comenius promptly complied. But what was the latter's surprise, not to say consternation, when some months afterward (1637) he received a package containing printed copies of his letter bearing the title *Connatuum Comenianorum praeludia!* Thus the greatest project which Comenius had undertaken was launched by an unauthorized publication of his private letter. To be sure, the second edition of it (*Pansophiae prodromus*) was published with his consent. Nevertheless, even this slight indication of his intended pansophic project was received with favor, and even with enthusiasm, although there was criticism as well. Comenius advocated an integration of all factual, inductively ascertained and verified knowledge into one encyclopedic system. It rested on three sources of knowledge: the study of nature (of objects themselves, rather than of books, or scientific study of nature); the use of reason in classifying and interpreting the data learned inductively; and an apprehension of moral and spiritual principles of the divine revelation in Scripture. Since all three ultimately derive from God, they must necessarily be capable of being harmonized with each other. It was in his insistence on harmonizing and integrating religion with science that Comenius differed from such of his contemporaries as René Descartes, who, although enthusiastic about the Comenian pansophic project in principle, repudiated what he regarded as confusing science with theology. But Comenius continued to hold the conviction that the whole truth may be found only in a harmonious unity of nature, reason, and religion. This was pansophy, the aim of which was to instruct all men in what is necessary for a worthy human existence, including a clear awareness of man's destiny here and hereafter. Comenius believed that such knowledge may be attained with clearness and certainty—a notion which reminds one of Descartes.

The circle of Comenius' English friends comprised, besides Hartlib himself, two archbishops, four bishops, several scholars and scientists, a few members of Parliament, and several private friends. Hartlib had repeatedly invited Comenius to England, but without success. It was not until 1641 that the latter was able to accept the invitation. He arrived in London on September 21, 1641, under the impression that it was the Long Parliament that had issued the request. Although it is clear from the Hartlib correspondence that the primary task expected of Comenius was the reform of the English school system, yet he thought that Parliament was interested in his pansophic plan as well. Since Parliament was not in session at the time of Comenius' arrival, he was persuaded, much against his inclinations, to stay until it reconvened.

In the meantime, his English friends, particularly Bishop Williams, exerted strong pressure on him in an attempt to persuade him to remove to England permanently. This, for reasons connected with his Church duties and his family, he refused to do.

Nevertheless, during his stay in England Comenius explained his pansophic principle in a book entitled *Via lucis*. First of all, there was to be established in London a "pansophic college" which would serve as the research and directing center of the whole, widely ramified educational system. Parliament actually assigned to it one of three existing institutions—Savoy, St. Cross at Winchester, and Chelsea—the last-named having been given preference. But unfortunately, the outbreak of the Irish rebellion (November, 1641) diverted Parliament's attention to the urgent tasks arising out of it. Comenius therefore left England. As one of Hartlib's correspondents expressed the disappointment to the English circle, "our Island is not yet worthy of that famous Oriental Professor." [26]

*Via lucis* details Comenius' concrete plans for the "pansophic college" that, in the first place, comprise the preparation of universal textbooks, embodying the pansophic principles. The aim of education, as defined here, is to train the pupil for an intelligent life. He must be enabled to learn all that is necessary for man to know for this and the future life.[27]

But to make these textbooks universally effective, there must exist a universal, free public school system of education. The curriculum of such schools would not be restricted to "secular" subjects, as is generally the case today. It would include everything needed for the training of pupils for a life conscious of its spiritual ends.

In the third place, Comenius demanded a fresh creative approach to education. This he hoped to derive from continuous, organized research. It was this part of the pansophic plan that called for a centralized research foundation, a universal college, located conveniently in a country easily accessible to all. London was chosen as the seat of the president. But the members of the body would be scattered all over the world and would keep in touch with the president by frequent correspondence. All members would be supported by public funds, and would devote themselves exclusively to the furthering of the college's pansophic aims.

In the fourth place, Comenius pursued a consciously international

[26] G. H. Turnbull, *Hartlib, Dury and Comenius* (Liverpool: The University Press, 1947), p. 362.

[27] J. A. Comenius, *The Way of Light*, E. T. Campagnac, tr., (Liverpool: The University Press, 1938).

goal. Consequently, the textbooks must be written in a new, universal language, a kind of "Esperanto." Latin was not regarded as quite adequate, for the new language must be completely regular.

Furthermore, the pansophic system aimed at bringing about not only a unified system of universal education, but also at securing universal peace and religious unity.

Such, then, was the grandiose, perhaps utopian, plan entertained by the Moravian exile who dared to dream it. As far as the English phase of it was concerned, it ended in failure, as we have seen. But he never abandoned it; single-handed, without the support of a body of scholars promised him in London, and often actually contrary to the wishes of his immediate employers, he persisted in his devotion to the ideal. The enormous task kept him busy to the end of his life. In 1645 he began the monumental work, *De rerum humanarum emendatione consultatio catholica*. It was to comprise seven volumes. Only the first two volumes and the Dedication were published during his lifetime (in 1656). He appears to have deliberately postponed the completion of the remaining volumes. The reason for the delay was partly his fear of criticism—which from some quarters was severe—but was mainly his "perfectionism." He was never satisfied with what he had written, and was everlastingly improving it.

The five remaining volumes of his *Consultatio* were not completed by the time of his death (1670), and he commended the task to his son Daniel, and his former assistant, Christian Nigrin. Actually, it was Nigrin and Paul Hartmann who organized the mass of material left by Comenius and who contributed to it whatever additional work was done. However, the volumes were never published. About the year 1700 all the manuscripts of the *Consultatio* came into the hands of one Justus Docemius, who placed them for safekeeping in the Orphanage at Halle a/d. Saale. There they were consulted by Budde for his edition of the *Panegersia* (1702), but were thereafter completely forgotten, and have since been considered lost. It is one of the modern literary romances that in 1935 Professor Dmitry Chizhevsky found the first six volumes, and in 1940 the seventh volume.[28] But even then the disturbed condition of the time prevented the publication of these five hitherto unknown Latin parts. Only the volumes IV and VI were translated into Czech and published by Professor Joseph Hendrich.[29] Moreover, just

---

[28] *Archiv pro bádáni o životě a spisech J. A. Komenského* (Brno, 1940), pp. 85-107.

[29] Josef Hendrich, tr., *J. A. Komenský, Vševýchova* (Praha: Státní nakladatelství, 1948); *J. A. Komenský, Všenáprava* (Praha: Orbis, 1950).

recently Chizhevsky at last published the Latin text (with a German translation) of Vol. IV, *Pampaedia*.[30]

The *Consultatio* is, from the pansophic point of view, Comenius' most important work. The first two volumes, published during his lifetime, are really introductory to the principal parts that were to follow. They bear the titles *Panegersia* and *Panaugia*. The former of these (The Universal Awakening), deals with the ground for the hope that human affairs, which had fallen into utter confusion, may be improved. For the world is one, human nature is the same everywhere; hence, all men are capable of being educated. Although confusion prevails in education, politics, and religion, a return to the original harmony is possible, and it is high time that it be made. No time is to be wasted and no hesitation is to be indulged in. The specific tasks confronting men of good will comprise man's conquest of nature by means of scientific knowledge; universal peace among men; and the spiritual transformation of men's religious and ethical motivation.

The *Panaugia* (The Universal Dawn) seeks the means for enlightening the human mind. Such means are found in education. God has provided men with three books through which they may learn wisdom: nature, reason, and revelation (Scripture). They may read these books by means of sense perception, intelligence, and faith. So far, many contradictions are to be found among them; but these may be removed through the syncretistic (comparative) method. What is lacking in one may be supplied from the other two. Thus the whole truth is to be found only in a synthesis of all three sources of knowledge.

The third part, *Pantaxia* (Universal Correlation) is identical with what Comenius formerly designated as *Pansophia*. In it Comenius equates scientific knowledge with a description of things as they are, and with the arrangement of them in the proper order in relation to other things. Knowledge, therefore, depends upon our perception of the true nature, character, and order of the material phenomena.

The fourth volume, entitled *Pampaedia* (Universal Education), presents Comenius' final reworking of his educational principles and methods, and as such should henceforth be taken into consideration in dealing with Comenian pedagogy, even though it does not supersede the *Great Didactic* and *The School of Infancy* because of its unfinished state. This final educational system of Comenius differs from his previous pedagogical works in so far as it extends the training from four to eight stages, or phases, of human life; while the *Great Didactic*

---

[30] Dmitrij Tschiżewskij *et al.*, *Johann Amos Comenius, Pampaedia* (Heidelberg: Quelle & Meyer, 1960).

divides the whole educational task into the kindergarten, elementary, secondary, and the university stages, the *Pampaedia* adds a prekindergarten and three adult stages, the latter comprising the School of Manhood, the School of Old Age, and a Preparation for Death. Thus Comenius aims at educating men from the cradle to the grave. The training is to make them intelligent both for this world and for eternity. As has been mentioned, the Latin text is now available in the Chizhevsky edition.

The fifth, *Panglottia* (Universal Language), is devoted to a discussion of the linguistic means best suited to convey the instruction to all the peoples of the earth.

The sixth volume is, fortunately, available in translation, and hence a more detailed description of its contents is possible. It bears the title of *Panorthosia* (Universal Reform), and as such is particularly pertinent to our principal interest in Comenius' pansophic principle. The book discusses the chaos caused by the lack of education, irreligion (we would perhaps say, secularism), bad government, and social evils. Comenius then offers concrete proposals for the removal of these evils; some of them echo his previously publicized schemes, but others are new.

Since Comenius consistently thinks of the universal reform under three aspects—cultural, political, and religious—he proposes as the principal instruments of reform three organizations: the Council of Light, which constitutes the ruling cultural body; the Court of Justice, which represents the highest judicial and political tribunal; and the Ecumenical Consistory, the governing body of the Universal Church.[31]

The Council of Light is charged with the stupendous task of educating the entire human race. Consequently, it has supervision of all schools and teachers. It must establish pedagogical principles and methods valid for the world, prepare and distribute textbooks for the schools, exercise censorship over all books and publishers. All textbooks must embody the pansophic principles. Hence, non-Christian books are "profitless." But not all books written by Christian authors are acceptable, either; some are surcharged with the humanist point of view. Furthermore, Christian books of former times are, as a rule, inadequate for modern use. Since the task of the Council of Light is global, the language employed by the body must likewise be universal. But this applies only to the intercourse at the highest level. Local schools would use the vernacular. Every village would possess an elementary school, every city elementary and secondary schools, and every country one or more universities.

---

[31] Hendrich, tr., *Vsenáprava*, chap. XV.

As for the Court of Justice, that institution is charged with the oversight of courts, judges, codes of law, civil administration, and everything which is conducive to the preservation of peace and justice. As Comenius pithily formulated it, "What is the aim of politics? Peace with all men, so that no harm be done to anyone." [32] Hence, all men possess equal rights before law, and an equal chance to secure a living and happiness. The ultimate aim is to secure universal peace, as far as possible without the use of force. Accordingly, all humankind must submit to the rule of law.

The Ecumenical Consistory, representing the unity of all Christian communions, counts among its duties the care of all the churches, of their ministers, and of religious literature. First of all, then, the unity of all existing separate bodies must be attained: this had been Comenius' endeavor throughout his life. He insists that all nonessential differences among Christians be eliminated: he deprecates the use of party names, such as the Lutheran, Calvinist, or Roman Catholic.[33] To that end he suggests a "*via media*" in theology for the removal of such stumbling blocks among the various theological camps as are the differing interpretations of the doctrines of the procession of the Holy Spirit, of justification by faith alone, of the sacraments, and of predestination.[34] The true "catholic" Christianity comprises everything that God has revealed, has commanded, and has promised to *all* His children. It is characterized by a minimum of dogmas, a simplicity of rites, and strictness of self-discipline. "Religious theory should be short, its practice life-long, its results eternal." [35] Among the duties of the Ecumenical Consistory, then, is the care for providing an adequate number of churches and ministers for the needs of all peoples. Likewise, provision must be made for the availability of Scripture in all the languages of the world. Missionary work both at home and abroad, characterized by persuasion rather than the use of force, must be undertaken. In the light of the present-day "ecumenical" attempts, how truly utopian all this sounds!

Each of these three tribunals is to be presided over by one person; but every continent is to have a regional presiding officer as well. But aside from these three organizations, there is to be organized one Universal Council,[36] which is to meet at least once in ten years and is to consist of three delegates from each nation—a scholar, a statesman,

[32] *Ibid.*, p. 191.
[33] *Ibid.*, p. 151.
[34] *Ibid.*, pp. 126-34.
[35] *Ibid.*, p. 188.
[36] *Ibid.*, chap. XXV.

and a theologian. This general gathering shall be convened by the heads of governments, who shall likewise provide for its expenses. The actual deliberations of the Council are to be carried on in common, rather than to be divided among the three constituent groups—the cultural, political, and religious.

The seventh and concluding volume, *Pannuthesia* (The Universal Admonition), is addressed to "the men of light," the learned men of the world, scientists, teachers, religious leaders, and statesmen. In this exhortation Comenius lays emphasis on the truth which is as greatly neglected in our day as it was in his, namely, that the spiritual transformation and reform is primary, and the environmental reform is secondary in the sense that it follows, not precedes, the former. Education lays upon its possessors the duty to pass it on. Moreover, there is a veritable "*terra incognita*" before humankind, which awaits discovery. How surprised would Comenius be if he could witness the tremendous mechanical progress of our day; but disappointed that this progress has not been accompanied by the kind of wisdom which to him was the supreme aim of education! His "point four" of the pansophic program is the enlightenment of the hitherto barbarous races, which must be made partakers of the cultural riches with the culturally more mature races. And he concludes by saying that this stupendous worldwide cultural program must be realized by means of humble, voluntary, zealous, and peaceful commitment to the task on the part of "the men of light."

In conclusion, let us raise the pertinent question as to the results of Comenius' lifelong labors and devotion: has it all ended in a noble failure? Much of it undoubtedly has, for it partook of the transient that characterizes every age. He had the misfortune, which is shared by many great men, of entertaining grandiose ideals which outran the pedestrian minds of his contemporaries. Some of his basic principles have been rejected by our modern world either unconsciously or deliberately. Descartes has proved far more influential for our age than Comenius. Integration of religion into general scientific and political culture has been largely ignored, if not repudiated. The result is secularism, which has reached in some instances the acute stage of militant atheism. We rely on political, economic, or scientific means for the creation of a good world; by implication we deny the truth which Comenius stressed—that the task is primarily spiritual.

But many of Comenius' contributions, fortunately, have proved practical and realizable. In the pedagogical reforms his proposals are generally recognized. But the long-lasting loss of the five volumes of *Consultatio* has deprived him of the credit for having been the pioneer of even greater reforms. Nevertheless, many have already been initiated, even though under different auspices. The ideal of universal popular education is fast becoming a reality. It is *not* unified in the way proposed by Comenius, but that is its defect rather than its merit. The United Nations Educational, Scientific, and Cultural Organization (UNESCO) somewhat feebly adumbrates his far more effectively conceived Council of Light. In the realm of political unification, we have begun to apply the concept of "one world" through the organization of the United Nations and of the Permanent International Court of Justice, as well as through the Charter of Human Rights. Although the religious unification is no more perfect than the political, astonishing progress has been made during the more than three and a half centuries since Comenius' birth; for most of the Protestant and some of the Eastern Orthodox communions have united in organizing the World Council of Churches of Christ. Thus, ideas which in Comenius' time seemed fantastic and utopian, have actually assumed concrete, although imperfect, forms. Their present state is undoubtedly marred by many faults. It is a pity that the non-availability of Comenius' pansophic writings has deprived him of a more direct influence upon these great accomplishments of our time. But at least we know that he deserves credit for his devotion in shaping them into concrete proposals at a time when very few were ready to accept them. Hence, Comenius *was* a pioneer of the new world, the dim outlines of which even to this day we see as in a glass, darkly, but which we hope shall be ultimately realized.

## Bishop Joseph Butler, the Rationalist Apologist for Christianity

Joseph Butler (1692-1752), who was the son of a Presbyterian linen merchant of Wantage, Berkshire, became the principal defender of the faith by turning the weapons of the Deists upon them. He was educated at the Presbyterian Academy of Tewkesbury, where he turned to the study of Locke. But having become convinced of the rightfulness of the Established Church, he joined it and went to Oriel College at Oxford for further study. He found the academic pabulum served there most unappetizing. He was ordained and in 1719 appointed preacher at the Rolls Chapel in London. There his congregation consisted mostly of lawyers and other professional men. He made his reputation there as an effective preacher. Some of his sermons were published under the title *Fifteen Sermons Preached at the Rolls Chapel* (1726) and comprise a system of ethics for which he became famous. In 1725 he received a rich benefice at Stanhope, where during the seven years of his residence, his *Analogy of Religion* (1736) was written. He then returned to London as the Clerk of the Closet to Queen Caroline; she was something of a blue-stocking, deeply interested in intellectual and religious currents of thought—in startling contrast to her boorish husband, King George II. She commanded Butler to attend her from seven to nine every evening, and read his *Analogy* every morning at breakfast. Lord Bolingbroke jibed at her in writing:

> Our learned queen . . . attends frequently to the controversy, almost fourteen hundred years old and still carried on with as much warmth, and as little success as ever, about that profound mystery the Trinity. She studies with much application the "analogy of revealed religion . . ." She understands the whole argument perfectly, and concludes, with the right reverend author, that it is not "so clear a case that there is nothing in revealed religion." Such royal, such lucrative encouragement must needs keep both metaphysics and the sublimist theology in credit.[37]

But such was not the judgment of that keenest-witted of the skeptics of the time, David Hume. He declared the *Analogy* to be "the best defense of Christianity he had ever known," although it failed to convert him. Nevertheless, he paid Butler the compliment of wishing to secure the latter's good opinion of his own work, *An Enquiry*, and even modified in it some passages and tenets in order to make it more palatable to the bishop. There is no evidence, however, that Butler was moved to regard Hume's opinions more favorably.

After the Queen's death (1737), Butler was offered the see of Bristol, but declined it as "not very suitable" (it was the poorest in England) and preferred the deanship of St. Paul's, which he held for ten years. After Archbishop Potter died in 1747, Butler was offered the primate's see, but declined. Nevertheless, in 1750 he did accept the wealthy bishopric of Durham, but held it only two years before he died.

Despite his excellent connections with the Court, Bishop Butler was not an ecclesiastical careerist and politician; in fact, he was quite strict in rebuking every appearance of simony. Although he held one of the

---

[37] Henry Saint-John Bolingbroke, *The Philosophical Works* (London: David Mollet, 1754), III, p. 443.

richest bishoprics in England, he distributed most of his income among charitable projects. He never married, and disapproved of married clergy. His manner of life was almost ascetic, considering the general looseness of morals prevalent even among the clergy. He was generally held in high esteem both for his purity of life, great learning, and generous heart.

Butler is philosophically a disciple of Locke, as are Berkeley and Wesley. Accordingly, he refrains on principle from any effort to prove the truths of Christianity as sure and certain, but only as *probable*. He embodies the spirit of the age, which was cautious—if not skeptical —coldly rationalistic, mortally afraid of the slightest appearance of the "enthusiasm" that to the men of that age was synonymous with fanaticism. Butler's use of analogy aims at a sober, meticulously reasoned statement about the unknown deduced from a careful observation of the known. "Probability is the very guide of life." And since so much in life depends upon probability rather than on clear knowledge of incontrovertible and provable truth, it is wise and prudent, for purposes of practical, ethical life, to choose the religious, rather than the irreligious alternative. To be sure, this prudential consideration, reminiscent of Pascal's "wager argument," is not a robust, exultant, and radiant kind of religion; but then the eighteenth century preferred the sober, unemotional, rationalistic type. Accordingly, Butler deliberately adopts the concept of Christianity in which he can fight the Deists on their own ground. When in effect the Deists treat religion as a system of rational propositions, Butler argues on the same basis for the adoption of religion as rationally acceptable and tenable. When they regard nature as perfect and scientific thinking about it as wholly reliable knowledge, he quietly and factually, without abuse or denunciation, points out that such thinking is subject to the same difficulties and uncertainties as is revealed religion. Hence there is no ground for rejecting the latter while relying upon and asserting the former. Religion, he wishes to demonstrate, affords a better basis for practical, ethical life than irreligion. With exquisite irony he ridicules the notion that Christianity is dead, as the skeptics of his day imagined:

> It is come, I know not how, to be taken for granted, by many persons, that Christianity is not so much as a subject of inquiry; but that it is, now at length, discovered to be fictitious. And accordingly they treat it, as if, in the present age, this were an agreed point among all people of discernment; and nothing remained, but to set it up as a principal subject of mirth and ridicule, as it were by way of reprisals, for its having so long interrupted the pleasures of the world. On the contrary, thus much, at least, will be here found, not taken for granted,

but proved, that any reasonable man, who will thoroughly consider the matter, may be as much assured, as he is of his own being, that it is not, however, so clear a case, that there is nothing in it.[38]

As has customarily been done by the Deists themselves, Butler divides the treatment of the subject into two parts: Natural and Revealed Religion. The first of these comprises such topics as are found even in Herbert of Cherbury's definition of natural religion: a future life, rewards and punishments in accordance with man's conduct, and the earthly life as probation and discipline. Revealed religion comprises such topics as sin, the proof from miracles, and the system of salvation as manifested by the Messiah and revealed to a part of mankind.[39]

Turning now to the actual development of the topics comprised under the heading of natural religion, and examining the author's treatment of future life, we find him arguing that man in his proper selfhood is not to be identified with his body. ". . . our organized bodies are no more ourselves or part of ourselves than any other matter around us." Hence, the destruction of the body does not involve the extinction of the ego. Clearly following Locke, Butler asserts that our perceptions are sensory and reflective; and argues that the sensory perceptions, destroyed by death, are not necessary to future life; while those of reflection are not destroyed. Thus

> Death may, in some sort, and in some respects, answer to our birth . . . ; death may immediately, in the natural course of things, put us into a higher and more enlarged state of life, as our birth does; a state in which our capacities, and sphere of perception and of action, may be much greater than at present.[40]

In the same manner, Butler then proceeds to point out analogies between the present states of pleasure and pain, which are largely "the consequences of our actions," and rewards and punishments of the future state, which likewise depend upon our conduct here. As God has appointed "satisfaction and delight to be the consequence of our acting in one manner, and pain and uneasiness of our acting in another," it follows logically that the same Author of Nature will reward or punish our conduct in the religious and moral spheres. But since divine punishments are mostly objected to, Butler points out that our miseries are in large part self-inflicted. He concludes:

---

[38] *The Works of Joseph Butler, D.C.L.,* W. E. Gladstone, ed. (Oxford: The Clarendon Press, 1896), I, pp. 1-2. By permission.
[39] *Ibid.,* pp. 16, ff.
[40] *Ibid.,* pp. 42-43.

And is there any pretence of reason, for people to think themselves secure, and talk as if they had certain proof, that, let them act as licentiously as they will, there can be nothing analogous to this, with regard to a future and more general interest, under the providence and government of the same God? [41]

As for the moral government of God, our author sums up his argument by asserting that "virtue and vice are naturally rewarded and punished as beneficial and mischievous to society." Hence, "The notion then of a moral scheme of government is not fictitious, but natural . . . ; they give a credibility to the supposition of their being rewarded and punished hereafter"; and in fact "in a higher degree than they are here." [42]

The foregoing considerations thus imply that our earthly life is probationary, and is intended to serve as moral discipline and as the means of improvement. "The general conduct of nature is not to save us trouble or danger, but to make us capable of going through them and to put it upon us to do so." Thus nature aims at moral discipline and character formation. Butler then concludes that since it is reasonable to hold that immortality is a fact, and that our future state shall be determined by our own conduct here on earth, he urges that it behooves men to live sober and righteous lives. For morality is firmly wedded to religion, while vice goes hand in hand with irreligion. He sums up the argument from natural religion by concluding:

It is absurd, absurd to the degree of being ridiculous, if the subject were not of so serious a kind, for men to think themselves secure in a vicious life; or even in that immoral thoughtlessness, which far the greatest part of them are fallen into. And the credibility of religion, arising from experience and facts here considered, is fully sufficient, in reason, to engage them to live in the general practice of all virtue and piety; under the serious apprehension, though it should be mixed with some doubt, of a righteous administration established in nature, and a future judgment in consequence of it: especially when we consider, how very questionable it is, whether any thing at all can be gained by vice; how unquestionably little, as well as precarious, the pleasures and profits of it are at the best; and how soon they must be parted with it at the longest . . . : so inducements to vice, from cool expectations of pleasure and interest so small and uncertain and short, are really so insignificant, as, in the view of reason, to be almost nothing in themselves; and in comparison with the importance of Religion, they quite disappear and are lost. [43]

[41] *Ibid.*, p. 63.
[42] *Ibid.*, pp. 92-93.
[43] *Ibid.*, p. 183.

Were this all to Butler's defense of Christianity, it would prove it to be merely moralistic Pelagianism, a religion of good works rather than of grace. But one must remember that he was here presenting the case for natural religion which he himself regarded as inadequate. It is the second part of the work, dealing with revealed religion, that was to supply the deficiency of the first, although he used it primarily as a defense against the Deists who rejected it as unnecessary. He affirms the necessity of revelation in the most explicit terms: "Some persons, upon pretence of the sufficiency of the light of nature, avowedly reject all revelation, as, in its very notion, incredible, and what must be fictitious." [44] But he goes on to point out how inadequate religious notions were prior to revelation, even on the part of "the greatest men." Revelation of God's commands, however, not only reinforces and reaffirms the precepts of natural religion, but supplements them by truths undiscoverable by unaided reason and by such additional proofs as miracles and prophecies. Miracles "afford mankind instruction additional to that of nature," hence are not incredible. Nevertheless, his caution intervenes, and lest he admit too much in urging the unqualified acceptance of revelation, he asserts: "Reason can, and it ought to judge, not only of the meaning, but also of the morality and the evidence, of revelation." [45] Accordingly Butler, following Locke too closely, subjects revelation to human reason, thus really giving away the case for revelation. It seems astonishing that a mind as keen as the bishop's failed to see the fallacy involved in this position.

Furthermore, by making the truth of revelation depend on miracles, Butler essentially weakened his own defense as well as that of the subsequent apologists using his argument. For the nonacceptance or repudiation of miracles thus became tantamount to the rejection of Christianity as a whole, as many Deists and skeptics quickly pointed out. The Church later paid an exceedingly high price for this position!

Besides these additions which Christianity makes to natural reason, the Church further strengthens the case by its admonitions, discipline, and public worship, thus affording men supernatural aid. To sum up: we may learn of the existence of God by means of natural religion; but it is only by revelation that we learn of Christ as the mediator between God and men, and of the Holy Spirit as our guide and sanctifier.

Butler further distinguishes between moral and positive precepts: the former are precepts "the reason for which we see"; the latter, "the reason for which we do not see." [46] But both are means to moral ends. The positive precepts, such as the Church imposes, cannot contradict or void moral precepts, as even our Lord taught on the occasion of his disciples' plucking of corn on the Sabbath day.

Butler goes so far as to concede that "Christianity is a scheme, quite beyond our comprehension. . . ." [47] Nevertheless, it is a truth of revelation that God had appointed in Christ a mediator between Himself and us, through Whom we are redeemed. The redemption is needed because man is under bondage to sin, occasioned by the fall of Adam and Eve, and persisted in by his own sinful nature. "Christ offered himself a propitiatory sacrifice, and made atonement for the sins of the world." [48] So whether some other means could have availed as well we cannot judge. At any rate, vicarious suffering is the order of nature.

The only valid objections to revelation, Butler admits, are those directed against the evidences for it; but he refutes them. This he does not claim to have done by some absolute proofs, but again only by analogy or on the grounds of probability—and occasionally of possibility. Thus he combats arguments against the credibility of Scriptures —incidentally, he holds to their plenary inspiration. He further argues against objections to the wisdom, justice, and goodness of God as presented in revelation by pointing out that the same objections apply to natural religion. All in all, Butler concludes that because revealed religion is not incredible—and that is all he undertakes to demonstrate— a prudent man of reason should accept such a practical proof as satisfactory (for other kinds of knowledge do not afford any more certainty) and live in accordance with its precepts. For thus alone may he live worthily and even happily.

Butler's treatise is intended to be an apologetic, not a systematic presentation of all the truth of Christianity. He admits with truly astonishing frankness that "It is most readily acknowledged, that the foregoing Treatise is by no means satisfactory; very far indeed from it: but so would any natural institution of life appear, if reduced into a system, together with its evidence." [49] His strongest argument for revealed religion then is that the objections to it are no different and no worse than could be made against natural religion, or against, let us say, medical science. But because physicians do not always make the right diagnosis and therefore fail in cures, men do not stop availing them-

[46] *Ibid.*, p. 202.
[47] *Ibid.*, p. 243.
[48] *Ibid.*, p. 268.
[49] *Ibid.*, pp. 362-63.

selves of the best medical care they can secure. Butler thus intends his work to serve as a lawyer's brief, a rebuttal of the opponents' charges, a legalistic defense against specific arguments of his Deistic and skeptical objectors. As such, Dr. Mossner regards it "on the whole shrewdly and adequately reasoned." [50] But as a "complete philosophy of religion, the *Analogy* must be held as of little permanent value except in the strength of incidental argument." [51]

## John Wesley and the Evangelical Awakening

John Wesley's answer to the Deistic, skeptical, and rationalistic movements of his day was not in terms of a new philosophical theory, as was Bishop Berkeley's case, nor in the turning of the Deists' weapons upon them, as in Bishop Butler's case, but in the revival of the religion of grace producing transformed lives. In this way Wesley made his greatest contribution by restoring the Reformation doctrine of justification by free grace through faith as against the current Anglican doctrine, which looked upon faith as a good work antecedent to justification; and by insisting upon sanctification as the necessary concomitant and consequence of justification, as against the moralism of the Deists and the rationalism of the skeptics—for whom these doctrines ceased to possess any positive meaning. Over against the efforts of the rationalists to prove or disprove God's existence by means of labored arguments based on logic or analogy, or by substituting nature for God, Wesley once more placed salvation at the center of the religious concern. The question "What shall I do to be saved?" outweighed in importance all merely theoretical speculation.

Wesley, born in 1703 in an Anglican parsonage, was brought up in strict conformity with the prevailing notions of religion. They were formulated most acceptably by Bishop George Bull in his *Harmonia Apostolica*, in which the doctrine of justification was couched in moralistic, largely Pelagian, terms: man must work out his salvation with fear and trembling, and is capable of doing so. He is justified by God on the ground of faith, to be sure; but it is in man's own power

---

[50] Ernest C. Mossner, *Bishop Butler and the Age of Reason* (New York: The Macmillan Company, 1936), p. 103.
[51] *Ibid.*, p. 104.

whether or not to believe. Thus faith is man's own act, not a gift of God. Moreover, faith is understood as an intellectual assent to the authoritative doctrines of the Church. As Bishop Bull expresses it: "Justification signifies that love of God, by which he embraces those who are already leading a holy life, and determines them to be worthy of the reward of life eternal through Christ." [52] Christ is in fact truly our Savior, because he has wrought satisfaction to God for our sins, and because he confers salvation on us. But although this logically makes salvation universal, yet it is in fact conditioned by man's acceptance of it. Hence, Bull concludes, "In the last analysis faith is really a work, for it involves man's own act of assent to the validity of the Gospel teaching, his willingness to engage in works of repentance, and his humble desire both to be good and to do good." [53]

When in 1725 Wesley decided to receive the holy orders, he commenced a period of earnest endeavor to fulfil the conditions of justification as he understood them. His views then were in full conformity with the current Anglican doctrine regarding justification, and he was far more serious in his efforts to realize the conditions than many another Anglican clergyman. He was then deeply influenced by such works as Jeremy Taylor's *Holy Living and Holy Dying* and later William Law's *Serious Call to a Devout and Holy Life*. Thomas à Kempis, among the mystics, also exerted a notable influence on him. His ascetic practices as a member and leader of the Holy Club are well known and bear witness to the zeal with which he sought to make his salvation sure. But by 1735 Wesley came to despair of his efforts, particularly after his disastrous American sojourn and his closer acquaintance with the piestistic Moravians. In London, he associated with Peter Böhler, under whose guidance he at last perceived the true meaning of the doctrine of justification by faith alone. The decisive experience came at the Aldersgate meeting on May 24, 1738. In his own memorable description of it he wrote: "About a quarter before nine, while he [the reader of Luther's preface to the Epistle to the Romans] was describing the change which God works in the heart through faith in Christ, I felt my heart strangely warmed. I felt I did trust in Christ, Christ alone, for salvation; and an assurance was given me, that he had taken away my sins, even mine, and saved me from the law of sin and death." [54]

---

[52] Quoted in William R. Cannon, *The Theology of John Wesley* (New York-Nashville: The Abingdon Press, 1956), p. 38.

[53] *Ibid.*, p. 41.

[54] *The Journal of the Rev. John Wesley, A.M.* (London: J. Kershaw, 1827), I, pp. 97-98.

Henceforth, the decisive experience of Aldersgate became normative for his theology throughout the rest of his life. There is still carried on a learned debate as to the relation of the experiences of 1725 and 1738: Father Piette regards the former date as that of a genuine conversion on Wesley's part, while Cannon and others vigorously deny such an interpretation and argue in favor of 1738. Wesley himself certainly joins the latter, for he vehemently and somewhat exaggeratedly declared immediately after Aldersgate that prior to it he had not been a Christian at all. Undoubtedly, he had not properly understood the doctrine of justification by faith alone, and in that sense his "evangelical" conversion of 1738 represents a stage of understanding and experience far in advance of his views of 1725. Perhaps we may designate his experience in 1725 as an awakening from a relative religious indifference and the whole period prior to 1738 as a preparation for the "evangelical" conversion occurring in that year.

At any rate, we are primarily concerned with his theological development since 1738—not that all his views remained unchanged for the rest of his life. Nor was he predominantly interested in elaborating a theological system; he was basically committed to the task of saving souls, and his theology was subordinated and subservient to this principal aim of his life. Nevertheless, his evangelical experience compelled him to formulate his views of justification and sanctification anew, and he proceeded to do so with astonishing dispatch. Thus only eleven days after Aldersgate he preached at St. Mary's at Oxford his famous sermon on "Salvation by Faith." In it, after enumerating inadequate and incomplete concepts of faith, he proceeds to define saving faith as completely and altogether a gift of God. Accordingly, the sinner can do nothing, absolutely nothing, to earn or deserve God's grace, and hence His forgiveness. The sinner is forgiven freely and without any works on his own behalf: forgiveness of sins is by God's grace alone. Faith, then, whereby we seize the proffered grace of God, is a gift, not an attainment or a compound of faith and works. Toward the end of his life he asserted that ever since his Aldersgate experience he has held to this doctrine "without any material alteration . . . from that very hour, I never varied, no not a hair's breadth." [55]

But has not Wesley, by abandoning the current Anglican doctrine, ceased to be an Anglican? Not in his own view. He declared in 1745 to Thomas Secker, then Bishop of Oxford, that he did not depart from the doctrines of *The Thirty-Nine Articles;* but that he held them—

---

[55] Quoted in Robert W. Burtner and Robert E. Chiles, eds., *A Compend of Wesley's Theology* (New York-Nashville: The Abingdon Press, 1954), p. 167.

particularly the one dealing with justification by faith—as they had been understood and interpreted in the Elizabethan, rather than in the Georgian, times. And although Wesley specifically attacked the great Bishop Bull's doctrine of justification as requiring good works in order to justify,[56] he nevertheless felt it his right to remain within the Anglican communion to the end of his life.

That communion since the days of Archbishop Laud held to a version of the Arminian interpretation of the doctrine of grace. Wesley retains this interpretation and thus places himself in opposition to the Calvinistic doctrine of double predestination. He vigorously denounces the latter as flatly contradicting the gospel and, indeed, as blasphemous.[57] For himself, he holds that God's grace is not limited to a particular group of the elect, predestined to salvation from all eternity, but is shed abroad upon all. Thus the prevenient grace, which is the potential source of justification, is available to all men without distinction. "Whosoever will, let him come," became the characteristic call to repentance in all Wesleyan evangelistic campaigns. It was on account of this doctrine, rejected by the strict Calvinists, that Wesley broke with George Whitefield. And although he shared with him the conviction that the Fall had robbed man of his original communion with God and vitiated his nature, he held that man still retained the prevenient grace—the ability, sometimes in a woefully attenuated degree, of accepting God's proffered grace extended to all; for Christ had died for all.

But it still remained a plain fact, evident to all, and to Wesley among the rest, that despite the possibility of man's salvation by the grace of God, not all men are saved. What, then, is necessary to make the prevenient grace effective? Man's faith, a voluntary acceptance on his part of what God has so graciously offered. Thus, Wesley goes beyond the Arminian doctrine in asserting that man is not only able to resist God's grace, and thus quench the work of the Spirit within him; he is able also to join with the Spirit in the work of grace begun and continued in him by the Spirit. Thus he may—yea, must—play a positive part in this process which eventuates in justification. This then is synergism. And Wesley clearly asserts it, quoting St. Augustine, in declaring, "He that made us without ourselves, will not save us without ourselves." [58] And in a sermon, "What is Man?" he declares: "And

---

[56] John Wesley, *Sermons on Several Occasions* (London: Wesleyan Conference Office, 1865), III, p. 512.

[57] *Ibid.*, III, p. 429.

[58] *Ibid.*, II, p. 319.

although I have not an absolute power over my mind, because of the corruption of my own nature; yet, through the grace of God assisting me, I have a power to choose and do good, as well as evil. I am free to choose whom I will serve; and if I choose the better part, to continue therein even unto death." [59] In this formulation of the doctrine, which may be regarded as his mature thought on the matter, Wesley occupies a position which differentiates him both from Luther and Calvin on the one hand, and Arminius on the other. Although he agrees with the former that justification is wrought by God's grace through faith, and in no sense by human deserts of any sort, yet he resolutely rejects their doctrine of predestination and limited grace; and on the other hand, although he agrees with the Arminians that grace is offered to all, he differs from them in making man's free will capable not only of quenching the Spirit, but also of cooperating positively in the work of grace.

But justification is only the beginning of the process of sanctification. It is in that sense truly a "new birth," which is the beginning of the life process. No life is possible without birth; but on the other hand, the whole span of life is not to be identified with birth alone. Salvation, therefore, is not limited to the "new birth" (except in case of death immediately after conversion), but includes sanctification, which is a lifetime process. In this task of transformation of a forgiven sinner into a saint, the cooperation of man's wholehearted efforts with divine grace is vigorously asserted. It is here that the Pauline exhortation, "Work out your salvation with fear and trembling" applies. Wesley rigorously demands of his converts that they subject themselves to an exacting regime of sanctification, which he himself exemplifies above all others by rules and methods which are nothing less than ascetic. They comprise early rising (at 4 in summer, at 5 in winter), prayer, devotional reading, meditation, and works of charity. It was not until his extreme old age that he mellowed enough to admit that a man who does not rise at an hour that could be called early may perhaps have a faint hope of being saved. Without regular prayers (three times a day) and Scripture reading accompanied by meditation no Christian can hope to keep his soul alive, any more than he can keep his body alive without food and drink. He insists upon fasting twice a week (Wednesday and Friday, in accordance with the early Church custom), during the forty days of Lent, on Ember days, and on the three Rogation days. He also insists on partaking frequently of communion. In

---

[59] Burtner and Chiles, *op. cit.*, p. 133.

1773 he wrote that "the Methodists, so called, observe more of the Articles, Rubrics, and the Canons of the Church than any other people in the three kingdoms." Of course, all card playing, theatre going, and idle talk are to be eschewed.

In order to provide devotional reading for the members of his societies, Wesley published a collection of fifty volumes called *Christian Library*. Among his selections were included authors like Pascal, Bunyan, Baxter, à Kempis, and Law—the latter two despite the very severe criticisms which he had levied against them earlier.

Can the process of sanctification reach its goal—that of sinlessness—in this life? Wesley was severely exercised over this problem, particularly immediately after his Aldersgate experience. Then he actually thought that a complete victory over sin might be attained. He wrote at the time in his *Journal:*

> After my return home, I was much buffeted with temptations; but cried out and they fled away. They returned again and again. I as often lifted up my eyes, and he sent me help from his holy place. And herein I found the difference between this and my former state chiefly consisted. I was striving, yea fighting with all my might under the law, as well as under grace; but then I was sometimes, if not often, conquered; now, I was always conqueror.[60]

This is indeed an astonishing claim, one which is not repeated ever after in this absolute form. Nevertheless, Wesley continues to hold firmly to the doctrine of perfection as the goal of the process of sanctification. But he defines it in terms of a motive. "Christian perfection, for Wesley, means, therefore, only one thing, and that is purity of motive: the love of God, freed entirely from all the corruptions of natural desire, and emancipated completely from any interest in self or in any other person or thing apart from God, guides unhindered every thought and every action of a man's life." [61] It does not mean freedom from ignorance or error and their consequences, nor perfect understanding or freedom from temptation. Has anyone ever attained it? Wesley asserts that it is not a state one can attain by moral effort, but comes as a free grace of God, just as justification does. One is to look for it in faith, and to strive for it throughout life. "If there is such a blessed change before death [i.e., entire sanctification], should we not encourage all believers to expect it?" Indeed we should. For "the more watchful they are against all sin, the more careful to grow in grace, the more zealous of good works, and the more punctual in their attendance on all the ordinances of God." [62] Nevertheless, for himself, he does not claim to have attained "entire sanctification," perhaps because it is not to be attained before death.[63] His less restrained spiritual progeny, such as the "Holy Rollers" of our day, profess the present realization of an aspiration which the great founder of the Methodist movement never dared to claim for himself.

What Wesley bequeathed to the Christian Church as a whole is the emphasis, often neglected if not altogether forgotten, that there can be no good society without spiritually transformed individuals composing it. Thus the notion that "individual" salvation necessarily stands in opposition to "social" redemption is seen to be gravely wrong, although either concept, taken in isolation, is likewise wrong. Only when practiced together do we have a full-orbed concept of Christian life.

[62] Burtner and Chiles, *op. cit.*, p. 183.

[63] R. N. Flew, *The Idea of Perfection in Christian Theology* (New York: Oxford University Press, 1934), p. 323. By permission.

# 5

# Emotion Undermines Rationalism

## Introduction: Jean Jacques Rousseau

Having considered in some detail the development of
rationalist-empiricist movements fathered respectively by
Descartes and Locke, we have concluded that they both
resulted in a relative failure. The empiricist movement
particularly ended in the debacle of Humean skepticism
with its radical denial of the possibility of knowing either
the material or the spiritual "substances." Hume reduced
"knowledge" to sensory perception, a mere "stream of
consciousness" of an ever-changing sensory kaleidoscope
without any permanent reality either of the sensation itself
or of the perceptive center of consciousness. The "Age of
Reason" thus having failed to justify the supreme confidence reposed in reason, a new approach to reality had to
be found if complete skepticism were to be avoided. It
was found in the principle of sentiment or feeling which
gave the movement it created the designation of Romanticism.

The earliest outstanding representative of this reaction
to the still dominant rationalist-empiricist culture of the
eighteenth century was Jean Jacques Rousseau (1712-78).
Beginning as a disciple of Voltaire and a close friend of
Diderot, Rousseau advanced to conclusions that were

contradictory to their rationalistic assumptions. His repudiation of the dominant presuppositions of the age is to be seen even in his earliest treatise, which attracted general attention: it was his *Discourse on the Sciences and the Arts* (1750), submitted in the essay contest conducted by the Dijon Academy. He describes the circumstances of its composition in a letter written thirteen years later, in which he tells a friend that he noticed the announcement of the contest accidentally, and that he had an instantaneous vision of the essay he would write: "Now the inner tension which he had hitherto felt but vaguely and dimly became a distinct and certain knowledge. Rousseau now *saw* where he stood; he not only felt, but he judged and condemned." [1] And although the essay he wrote was the most eloquent piece of writing he ever penned, and not only won him the Dijon Academy prize but made him a famous man of letters almost overnight, the argument he presented was philosophically not without weaknesses. He himself acknowledged the fact, and later rewrote the thesis in a more acceptable form in his *A Discourse upon the Origin and the Foundation of Inequality among Mankind.* Taken together, these essays advance the radical thesis that the reason for the moral decay of the times is to be sought in civilization itself. He turned savagely upon the existing *mores* and denounced them root and branch; society is in decay because it rests upon artificial foundations.

> There prevails in our morals an abject and deceptive uniformity, and all minds seem to have been cast in the same mold. Endlessly, politeness makes demands, decorum gives orders, we follow customs, never our own bent. We no longer dare seem what we are; and in this perpetual constraint the men who form this herd which we call society will all do the same things under the same circumstances.[2]

And the remedy? Not more artificial culture, but a return to nature. "Retire to the woods," Rousseau cried passionately, "there to lose sight and remembrance of the crimes of your contemporaries, and be not apprehensive of degrading your species by renouncing its advances in order to renounce its vices." Actually, Rousseau himself finally left society and retired "to the woods." And in his treatise on education, entitled *Émile,* he prescribes that the pupil be scrupulously guarded against any contact with society lest he be contaminated by its vices

---

[1] Ernst Cassirer, *The Question of Jean-Jacques Rousseau,* Peter Gay, tr. (New York: Columbia University Press, 1954), p. 48. By permission.

[2] Quoted in *Ibid.,* p. 45.

and corruption. Cassirer, whose interpretation of Rousseau differs fundamentally from nearly all the other writers on the subject, insists that Rousseau did not mean that man should return to savagery or his primitive condition, but that by "nature" he meant the unspoiled impulses of the human heart which he held to be good. Later Rousseau stated that it had never been his intention to return to the past, since human nature does not go back. In *The Social Contract* he further remarks that his aim had been not a return to the primitive conditions of society but to its primitive function, which he defined as "the administration of law and the establishment of justice." In other words, Rousseau contrasted man as he was in the admittedly artificial society of his day with the man he ought to have been. Nevertheless, it must be conceded that Rousseau's example and his various writings have been understood by many of his disciples and admirers as literally "going back to nature"—as witness Thoreau's *Walden*, the vogue of the "noble savage" in Chateaubriand, not to speak of James Fenimore Cooper!

But even the briefest sketch of Rousseau's central theme would be incomplete without a mention of his last great work, *The Social Contract* (1762), in which he presents his theory of the state. He declares in his *Confessions* that "I had come to see that everything was radically connected with politics, and that . . . no people would be other than the nature of its government made it.[3] Thus in *The Social Contract* in which he restates the Hobbesian and Lockean theories of the origin of the state, tracing it back to the emergence of property, Rousseau "writes the code for the very society which he has rejected and castigated as the cause of all the depravity and unhappiness of mankind." [4] Moreover he proclaims that since the state represents the "general will" (*volonté générale*), all members of society must submit to it voluntarily but unconditionally. Thus he stands for a rigid and universal reign of law —not man's autonomy, not to say license. The famous phrase, "Man, born free, is now everywhere in chains," must not, accordingly, be understood in an anarchistic sense, as if it were a call for the abolition of all government. But the equally vital distinction which Rousseau makes between the existing and the ideal state he advocated is that the latter represents the general will while the former does not. How the general will is to be ascertained and made to prevail, however, he does not say. Therefore, his political masterpiece remains as much a theoretical construct as is Plato's *Republic*, which Rousseau carefully

[3] Lester G. Crocker, ed., *The Confessions of Jean Jacques Rousseau* (New York: Pocket Library, Inc., 1956), p. 207. By permission.
[4] Cassirer, *op. cit.*, p. 52.

studied and imitated. But how can one produce social harmony by compounding wholly selfish individual wills into an equally selfish "general will"?

Since in the ideal state any deviation from the "general will" would destroy social harmony, the state dictates everything, including religion. The concluding chapter of *The Social Contract* deals with the subject of civil religion obligatory upon all. Anything that is regarded as irrelevant to social life is not subject to restriction; but all the rest is strictly defined, imposed, and enforced—even punished by expulsion from society. The dogmas comprise faith in the Supreme Being, providence, immortality, and the last judgment. But aside from the dictates of the state, Rousseau also recognizes, somewhat inconsistently, the freely avowed individual conviction, best expressed in the famous "Profession of Faith of the Savoyard Vicar" that is included in *Émile:*

> Conscience! Conscience! thou divine instinct, immortal and celestial voice: thou certain guide of an ignorant and limited being, though intelligent and free; thou infallible judge of good and evil, who renderest man to resemble God! In thee consist the excellence of his nature and the morality of his actions. Without thee I perceive nothing in myself that should elevate me above the beasts, but the sad privilege of wandering from error to error by the aid of an ill-regulated understanding and unprincipled reason.[5]

The conscience, the voice of God in man's heart, is thus the true and only source of religion.

These principles, often misunderstood and perverted into mere naturalism—asserting that whatever is natural is good—have created the new era of Romanticism.

## F. D. E. Schleiermacher, the Theological Exponent of Romanticism

The principal religious representative of Romanticism is Friedrich Daniel Ernst Schleiermacher (1768-1834), who is regarded as the father of modern liberal theology. His father, a Reformed army chaplain

---

[5] Jean Jacques Rousseau, "Profession of Faith of a Savoyard Vicar," in *Oeuvres de J. J. Rousseau* (Paris, chez Deterville, 1817), VI, p. 70. My translation.

deeply skeptical toward religion, sent his son to be educated at Moravian schools. Young Friedrich spent four impressionable years in two of their institutions, and ever after remained influenced by their pietism, which was akin to Romanticism only in stressing feeling against arid intellectualism. He always remained "a higher kind of Moravian," for these ardent pietists had taught him how to enrich religion with the warmth of feeling. ". . . Zinzendorf and Schleiermacher laid their religious emphasis on peace, on receptivity, on dependence, on the immediate touch of God on the human heart." [6] Schleiermacher's appeal to subjective religious feeling of dependence begins a new epoch in the history of evangelical Christianity. Even Brunner and Barth regard him as one of the really significant theologians of the nineteenth century.

When in 1787 he left the Moravian seminary at Barby—because of its "theological rubbish"—for the University of Halle, he encountered at this latter place the philosophy of Kant. But he never became entirely a Kantian. Nevertheless, the rigorous intellectual discipline necessary for the study of Kant taught him how to think. He was in agreement with the great philosopher's rejection of hedonism and accepted the conclusions of *The Critique of Pure Reason*. But Kant's definition of the *summum bonum* in terms of morality alone did not satisfy Schleiermacher. He missed in Kant the strong sense of the divine presence, the very qualities of the religious emotions in which he had been nurtured among the Moravians.

> Kant called himself a Theist and found that the moral law within filled him with wonder. It was, therefore, easier for one so acute and at the same time so profoundly religious as Schleiermacher, to perceive that the traditional rationalist theology, with its proofs of the existence of God, had suffered a deadly blow at the hands of Kant. Religion, he saw, could not be appropriated by purely intellectual means. In fact the central point of religion was not in the intellect at all.[7]

But it was his removal to Berlin in 1793 where three years later he became the preacher at the Charity Hospital that brought him into the very vortex of Romanticism. He became intimately acquainted with Friedrich Schlegel's and Novalis' circle and accepted enthusiastically the principal tenet of that movement—the rediscovery of feeling as against the centrality of reason. Even prior to this period, Spinoza had exerted a decisive influence upon him. He had been particularly im-

[6] Flew, *The Idea of Perfection*, p. 343.
[7] *Ibid.*, p. 347.

pressed with the Spinozan doctrine of the infinite substance, with which he roughly identified Kant's noumenal *ding an sich*. This then was further combined with the Romanticist emphases and Goethe's influence. Both stressed man's natural goodness as the highest manifestation of the spiritual universe. "The infinity of the human soul," wrote Schlegel, "the divinity of all natural things, and the humanity of the gods, remain the great eternal theme of all these variations." [8] Likewise Goethe's writings seemed to Schleiermacher

> like the revelation of a new ideal of life. . . . There was more than a touch of Pantheism in the outlook of the school. Spinoza's doctrines gave satisfaction to Goethe. . . . The world-spirit was conceived as unfolding itself in a genetic development from unconscious Nature to the highest forms of self-consciousness. Out of this conception grew the new Pantheism apparent in the systems of Schelling and Hegel.[9]

The first fruits of Schleiermacher's new religious *Weltanschauung*, written expressly for his Romantic friends, appeared in 1799 in his first important work, entitled *On Religion: Speeches addressed to its Cultured Despisers*. It was republished in a modified form in 1806. The *Speeches* were followed in 1800 by his *Soliloquies*, a collection of philosophical essays dealing with various topics. The first of these works, proving the serious apologetic intention of one educated man who understood the high value of religion toward others who did not, affords us a truly eloquent, even passionate, defense of religion in general: religion is not "a patchwork of ethical and metaphysical crumbs, but a sense and taste for the Infinite." [10] As such, it is feeling and intuition, and thus it is subjective. One without the other "is nothing." But in the second edition of the *Speeches* he omitted intuition as suggesting intellectual activity, and restricted the realm of religion wholly to feeling, which he understood as an "immediate self-consciousness," the doctrinal tenets being derivative from this essentially ineffable state. Thus "The pious mind as such knows nothing and does nothing. . . . No account is taken of the constitutive function of *belief* in religion as we actually know it." [11] But what then is the object of this feeling?

---

[8] Quoted in Richard B. Brandt, *The Philosophy of Schleiermacher* (New York: Harper & Brothers, 1941), pp. 61-62. By permission.

[9] Flew, *op. cit.*, pp. 347-48.

[10] John Oman, tr., Schleiermacher, *On Religion* (London, 1894), pp. 31, 39.

[11] Hugh Ross Mackintosh, *Types of Modern Theology* (New York: Charles Scribner's Sons, 1937; London: James Nisbet and Company, Ltd., 1937), pp. 48-49. By permission.

In the first edition of the *Speeches* he refers to it as "the Universe" and "the World-All." Since the Universe exhibits purposiveness of a cosmic mind, one may think of it as a personal God. But Schleiermacher repudiates such a theistic interpretation: "God is not everything in religion . . . and the Universe is more." [12] In the second edition the essentially Spinozan terms are replaced by such appellations as "the Divine" and "God," thus showing a greater distinction between God and the world. But even so it must not be supposed that Schleiermacher had passed over to the belief in a personal God. In fact, although he admitted that the theists are as justified in their views as the nontheists, he personally joined the latter. He went even so far as to repudiate the idea of "no God, no religion," [13] and thus asserted that an atheistic religion was a possibility. But how that can be in view of his own definition of religion as the sense of the Infinite, he does not explain.

In the second place, Schleiermacher places emphasis upon the individual. Each human being is a microcosm, an embodiment of the All. He writes in the *Soliloquies:*

> For a long time I too was content with the discovery of a universal reason; I worshipped the one essential being as the highest, and so believed that there is but a single right way of acting in every situation, that the conduct of all men should be alike, each differing from the other only by reason of his place and station in the world. . . . [But] there dawned upon me what is now my highest intuition. I saw clearly that each man is meant to represent humanity in his own way, combining its elements uniquely, so that it may reveal itself in every mode, and all that can issue from its womb be made actual in the fulness of unending space and time.[14]

This is a reaffirmation of the familiar emphasis of the entire humanist era, placing man at the center—Schleiermacher's anthropocentric focus in Christian theology. But at the same time the individual must be united with humanity through love. The goal of human history is bound up with the spiritual growth of humankind through the development of each individual. It is truly remarkable that with this high appreciation of man's individuality Schleiermacher rejects and even ridicules the belief in immortality conceived in terms of the survival of personality. At that time his concept of "eternal life" takes the form of the absorption of one's personality into the Infinite.

---

[12] Schleiermacher, *Reden*, first ed., pp. 132-33.
[13] *Ibid.*, p. 124.
[14] Horace Leland Friess, tr. *Schleiermacher's Soliloquies* (La Salle, Illinois: The Open Court Publishing Company, 1926), pp. 30-31. By permission.

To sum up, then, Schleiermacher's view of religion during the period of 1799-1800: he understands it as feeling and intuition. Intuition without feeling is nothing and so is feeling without intuition. As such, religion is a natural instinct for the Infinite, which does not require the holding of any particular doctrines or of any given ethical system. Nor is religion a particular philosophy or science. The religious man is not primarily a moral or ethical personality (Kant), or a thinker (Hegel), but possesses a deeper level of self-consciousness beyond that of reflection. Thus to be religious is to possess a sense of the Infinite as existing in all finite manifestations—"to see in all things, no matter how repugnant they may seem, an underlying relation to the perfection, beauty, and harmony of the universe." [15]

However, Schleiermacher's views underwent a rapid development during the next six years, particularly after he became professor of theology at Halle, where he devoted himself to the task of translating Plato. In 1809, when the University of Berlin was founded, he became the founding member of the Faculty of that important institution, but also accepted the post of preacher at the Holy Trinity Church—thus choosing to engage in the active ministry of preaching, instead of the academic functions alone. During the next eleven years, until 1821 when he published his *Glaubenslehre* (the English translation is entitled *The Christian Faith*), he not only arrived at views considerably removed from those published more than twenty years earlier, but expressed them in a language more acceptable to Christians generally. To be sure, the controversy about Schleiermacher's "pantheism" still rages, and opposing views of it are taken by distinguished representatives of different theological traditions. All that needs to be affirmed, however, is that he did not intend to be a pantheist, even though he was not always successful in carrying out his intention, nor was he always consistent in holding the intention.

Nevertheless, one does not always know when the changed terminology represents an attempt at accommodation to what he regards as the current attitude of the Church (for after all he is dealing with the Christian faith, not necessarily with his own private views), and when it represents a genuine change of thought on his own part. For to begin with, Schleiermacher defines the task of the Christian theologian as that of depicting Christian experience, of interpreting the believer's self-consciousness of God, and *not* the search for or formulation of an objective system based on an external criterion, such as the Scriptures. Thus all that he deals with—all that he has to say about God, sin, and

[15] Brandt, *op. cit.*, p. 97.

redemption—is viewed from the subjective side. It is an effort to describe our own feelings, not the objective reality of God as He exists irrespective of our emotions about Him. Schleiermacher asserts that theology as knowledge of God is forever impossible, for all we can ever *know* are our feelings concerning Him. Thus he practically identifies the concept of revelation with this subjective experience of Christians. Moreover, he often describes what he thinks is the self-consciousness of the Christian community, rather than his own emotional states, which he formerly described almost exclusively in the *Soliloquies*. And since the religious consciousness of Christian believers differs from time to time, no formal doctrinal tenets can ever be of permanent validity. It is while bearing this in mind that one must approach the study of Schleiermacher's great work of his maturity, of which Mackintosh writes that "Next to the *Institutes* of Calvin, it is the most influential dogmatic work to which evangelical Protestantism can point. . . ." [16] Furthermore, another important difference between this work and Schleiermacher's earlier writings about religion is the fact that it is devoted to the exposition of the Christian faith in particular, rather than to religion in general. Religion is still defined as feeling (intuition is no longer mentioned), but now it is specifically identified with the feeling of absolute dependence upon God. Piety is "neither a Knowing nor a Doing, but a modification of Feeling, or of immediate self-consciousness." [17] And furthermore, Christianity as a particular expression of religion differs from other forms of historical religions, and particularly from Judaism and Islam, the other two "highest religions," insofar as it is "a monotheistic faith, belonging to the teleological type of religion and it is essentially distinguished from other such faiths by the fact that in it everything is related to the redemption accomplished by Jesus of Nazareth." Furthermore, Christianity is ". . . the most perfect of the most highly developed forms of religion." [18]

Although the basic concept of religion defined by Schleiermacher as the absolute feeling of dependence is considerably more concrete than the earlier formula of feeling pure and simple (even though intuition was mentioned along with feeling in the first edition of the *Speeches*), it still proves inadequate. His distinguished colleague at the University, the famous philosopher Georg Hegel, made fun of it by asserting that in such a case a dog would be the most religious of all creatures, since he possesses the feeling of absolute dependence to an extraordinary

---

[16] Mackintosh, *op. cit.*, p. 60.
[17] F. D. E. Schleiermacher, *The Christian Faith*, H. R. Mackintosh and J. S. Stewart, trs. (Edinburgh: T. & T. Clark, 1928), p. 5. By permission.
[18] *Ibid.*, pp. 52, 38.

degree. Moreover, it appeared obvious to his contemporaries and subsequent thinkers that Christianity has a doctrinal content, that Christians believe something objective about God, man, and redemption; and furthermore, that they are also bound to observe a moral code, to live in accordance with certain ethical principles. If religion is not *exclusively* a matter of knowledge and ethics—and it is not—it is not *exclusively* a matter of feeling, either. It partakes of all three elements in a necessary coordination, and a denial of any one of the three distorts, in fact destroys, the harmonious whole.

This aspect of Schleiermacher's concept of Christianity—no matter how valuable at the time when rationalism and moralism denied the emotional element—proved to be unsatisfactory as being both one-sided and vague. The principal modern exponent of the Schleiermacherian tradition, Rudolf Otto, redefined it more adequately by making the sense of the "numinous" to connote the specifically religious emotion, uniquely perceptible in religious experience. It is the *mysterium tremendum et fascinans*. As such it is *sui generis* religious. Only in it do men feel awe in the presence of something mysterious and overwhelmingly fascinating. Response to it on man's part is nonmoral and nonintellectual; hence, it constitutes an *a priori* religious category. But despite this nonintellectual character, religious response to the numinous also possesses a cognitive aspect: it apprehends the reality as "wholly other" or divine. In Otto's own words:

> It is an immediate appraisal of the universe as the one and the whole, transcending the mere parts which science may grasp, and at the same time, the profound spiritual experience of its underlying ideal essence.[19]

And further stressing the uniqueness of this experience, he writes:

> All this teaches us the independence of the positive content of this experience from the implications of its overt conceptual expression, and how it can be firmly grasped, thoroughly understood, and profoundly appreciated, purely in, with, and from the feeling itself.[20]

Returning now to Schleiermacher's own views, we may consider, first of all, his treatment of the concept of God. We must bear in mind

---

[19] Rudolf Otto, *Religious Essays* (New York: Oxford University Press, Inc., 1951), p. 75. By permission.
[20] Rudolf Otto, *Idea of the Holy* (New York: Oxford University Press, Inc., 1943), p. 34. By permission. Also cf. Robert F. Davidson, *Rudolf Otto's Interpretation of Religion* (Princeton: Princeton University Press, 1947).

what has already been mentioned; that we can never know what God is in Himself, but only what is involved in our own consciousness of Him. For to be absolutely dependent upon Him is identical with being in relation to Him. Had Schleiermacher developed the concept of our relation to God, he could hardly avoid ascribing personality to Him. This Schleiermacher does not do. He still speaks of God as the absolute Unity behind and beyond all things. He is the ultimate Source of all being—the cosmos, man, spiritual realities, including religious consciousness of man. Man can have no personal contact with this impersonal force. To regard God as personal would be to reduce Him to human, finite level. Accordingly, to think of Him as Father and to repose a childlike trust in Him is absent from Schleiermacher's thought. Schleiermacher indeed goes on to say that God is the creator and sustainer of all that exists, but refuses to amplify this assertion by any reference either to the biblical or to other accounts of it. Such questions, he asserts, have nothing to do with our consciousness of dependence, and therefore "we can take no particular interest" in them.[21] However, by insisting that creation and preservation must always be held together, he betrays his immanentist tendencies, which logically lead to the assertion that God and the world are one. This amounts to a refusal to distinguish between God and the world—the very essence of pantheism.

Nevertheless, he does speak of attributes of God, and distinguishes three sets of them. They do not tell us anything about God himself, with the exception of the third set, but only describe the conclusions drawn from our own consciousness of God. Thus the first set of these attributes refers to our consciousness of God's relation to the world: it comprises God's eternity, omnipresence, omnipotence, and omniscience. In the second place, there are the attributes of holiness and justice which are derived from God's relation to our consciousness of sin. And finally, he names the attributes of wisdom and love, which we deduce from the redemption wrought in us by God.[22] Of these attributes, only love and wisdom "can claim to be not mere attributes but also expressions of the very essence of God." Thus, after all, we appear to have a knowledge of the essence of God, despite Schleiermacher's earlier denial of it. And of the two, love is primary, for "we have the sense of divine love directly in the consciousness of redemption, and as this is the basis on which all the rest of our God-conscious-

21 *The Christian Faith*, p. 150.
22 *Ibid.*, pp. 194 ff., 345 ff., 723 ff.

ness is built up, it of course represents to us the essence of God." [23]
But it is difficult to conceive why, if we have consciousness of God's
attributes, Schleiermacher refuses to acknowledge them as describing
God. Does he doubt the existence of a reliable nexus between our feeling and reality? That would bring into question his basic principle of
the reliability of self-consciousness. And above all, in affirming that love
is not only an attribute but that it "represents to us the essence of
God," how can he then fail to assert the personality of God? Can he
conceive of love—any love, human or divine—as impersonal or less
than personal? One regrets finding this basic inconsistency in Schleiermacher's thinking, for it indicates his inability to free himself from
his earlier pantheistic or semi-pantheistic tendencies.

Naturally, the traditional doctrine of the Trinity has but a slight
hold, if any, upon Schleiermacher's mind; he writes that "the doctrine
itself, as ecclesiastically framed, is not an immediate utterance concerning the Christian self-consciousness . . ." [24] However, he suggests
a reconstruction of the doctrine that would make it acceptable to him.
In his view, it should affirm the fact that God was in Christ and that
His Spirit abides in the Church. However, he speaks of the Spirit in
the same way as he would of the spirit of humanity—hardly the same
concept as that of the New Testament or the Creeds.

As has already been indicated, the distinctive feature of Christianity
in comparison with other religions is the fact that everything in it is
related to the redemption wrought by Jesus Christ. Thus Schleiermacher's theology is Christocentric. He goes so far in stressing this
fact as virtually to reject the Old Testament. Jesus, although by nature
human, as we are, possessed a unique degree of God-consciousness.
Nevertheless, His "incarnation" is a natural, even though a supra-
rational (although not an *absolutely* supra-rational) fact, for all men
are capable of "taking up the divine" into themselves. [25] In this sense,
the difference between man and Jesus is one of degree, not of kind. He
becomes the Redeemer of humankind by communicating to them the
God-consciousness of which He is the supreme revelation in history,
thus saving them from the self-centeredness of their condition. But He
is unlike other men in the sense that His impulses and motivations
were always dominated by God-consciousness so completely as to be
unfailingly victorious over temptations. This is what is meant by His

[23] *Ibid.*, pp. 731-32.
[24] *Ibid.*, p. 738.
[25] *Ibid.*, pp. 64-65.

sinlessness: ". . . that from the beginning He must have been free from every influence from earlier generations which disseminated sin and disturbed the inner God-consciousness . . ." [26] However, Schleiermacher goes so far as to reject the historic doctrine of the two natures in Jesus Christ—human and divine—united in one person, and the pre-existence of the divine nature—Christ—and urges that "both the expressions, divine nature and the duality of natures in the same Person . . . shall be altogether avoided." [27] This obviously constitutes the denial of Jesus Christ's divinity as traditionally understood. Christ is, therefore, the archetypal man; we are to become what He is. Thus the redemptive work of Jesus Christ consists in communicating to men the God-consciousness of which He was wholly possessed. This is accomplished by means of a "mystical union" of the believer with Christ and is mediated through the community He founded for that purpose—the Church.

Schleiermacher's concept of man has proved extremely influential for modern thinking, for along with all Romanticists, he thought of man as essentially good; that is, as naturally predisposed to God-consciousness, which he has never completely lost. Accordingly, Schleiermacher resolutely repudiates the Augustinian-Calvinistic anthropology with its emphasis upon man's innate sinfulness—the original sin. This inadequate realization of the fact and power of sin in human life and society is indeed the principal defect of his system. He seems to have lacked any fundamental understanding of the tragic and terrible consequences of sin and evil upon the souls of men; he regards sin essentially as an inadequately developed God-consciousness—the initial stage of man on the way to redemption. In fact, to begin with, he has considerable difficulty in accounting for the origin of sin at all—the willful turning away from God—for this "must like all else be ordained of God." [28] Sin is ordained by God in so far as it exists as a necessary concomitant of the conditions under which mankind must live. There are, however, other passages in which Schleiermacher argues that sin is nonexistent for God, and therefore unreal. But setting aside these difficulties, he defines sin as "a positive antagonism of the flesh against the spirit." We must "reckon everything as sin that has arrested the free development of God-consciousness." [29] This he accounts for by saying that it is "a result of the unequal development of insight and will-power" as against the prior development of the physical body,

[26] *Ibid.*, pp. 388-89.
[27] *Ibid.*, pp. 391-92, 397.
[28] *Ibid.*, p. 269.
[29] *Ibid.*, p. 271.

with its overpowering natural drives and demands. Nevertheless, this must be regarded as "a derangement of our nature," [30] despite the fact that it is necessary as a stage toward the good. Thus it is not a positive evil, but an immature good, as a green apple is not a bad apple, but only an unripe one. What Schleiermacher wholly ignores is the fact that sin involves guilt, i.e., a consciousness of wrong in rebelling against God's will. The sense of "Against Thee, Thee only, have I sinned," is strangely absent from his concept; and without it, the deepest conviction of Christians—for after all, he was supposed to be describing their God-consciousness, not exclusively his own—that they ever stand condemned as sinners in the sight of God, is lacking. Mackintosh passes the severe judgment upon him that "in a Christian thinker this may well be thought the unpardonable sin." [31]

Accordingly, there is no necessity for a radical change of human nature, such as is demanded in traditional theology. Nor does divine grace miraculously restore the lost Christian virtues of faith, hope, and love. A modicum of these virtues has never been wholly lost by man. Schleiermacher writes: "Religious experience, however, consists precisely in this, that we are aware of this tendency to God-consciousness as a living impulse; but such an impulse can only proceed from the true inner nature of the being which it goes to constitute." [32] Redemption then is essentially a matter of growth in God-consciousness. It is gained

> as the individual's sense of God grows stronger. Atonement, reconciliation, is the sense of blessedness, which follows on a deepened consciousness of God. . . . Schleiermacher says quite plainly that the change in spiritual life which comes to pass as the soul's consciousness of God is deepened, is the real meaning of that which is called atonement.[33]

Men thus redeemed constitute the Church. The Church is the communion of those who participate in the common religious life derived from Christ. Membership in this body therefore is conditioned by faith in Christ as the Redeemer; such faith "leads necessarily . . . to fellowship or communion, a communion which, on the one hand, is variable and fluid, and, on the other, has definite limits, i.e., is a Church." [34] Outside this fellowship salvation is not available to the same degree

[30] *Ibid.,* p. 275.
[31] Mackintosh, *op. cit.,* p. 96.
[32] *The Christian Faith,* p. 244.
[33] Gustaf Aulén, *Christus Victor* (London: S.P.C.K.; and New York: The Macmillan Company, 1945), p. 152. By permission.
[34] *The Christian Faith,* p. 26.

because the God-consciousness originating in Christ and mediated through the Holy Spirit is absent. In this sense redemption comes to the believer through the Church, in which the divine Spirit dwells, and not from within himself; this is what is meant by the traditional phrase that men are "saved by grace." Thus no one is saved in a vacuum, by himself, nor unto himself, but only in the fellowship of Christ's Church.

The aim of Christian life is holiness, that is, the enjoyment of perfect God-consciousness. This cannot be developed except in the fellowship of the Church. This is the principal task of the Church. "That a Church is nothing but a communion or association relating to religion or piety, is beyond all doubt for us Evangelical (Protestant) Christians, since we regard it as equivalent to degeneration in a Church when it begins to occupy itself with other matters as well, whether the affairs of science or of outward organization." [35] Schleiermacher thought that holiness may be attained in this life. Yet, he recoiled from asserting that one may reach a stage of perfection in which all differences between him and Christ would disappear: for no one has experienced *throughout* his life the uninterrupted communion with God that Christ had. Nevertheless, the difference is one of degree, not of kind.

Schleiermacher stands at the beginning of a new period of Christian theology. Barth writes of him in high admiration that "the first place in a history of theology of the most recent times belongs and will always belong to Schleiermacher, and he has no rival." [36] Among Schleiermacher's new emphases are those on the individual believer and the communion of believers. Both are the logical consequences of the basic presuppositions of his system. Since religion is essentially a feeling, it is necessarily experienced in the individual consciousness. This emphasis on the uniqueness and the worth of each individual is rooted in his earlier Romanticism, as has already been noted. But along with this emphasis, Schleiermacher also stresses the importance of the community of believers in the Church without which, as we have seen, no individual could participate in the God-consciousness passed down through the ages in that fellowship. In this respect, Schleiermacher is a pioneer in a new appreciation of the Church, later further developed by Ritschl. It presaged the modern emphasis on the social implications of the gospel.

Nevertheless, Schleiermacher has exerted his most potent, but not altogether beneficial, influence in those aspects in which he restricted

---

[35] *Ibid.*, p. 5.
[36] Karl Barth, *Protestant Thought from Rousseau to Ritschl* (New York: Harper & Brothers, 1959), p. 306. By permission.

the sphere of theology to such doctrines alone as are derived from the feeling of absolute dependence. This "theological empiricism" is evident in all subsequent development of liberal theology. In the first place, then, this influence is seen in the rejection of the historical tradition of the authority of the Scriptures as based on miracles and prophecies concerning Christ. Indeed, Schleiermacher inverts the argument by asserting that the acceptance of the Scriptures follows, rather than precedes, faith in Christ. He further limits Christian testimony to the New Testament, since according to him its writers alone could be said to have been inspired by Christ. That is the only sense in which Schleiermacher thought of "inspiration." He regards the Old Testament as not essentially different from the religious books of the Greeks.

From the same point of view, Schleiermacher found no integral place in his system for the doctrines of the Virgin Birth, the Resurrection, Ascension, the Second Coming, Trinity, eternal damnation, angels and devils. All these doctrines, it may be remarked, have set but loosely in the liberal tradition ever since.

Furthermore, since Christian theology is a description of the God-consciousness of believers in a given historical period, no one of these changing descriptions of the content of the Christian faith may claim final authority. It is ever becoming, never completed. There can, therefore, be no authoritative, final statement of faith, no "faith once delivered to the saints," the same now and ever more. Consequently, any attempt to distinguish between "orthodoxy" and "heterodoxy" is meaningless. This is particularly true if we restrict the term "orthodoxy" to a conformity "with the matter fixed in the confessional documents." [37] Since these can never become universally valid, the demand for conformity with them ceases to be valid. All that can be done is to contrast the faith of today with its various formularies in the past. But one is no more authoritative than the rest. Schleiermacher ranged himself on the side of the "heterodox" in respect to the confessional standards, although "it is the kind of heterodoxy that will soon enough be orthodox." [38]

In summing up our consideration of Schleiermacher, we may safely assert that he has exerted an enormous influence, either directly or indirectly, on all theologians since his day. His positive contribution consists in opening up new avenues of understanding of religion for those to whom the traditional rationalistic orthodoxy or the Kantian moralism are unacceptable. The age, with its romanticism and incipient

---

[37] *The Christian Faith*, p. 110.
[38] Quoted in Mackintosh, *op. cit.*, p. 83.

scientism, found his approach more congenial, particularly in so far as it provided an escape from arid rationalism. Therefore, largely as the result of his work, many Protestant theologians of the succeeding generations have found his views suggestive and helpful. His emphasis on the subjective side of religion has led to the development of psychology of religion. His undoubted loyalty to Christ—an evidence of the abiding influence of Moravianism—has also served as a corrective to the former comparative neglect of Christology; this is likewise true of his emphasis on the Church as a fellowship of believers.

Nevertheless, Schleiermacher's interpretation of Christianity also manifests grave inadequacies and positive faults. In its exclusive emphasis on feeling it is as one-sided as the rationalism and moralism which it opposed. Instead of conceiving religion as a response of the whole personality to the impact of God's grace, Schleiermacher singled out one of the "faculties" as the sole active part of man in the religious experience. This has led to the inevitable denial of the rest of man's personality and its rightful place and function in the religious experience. Another result of his views has been the weakening of faith in, and in some instances an abandonment of, some basic Christian tenets. In the first place, the Schleiermacherian tradition shows a tendency toward pantheism or semi-pantheism, as a result of which it often places insufficient emphasis on the personality of God. In its most extreme modern form, this tendency manifests itself in naturalism and humanism, the latter even denying the existence of God altogether. Moreover, the tradition lacks clarity in distinguishing between man and God, particularly as far as Christology is concerned; generally, the distinction has been said to be one of degree rather than of kind. But among its most serious failures is the wholly inadequate concept of sin, and consequently of redemption and salvation. In all these aspects, Schleiermacher's interpretation of Christian faith is clearly at variance with the central gospel message of Jesus Christ as well as with the teaching of the Protestant Reformers. Thus Schleiermacher exhibits to a very notable degree the impact of the secularist culture of his day upon Christian theology.

# 6

# Reality—Ethical Imperative or Absolute All-Unity?

## Immanuel Kant and His "Critiques" of Philosophy and Religion

The greatest revolution that occurred in philosophical thinking after the debacle of empiricism caused by Hume was the work of Immanuel Kant (1724-1804). He was born in Königsberg, East Prussia (at present Kaliningrad in the Soviet Union), of a poor family. His father was a saddler. Both parents were ardent pietists, and it was in that spirit that they brought up their son. But the greatest single influence in the life of young Kant was exerted upon him by the pietistic pastor of his parents, Schultz. He persuaded them to send their eight-year-old son to the *Collegium Fridericianum* of which he was principal; there young Kant was trained under strict pietistic influences and pressures. But like Schleiermacher later, Kant revolted against the regimentation to which he was subjected at school. At the age of sixteen, he entered that "most undistinguished of the German universities," Königsberg (Berlin was not in existence then), enrolling in the faculty of theology, of which Pastor Schultz was the leading member. But it was philosophy which attracted him most. Under the influence of his teacher, Martin Knutzen, the best professor the university could boast, Kant became an adherent of the rationalistic school of Wolff, that Philistine philosopher of barren Reason. It was under such circumstances that Kant developed a strong distaste for, or rather aversion from, all emotional and mystical elements of pietism which prevented him ever after from comprehending their proper place in religion. He was mortally afraid of anything that smacked of "enthusiasm," or as he terms it, "*Schwärmerei.*" He retained, however, the pietistic emphasis on moral earnestness. His own religious views, further affected by Rousseau, developed in the direction of moralism, the sense of the ethical foundations of human life conceived in terms of imperative duty, of reverence for "the starry heavens above and the moral law within."

After graduating from the university, he was obliged to support himself by tutoring. It was not until 1755, at the age of thirty-one, that he was appointed a *privat-dozent* at the University. Fifteen years later he at last was promoted to the full rank of *professor ordinarius*. The delay was caused by a distrust of his religious views, for the pietistic element among the faculty members was still strong.

Contrary to the popular caricature of him as a pedantic "*Gelehrte*" and a human clockwork, he was actually widely regarded as a fascinating conversationalist and popular lecturer who possessed, besides his academic abilities, social graces and talents of a high order. He was a welcome guest in many socially prominent families. Herder, who was Kant's pupil, wrote of him "with greatest thankfulness and reverence."

In his philosophical thought Kant matured slowly. He began, as has already been mentioned, as a Wolffian; but soon added to rationalism adherence to the tenets of Lockean empiricism, which, however, he knew mainly through David Hume. It was Hume, Kant confessed, who was instrumental in "waking him from his dogmatic slumbers." But Rousseau exercised even greater influence upon his thinking. It is not without significance that the only portrait that hung on the walls of his study was that of Rousseau and that he—the most methodical and punctilious of men—missed his daily walk only once, when Rousseau's *Émile* came off the press and he was immersed in reading it!

Ernst Cassirer, to whom we principally owe the discovery of Rousseau's influence on Kant,[1] points out that this is to be seen particularly

---

[1] Ernst Cassirer, *Rousseau, Kant, Goethe* (Princeton: Princeton University Press, 1945).

clearly in Kant's recognition (in his *Critique of Practical Reason*) of the ethical realm as the noumenal reality. Rousseau's notion of conscience as opposed to all external authority of the current *mores* became basic for Kant in the form of the "categorical imperative." Kant also credited Rousseau with teaching him "the gospel of man," understanding man as an essentially moral being, ethically autonomous and therefore free. Man was thus part of the noumenal realm, and as such was a being of infinite worth—not merely of temporal value. For value has its equivalent in a price; worth is above all price.

Confronted with the debacle of Lockean empiricism as presented in the skepticism of Hume, Kant set himself the task of reconstruction. Without surrendering the basic principles of empiricism, he thought he saw an escape from the faux pas that had led to the Humean debacle. At first he hoped to put the whole matter right in one volume. But as he worked away at the critical problem, the subject matter differentiated itself into three *Critiques* and later into his *Religion within the Limits of Reason Alone*. It took him the greater part of his remaining life to accomplish the task he had blithely thought of completing in a relatively short time.

The *Critiques* form a unity, dealing with a single theme; as such they must be considered together. The questions he sought to answer have to do, first of all, with the limits of scientific—what he calls pure —knowledge; since this is derived from experience plus reason and understanding, it is necessarily limited to the empirical—or what he calls the phenomenal—realm. This is the burden of his *Critique of Pure Reason*, on which he worked for eleven years and which was at last published in 1781. But since noumenal reality, being immaterial, is not capable of being subjected to empirical inquiry, a different method of treatment is required: it is the practical reason, or morality, which yields answers to the metaphysical problems. This is then the theme of the *Critique of Practical Reason* published in 1788. And finally his attempt to deal with esthetics and religion (as distinct from morality) is the subject not only of his *Critique of Judgment* but also of his *Religion within the Limits of Reason Alone*.

First of all, let us examine the arguments of his first *Critique*, the importance of which for philosophy it would be difficult to overestimate. Professor Lindsay characterizes it as among the most illuminating books in the world, if one understands it! Since no further development of the empiricist line of argument was possible after the Humean debacle, Kant had to introduce into it the saving notion that mind is not passive but active. Mind is not a mere receiving set for sensory impressions, but seizes upon them and transforms them before we become aware of the result of this process. Knowledge then represents the combination of the raw sensory impressions that we perceive —or to use his own term, that we intuit—and the understanding and reason that the mind adds. The functions of intuition, understanding and reason are disparate and cannot be interchanged. But all three are absolutely essential to the process of knowing.

In what then does the inherent a priori mental activity consist that transforms the sensory data into the aspect under which we know them? Kant distinguishes two kinds: forms and categories. Forms affect exclusively our intuition of sensory objects and consist of space and time. We intuit all objects under these forms; they are not inherent in the objects themselves, but are added to them by our minds. Accordingly—although without the forms of space and time we cannot intuit any object whatsoever, and these forms appear real to us—they are not noumenally real. As for the categories, they apply to the understanding, not to intuition. They are quantity, quality, relation (cause and effect), and modality (possibility, actuality, and necessity). Since, then, in knowledge our awareness includes only the end result of this amalgamation of the sensory data with the categories and understanding, we can never know what the object which was intuited by us was in itself (*ding an sich*) before it had undergone the transforming process. Thus we know things as they appear to us (as phenomena), not as they are in themselves (noumena). And as long as the human mind is constituted in the way Kant describes, it is obvious that we shall never know things otherwise than as they appear. It is not a matter of imperfect knowledge which can, in time, be overcome; our scientific objective knowledge—knowledge of matter, of things—can never be other than "phenomenal." After all the only instrument of knowledge we possess is the mind, such as it is. We cannot "get out of our mind" in order to gain better knowledge. To be "out of one's mind" is to be insane.

But does that mean that if we cannot know the object "in itself" (*ding an sich*), it does not exist or that our minds create it? Kant never doubted or denied the existence of reality outside our minds, nor did he ever assert that our minds *create* objects. This was the step taken by his successors, such as Fichte and Schelling.

Furthermore, it must also be made clear that Kant makes an important distinction between understanding and reason: "All our knowledge starts with the senses, proceeds from thence to understanding, and ends with reason, beyond which there is no higher faculty to be found in us for elaborating the matter of intuition and bringing it under the highest unity of thought." [2] Thus the function of reason is to unify the data given us in intuition and understanding into ever enlarged concepts; for otherwise our knowledge would consist of innumerable fragmentary and unintegrated experiences.

Since our knowledge is wholly of the phenomenal world and never can reach the noumenal reality, it can deal only with the sensory data, and "cannot prove anything regarding man's immortality, transcendental freedom, an intelligible world, or an unconditioned Being. . . . Speculative reason can never afford us knowledge of the nature of ultimate reality; but for identical reasons materialism, too, can never prove its case." [3] Accordingly, Kant proceeds to attack and to reject the three traditional arguments (long held to be proofs) for the existence of God, since they rest upon the objective, i.e., phenomenal grounds. "I have therefore found it necessary to deny knowledge, in order to make room for faith," he writes in the Preface to the second edition of his *Critique of Pure Reason*. The ontological arguments of Anselm which he knew only in the Cartesian version, he declares to be fallacious as resting on "a confusion between the logical necessity of thought and the ontological necessity of existence." [4] The cosmological argument of Thomas Aquinas—that is, the argument from various contingencies of particular things depending for their existence upon a self-existent Being—is inapplicable, because the category of causality belongs only to the phenomenal world, not to God, Who is of the noumenal realm.

The teleological argument is dealt with in the *Critique of Judgment;* nevertheless, we may consider it here for the sake of completeness. Nature exhibits, Kant writes, countless examples of purposiveness. A tree, for instance, is self-perpetuating, having within itself power to develop from the seed to maturity and then to reproduce itself. Viewed as a fortuitous result of chance, it is incomprehensible and inexplicable. To explain it, we must presuppose a supranatural power working purposefully toward a goal. As Tennyson expressed it in regard to the "flower in the crannied wall," "if I knew what thou art, root and all and all in all, I would know what God and man is."

But when we suppose such a purposeful power working in nature, we come into conflict with the mechanical principle held as operative

---

[2] Kant's *Critique of Pure Reason*, translated by Norman Kemp Smith, by permission of St. Martin's Press, Inc. and Macmillan & Co., Ltd., London, 1929, p. 300.

[3] Theodore M. Greene, tr., *Kant's Religion within the Limits of Reason Alone* (La Salle, Illinois: The Open Court Publishing Company, 1934). Introduction, p. xli. By permission.

[4] *Ibid.*, xlii, n. 1.

in nature ever since the days of Descartes. And yet, Kant continues, "That crude matter should have originally formed itself according to mechanical laws, that life should have sprung from the nature of what is lifeless, that matter should have been able to dispose itself into the form of a self-maintaining purposiveness—this . . . [is] contrary to reason." "Absolutely no human reason . . . can hope to understand the production of even a blade of grass by mere mechanical causes." [5] How then shall the teleological argument by regarded? Kant, rejecting both the mechanical and Spinozan hypotheses, inclines to accept the theistic explanation as the most satisfactory, not as knowledge, however, but as faith. Nevertheless, he declares that theism is "certainly superior to all other grounds of explanation." [6]

To sum up: neither scientific knowledge nor speculative reason is able to prove the existence of God, for God is not part of the objective world with which our cognitive apparatus deals. This is not to say that God cannot be apprehended by man at all; only that He cannot be known by human mind. For Christian theology this is nothing new. The anonymous fourteenth century English mystic who wrote *The Cloud of Unknowing* expressed it by saying, "By love He can be gotten and holden; by thought, never." Pascal also discovered that "the heart has its reasons which reason does not know." And Kant points out that were it otherwise, it would be detrimental to religion:

> Once prove God's existence out of the mouth of non-moral nature and you have a non-moral God of no use to the religious consciousness. In Kant's opinion, then, it is all to the good that man is forced to depend upon moral proofs of God's existence and nature for an adequate theology and a sound basis for religious faith." [7]

Such a new, and in his judgment sound, basis for the existence of God and the moral realm Kant provides in his *Critique of Practical Reason* (1788), which establishes not only the existence of the noumenal realm, but also asserts the method for our attaining it. This then places Kant, along with Plato, among the few outstanding philosophical dualists. In the opinion of Nicolas Berdyaev, these dualist philosophers were the greatest minds of the entire history of Western thought, for they distinguished by a philosophical method the two kinds of reality—material and metaphysical. To be sure, Kant's successors (just as Plato's) quietly

---

[6] *Kant's Critique of Judgment*, J. H. Bernard, tr. (London: Macmillan and Co., Ltd., 1914), p. 326. By permission.
[6] *Ibid.*, p. 305.
[7] *Religion within the Limits of Reason Alone*, p. li.

subverted the master's dualism into monism. Nevertheless, it is Kant's glory that he provided on philosophical grounds the proof of the metaphysical (or as he called it, the noumenal) reality, even though from the point of view of Christian faith it is not adequate; nevertheless it makes the adequate statement possible.

Kant's own characterization of the noumenal realm is exclusively ethical, and he finds an empirical basis for it in man's moral sense. All normal human beings possess a sense—no matter how rudimentary—of right and wrong. This moral faculty, potential or developed, is an ultimate fact. In words irresistibly reminiscent of Rousseau's apotheosis of Conscience as the voice of God in the human heart, Kant hymns the praises of Duty:

> *Duty!* Thou sublime and mighty name that dost embrace nothing charming or insinuating, but requirest submission, and yet seekest not to move the will by threatening aught that would arouse natural aversion or terror, but merely holdest forth a law which of itself finds entrance into the mind . . ." [8]

One recognizes a profound religious attitude rather than mere legalism in Kant's apostrophe to Duty. This *sense of oughtness,* empirically discerned, not merely deduced or asserted on a priori grounds, he calls "the categorical imperative." Kant, who has a perfect horror of hedonism—doing what one does for one's own satisfaction or pleasure—resolutely insists that this sense of duty goes contrary to our natural lusts or selfish desires: it "embraces nothing charming or insinuating," but requires submission. Hence he preaches duty for duty's sake. No action is good unless it be motivated *solely* by the sense of duty, a pure respect for the law of reason without fear of punishment or hope of reward. Moreover, it is binding upon all men impartially, since it is possessed by all. No distinction is made between the religious and the irreligious; all ought equally to obey the categorical imperative of their moral nature. Likewise, it is universal: "Act in conformity with that maxim, and that maxim only, which you can at the same time will to be a universal law." This is recognizably Kant's version of the Golden Rule. Furthermore, in the greatest aphorism coined by Kant, he requires respect for every other personality as of the highest worth: "Act so as to use humanity, whether in your own person or in the person of another, always as an end, never as merely a means." [9] Ac-

---

[8] Quoted in *ibid.,* pp. li-lii.
[9] John Watson, *The Philosophy of Kant—Extracts from his Own Writings* (New York: The Macmillan Company, 1891), pp. 241, 246.

cordingly, the ideal of human society is that of "a moral kingdom of ends."

In developing the implications of the categorical imperative, Kant holds it as axiomatic that the moral obligation necessarily implies moral freedom, without which it would be a mere mockery. If we felt compelled to live virtuously without being able to do so, it would imply a radical evil in the moral universe. Hence he concludes, "I ought, therefore I can." But this in turn necessarily implies not only that the realm of moral freedom—the noumenal realm—exists, but that man is part of it. Thus man is an intersection of two realms, the phenomenal and noumenal, the only being in existence whom we know to be so placed. By his physical nature he belongs to the former; by his moral nature, to the latter. If by the limitations of our minds we are restricted to a knowledge of the phenomenal realm, by means of our moral nature we become aware of the noumenal reality. In the phenomenal realm we are subject to physical necessity that we loosely term natural laws; in the noumenal realm we are morally free. Or to put it in another way, on its positive side, moral freedom is the ability to live in accordance with the moral requirements; on the negative side, it is independence from the natural law. Although Kant's concept is not to be identified with the fully developed theological concept of the spiritual realm, it is obviously congenial to it and affords an empirical ground for it.

Yet virtue is not *wholly* its own reward, but is a condition of happiness. For, if virtue deserves to be crowned with happiness, it is a matter of common and fairly frequent observation that a life of virtue is not always so rewarded. Is, then, moral law a mockery, an illusion, a sorry jest of some cosmic demiurge? Never! In order to remove the intolerable doubt as to the integrity of the moral law, moral consciousness must postulate the existence of God as the guarantor of the ultimate and inevitable fulfilment of happiness, and of the eternal life in which the tragic shortcomings of our earthly existence shall be made good. These "moral" arguments for the existence of God and for immortality are Kant's substitutes for the ontological and cosmological "proofs" he had rejected.

The argument suffers from the fatal weakness that it is a deduction from the premise of the sense of moral law, rather than a self-sufficient fact. Anyone who does not acknowledge the premise, or does not make the deduction from it that Kant made, need not acknowledge the existence of God and immortality. Furthermore, if one acts solely from a sense of duty, then it must be without regard to whether happiness or unhappiness result. And if happiness is necessarily presupposed either in this life or the next, then the sense of duty is no longer the *sole* motive. On the other hand, if virtue need not necessarily result in happiness, neither God nor immortality is essential to the scheme. Nevertheless, for himself, Kant did make the deduction. He furthermore asserts that God, in order to satisfy the conditions implied by the moral sense, must be possessed of perfection. But in asserting it, he rigorously excludes all finite attributes and anthropomorphisms and rejects all arguments from "natural theology" on the ground that religion, i.e., morality, is not "natural," does not belong to the phenomenal, but to the noumenal realm. As for immortality, Kant has but little to tell us about it. We "know nothing of the future," he writes, "and we ought not to seek to know more than what is rationally bound up with the incentives of morality and their end." [10] In general, Kant conceives of the future life as continuation of the earthly.

It is in the moral realm, then, that man has transcended the limitation of the phenomenal world and has entered into the freedom of the noumenal. Thus it happens that Kant, quite unwittingly, I believe, affirms the fundamental postulates of the Augustinian-Anselmic tradition that faith is more fundamental than knowledge, as expressed in the formula *Credo ut intelligam*. But for Kant there is a gulf fixed between the phenomenal and noumenal world which cannot be crossed. For him, man apprehends reality only in the realm of moral consciousness. This will never enable him to acquire knowledge of objective reality in the material realm. Science is destined forever to deal only with the functions of matter, not with its essence. This is the conclusion—on vastly different grounds—of Albert Einstein as well.

Kant's third volume in the series, *Critique of Judgment*, appeared in 1790 and was devoted to his treatment of the esthetic sense. It also includes the much more important subject of teleology, which has already been dealt with. These two subjects are treated together because Kant discerned an affinity between them: beauty and teleology both comprise significance or meaning above and beyond the underlying physical fact. For Kant as for Wordsworth, the yellow primrose along the water bank is not merely "a primrose and nothing more." It comprises meaning which lies "too deep for tears."

Thus at last we come to the work devoted to Kant's consideration of religion, entitled *Religion within the Limits of Reason Alone* (1793). To begin with, Kant claims in the preface to the second edition "that

[10] *Religion within the Limits of Reason Alone*, p. 149, n.

reason can be found to be not only compatible with Scripture but also at one with it . . ." [11] In Book One he breaks with the fundamental assumption of the Enlightenment that man is good by nature and is corrupted (if at all) solely by environment. Kant, on the other hand— *mirabile dictu*—asserts the long reviled and uncongenial doctrine of the original sin, or something suspiciously close to it, "not as a revealed dogma, but as an implication of our moral experience, making it the foundation of his whole theory of the nature and function of religion in human life." [12] No wonder that he was denounced by Goethe as having soiled his philosophical cloak by it! [13] Since every man is subject to the categorical requirement of the moral law, this radical tendency toward evil constitutes an original defect of man's nature. Nevertheless, every man is likewise potentially capable of good by obeying the voice of duty. Nor does Kant admit that the source of corruption is outside man's will, in his ancestry, his environment, or his finiteness; it is within himself. He identifies it with self-love, as the traditional Christian theology has always done. Man is evil, i.e., despite being conscious of the moral law, he nevertheless deviates from it; and he is evil *by nature*, by a *radical innate evil*, because this tendency inheres in humankind generally, not by an exception here and there. [14] Nevertheless, considering this teaching of Kant regarding the radical evil of the human nature against the general tenor of his philosophy, it must be regarded as contradictory.

Having asserted the essentially Christian doctrine of the natural state of corruption of human nature, Kant follows it by the equally traditional doctrine of the new birth or the new creature—a revolutionary change caused by what is the effect of divine grace in man's basic motivation. To be sure, he departs from this traditional doctrine in some basic particulars; but the doctrine of redemption is asserted nevertheless. Since man is capable of doing what he *ought* to do, this moral change is to some degree man's own act. And yet, it cannot be accomplished by human powers alone, but requires supernatural aid. However, once that is received, man then can and must persevere in the effort of moral growth. For man thereafter makes himself into whatever he is to become, whether good or not. An adequate consideration of the role the divine aid plays in the drama of man's moral transformation is not attempted by Kant on the ground that it

[11] *Ibid.*, p. 11.

[12] C. C. J. Webb, *Kant's Philosophy of Religion* (Oxford: The Clarendon Press, 1926), pp. 92-93. By permission.

[13] Karl Barth remarks in his *Protestant Thought* that "It is in fact the last thing one would expect of Kant!" Cf. p. 176.

[14] *Religion within the Limits of Reason Alone*, pp. 27-28.

does not belong to the treatment of religion "within the limits of reason alone."

Thus the aim of God in creating man is man's complete moral perfection. This archetypal ideal perfection existed in God's mind from the beginning, and Kant applies to it the terms used in the Prologue of the Fourth Gospel regarding the Logos. As such, he "is no created thing but His [God's] only-begotten Son, 'the Word (the *Fiat!*) through which all other things are . . .' This archetype has *come down* to us from heaven and has assumed our humanity. . . . Man may then hope to become acceptable to God (and so be saved) through a *practical faith in this Son of God* (so far as He is represented as having taken upon Himself man's nature)." [15] And since we *ought* to conform to this exemplar, with God's aid, we *can* do it.

Since Kant himself quotes the Prologue to the Fourth Gospel in the very characterization of the Son of God as the Logos, one would naturally suppose that he also accepts the further statement of that Gospel that "the Word became flesh and dwelt among us." He not only does not say so, but actually rejects the basic Christian doctrine that the Logos, the Word "is incarnate in our Lord Jesus Christ." This comes about as close to a misleading act on Kant's part as one finds anywhere in his writing. To be sure, he makes his position quite clear in the pages following his use of the quotations from the Fourth Gospel; and yet it is difficult to see how he can properly use the phrase "assumed our humanity" if he does not mean Christ thereby. Moreover, he must have known that the writer of the Fourth Gospel applied the term Word to Jesus Christ, and that the radical reinterpretation of his terms is hardly a fair use of those terms! It is to be noted that Kant never uses the designation "Jesus Christ" in connection with our Lord. The term "Son of God," commonly applied to Christ, Kant reinterprets to mean the eternal ideal of humanity, and the "*archetype* of such a person is to be sought nowhere but in our own reason." The historic Jesus is not the manifestation of such an eternal ideal, and must himself be judged by that exalted criterion. We "have no cause for supposing him other than a man naturally begotten." He has indeed "produced immeasurably great good upon earth," and has given "through his teachings, his conduct, and his sufferings, as perfect an *example* of a man well pleasing to God as one can expect to find in external experience. . . ." [16] But that does not, in Kant's estimation, make him the Incarnate God of the Nicene Creed.

In the Third Book of his work Kant deals with the Kingdom of God

[15] *Ibid.*, pp. 54-55.
[16] *Ibid.*, p. 57.

on earth, which he asserts to have been founded by God, even though its human members are responsible for its organization. This leads him first of all to discuss the concept of the Church, which he defines as "an ethical commonwealth of a People of God." The *visible* Church (the only one he finds possible to deal with, for the *invisible* is identical with the Kingdom of God) must be universal, pure, free, and unchangeable. The universal Church must be based on reasonable grounds in order to be accessible and acceptable to all reasonable men. It excludes sectarian divisions. The only pure worship of God is doing God's will, i.e., living a moral life. He rejects the ecclesiastical (or what he calls "statutory") requirements on the ground that they are extra-moral. They are at best human devices accessory to purely moral religion, although they may be useful since men are generally not swayed by reason alone. Purity of the Church also excludes superstition and fanaticism. The Church must likewise be free both as regards its relation to the state and of one member to another. Kant rejects further any autocratic (papal), aristocratic (episcopal), or democratic organization of the Church as incompatible with the demands of freedom. Essentially, it must be patterned on the family, ruled by God through His Son. And finally, the Church must remain unchangeably loyal to its basic idea, its ultimate moral aim. The "ecclesiastical" religion, by which Kant means the historic Church, will in course of time be transmuted into pure faith—i.e., an exclusively ethical concept of religion. The present time, Kant asserts, is most conducive to such a transforming process:

> . . . if the seed of the true religious faith, as it is now being publicly sown in Christendom, though only by a few, is allowed more and more to grow unhindered, we may look for a continuous approximation to that church, eternally uniting all men, which constitutes the visible representation (the schema) of an invisible kingdom of God on earth.[17]

He concludes his treatment of the subject in the Fourth Book, devoted to a discussion "concerning religion and clericalism." Once again he asserts: "Religion is (subjectively regarded) the recognition of all duties as divine commands." [18] He further defines rationalists in religion as those who regard the "natural religion alone as morally necessary, *i.e.*, as duty." A naturalist in religion is he who "denies the reality of all supernatural divine revelation." And a supernaturalist is he

---

[17] *Ibid.*, p. 122.
[18] *Ibid.*, p. 142.

who holds "that belief in it is necessary to universal religion." [19] As for Christianity considered as a natural religion, the duties of it are laid down by its founder, Jesus Christ, in the Sermon on the Mount. Kant seriously assumes that this constitutes the ethical standard of "rational" Christians. First of all, our Lord teaches that

> not the observance of outer civil or statutory churchly duties but the pure moral disposition of the heart alone can make man well-pleasing to God (Matthew 5:20-48); that sins in thought are regarded, in the eyes of God, as tantamount to action (5:28) and that, in general, holiness is the goal toward which man should strive (5:48); that, for example, to hate in one's heart is equivalent to killing (5:22); that injury done one's neighbor can be repaired only through satisfaction rendered to the neighbor himself, not through acts of divine worship (5:24); and that, on the point of truthfulness, the civil device for extorting it by oath does violence to the respect for truth itself (5:34-37); that the natural but evil propensity of the human heart is to be completely reversed, that the sweet sense of revenge must be transformed into tolerance (5:39-40) and the hatred of one's enemies into charity (5:44). . . . Finally, he combines all duties (1) in one *universal* rule (which includes within itself both the inner and the outer moral relations of men), namely: Perform your duty for no motive other than unconditioned esteem for duty itself, *i.e.,* love God (the Legislator of all duties) above all else; and (2) in a *particular* rule, that, namely, which concerns man's external relation to other men as universal duty: Love everyone as yourself, *i.e.,* further his welfare from good-will that is immediate and not derived from motives of self-advantage." [20] Here then is a complete religion, which can be presented to all men comprehensibly and convincingly through their own reason.[21]

Nevertheless, although the true service of God is the service of the heart, yet it may be aided by outward means. Kant summarizes them as follows: (1) private prayer, "to awaken the disposition of goodness in the heart"; (2) church attendance, to spread abroad the goodness through public assembly; (3) baptism, the reception of new members into the group; and (4) communion, the maintenance of this fellowship. It is however to be noted that Kant himself never attended church services except when he served in an official academic capacity. At other times, even though he joined the academic procession when the faculty attended the church on the "academic day," he left it at the church door.

Kant's grandiose project of effecting a new "Copernican revolution"

[19] *Ibid.,* p. 143.
[20] *Ibid.,* pp. 147-48.
[21] *Ibid.,* p. 150.

in philosophy by reconstituting empiricism—discredited by Hume—
by his dualistic critical idealism, was now at last completed. But toward
the end of his life Kant himself developed doubts as to the validity of
his reconstruction, as is evident from his unfinished *Opus postumum*,
found on his desk after his death and published in 1920 by Erich
Adickes. About this work Adickes asserts, "The whole teaching of
the highest good, together with the proofs based thereon of God
and immortality has now . . . practically disappeared." [22] Kant now
recognizes that the dreaded principle of hedonism (seeking happiness
as a reward of virtue) has crept into his system. In the expurgated and
rigorously revised system, Adickes says:

> the moral individual is to do what is good *only* because it is good;
> he is thus to act without reference to any external ends whatsoever,
> in this life or the next, but absolutely autonomously, conformable
> to . . . the categorical command of his practical reason. As a religious
> person, however, he simultaneously recognizes that the ideals and
> ends which he has himself chosen, and the laws which he has himself
> imposed, are also God's ideals, ends, and laws, and through this
> recognition his motives to do good are appreciably strengthened.[23]

Moreover, since Kant's previous argument for the existence of God
has been thereby considerably weakened, if not entirely undermined, he now suggests in its place "that the moral experience *itself*
may legitimately be regarded an an experience of the Divine." "The
categorical imperative leads directly to God, yea, serves as a pledge of
His reality." Thus, at last, Kant provides what is essentially an
existential proof of God; he comes close to asserting that God is present
to consciousness and thus intuitively known, instead of deduced by a
process of reasoning from moral grounds.

In conclusion, then, what is Kant's contribution to religious thought
in general, and Christian apprehension of it, in particular? First of all,
as Berdyaev has recognized, Kant established, on empirical grounds,
without recourse to religious presuppositions, the existence of two
kinds of reality—phenomenal and noumenal. It was the latter that
provided the ground for a spiritual interpretation of the cosmos congenial to the religious view of life. To be sure, Kant's successors immediately proceeded to convert his dualism into monism—either of
the idealistic or the materialistic kind. But Kant's own conclusion,

[22] Quoted in *ibid.*, p. lxv.
[23] Quoted in *ibid.*, p. lxvi.

that scientific (pure) reason cannot perceive true reality (*ding an sich*), but possesses knowledge only of the phenomenal world, is a solid achievement, although some scientists and most nonscientists still look upon scientific knowledge as the only "objective" kind there is. Nevertheless, since God is Spirit, and therefore not an object perceivable by sense-perception, He cannot be "known" scientifically. Kant thus repudiates the Thomistic assumption that knowledge of God's existence is inferential from sense-perception (*per ea quae facta sunt*). He grounds such inference upon the moral sense of mankind, although in his last unfinished work he comes close to holding that man may know God intuitively. Nevertheless, his lifelong mistrust of mysticism and "enthusiasm" have kept him from acknowledging rightly this approach to the question which would have resulted in some form of existentialism. Accordingly, his critical reconstruction has led him to regard religion as morality, and his essential Pelagianism ("I ought, therefore I can") has caused him to assume that all men are potentially capable of realizing, as a duty dictated by rational morality, the Sermon on the Mount. And although he occasionally has conceded the need of "supernatural aid" in the process of transforming the evil nature of man into one animated by altruistic motives, he has remained a stranger to the insights of Paul and Augustine in regard to the antinomy of law and grace. His influence on theological thinking of his and subsequent periods has been profound, but has been fraught with a preponderance of philosophical over purely theological concepts. This illustrates the impact of the secular over the religious concern characteristic of the entire humanist era. But despite all these inadequacies, Kant has rendered religion most valuable service.

## *The Idealistic Monism of Georg W. Friedrich Hegel*

Perhaps equally important, if not even greater than Kant's, has been the influence exerted by Hegel upon theology. He was a monist; in this respect he abandoned the dualism of Kant for the sole reality of the Absolute Idea, for he along with others found Kant's assertion of the unknowableness of the noumenal reality unendurable. Thus in the rational manifestations of the Absolute Idea the noumenal reality becomes capable of being known by reason, since our finite reason is but an infinitesimal manifestation of the Absolute Reason. It was Hegel's proud boast that in his philosophy the absolute stage of this development was reached.

Hegel was born in Stuttgart in 1770, the son of an official in the service of the King of Württemberg. He received his earliest education in his native city and later studied at Tübingen, where the earlier Enlightenment tendencies were modified by Kantian rationalism. He there succumbed to Greek classicism and tried to combine the Greek ideal of beauty with Kantian reason. Having matriculated in the theological faculty, he planned to prepare himself for the Lutheran ministry. Later he gave up this intention, but never ceased to be interested in religious problems; his philosophy may be basically understood as an attempt to explain religion intellectually. One of his earliest published works is *The Spirit of Christianity*, in which he shows ". . . deep sympathy for the doctrine of the Gospel, which had come to Hegel as the result of his inner struggle." [24] Next he became deeply influenced by the Romantic Movement, particularly of the Schelling, Fichte, and Schleiermacher varieties. But by 1801 he had already developed his own critique of Fichte and Schelling by arriving at his basic concept of the *modus operandi* of the mind, whether absolute or finite; namely, the dialectical relation of the thesis, antithesis, and synthesis. "The spirit is operative in its method. The intellect separates and objectifies, but spirit reunites and resubjectifies." [25] It was in this concept that Hegel found connection ". . . between mind and spirit, between the human and the divine." He discovered that what is real is rational, and what is rational is real. "This is the greatest of all his discoveries." [26] It culminates in the notion of the Absolute Mind. Thus the only adequate understanding of religion is philosophical—a subversion of his earlier thinking. "Philosophy is called upon to do what faith alone can never achieve: the absolute reconciliation of absolute opposites." [27]

It was during the Jena period (up to 1806, when Napoleon closed the university) that Hegel worked out his mature system, as seen in his *Phenomenology of Mind*—an elaboration of his concept of the Absolute Mind. Reality is defined as the development of the Absolute by the mode of dialectical self-differentiation; the cosmos, which is a living, unfolding organism, manifests this process through stages from

[24] T. M. Knox and Richard Kroner, trs., *G. W. F. Hegel, Early Theological Writings* (Chicago: The University of Chicago Press, 1948), p. 9. By permission.
[25] *Ibid.*, p. 31.
[26] *Ibid.*, p. 33.
[27] *Ibid.*, p. 38.

nature to self-conscious spirit. At the lowest it is unconscious of its own workings or aims, but is subject to laws of which it itself is unaware. Only in man does nature become conscious of itself. Thus nature, contrary to Fichte, is not "created" by our ideas, does not exist merely in our consciousness, but is a phase of the Absolute—although an unconscious phase. Its conscious stage is reached only in man, in whom the Absolute Spirit finds a momentary objectivization of its own self-consciousness in intelligence, morality, and religion. This aspect of Hegel's teaching is particularly difficult to accept, for it makes the Infinite Spirit dependent for its self-consciousness upon the finite creature of its own making. According to Hegel, then, all reality, whether physical, mental, or spiritual, is but a phase of the development of the Absolute Mind or Spirit, which is the immanent cause of this developing process. Reality is thus not static, but dynamic.

Reason is the highest stage of this development; hence, in relation to religion it is the task of philosophy to purify theology of inadequate representational images and anthropomorphic notions and to substitute for them ultimate concepts of pure reason. Thus Hegel had nothing but contempt for his colleague at the University of Berlin, Schleiermacher, who made feeling basic in religion. At best, religion conceived as an imaginative representation of reality is a lower form of apprehension of truth; only philosophy attains its adequate understanding by formulating it in exact concepts (*Begriffe*). When that is done, theology is as thoroughly rational as any other intellectual human discipline. True religion then is true knowledge of God. This conclusion may, in Hegel's view, be regarded as the highest achievement of the strivings of the best minds among the rationalist thinkers, because it resolves the conflict between reason and revelation.

Hegel's aims were by no means inimical to Christianity; in fact, he flattered himself that his philosophy was the only adequate explication and defense of it in his era. Thus he never surrendered his original aim of presenting Christianity in a form acceptable to the educated men of his time. Christianity, understood from the Hegelian point of view, is the absolute religion. His most extensive exposition of his religious concepts is to be found in his *Lectures on the Philosophy of Religion* published posthumously.[28] In dealing with God, Hegel first of all distinguishes between our subjective religious consciousness and scientific knowledge. For the former, God is knowable, but not for the latter. "What God is, is for us who are religious a known content of the

[28] "Vorlesungen über die Philosophie der Religion," in *Sämtliche Werke*, xv. (Stuttgart, 1928).

subjective consciousness; but considered scientifically, God is a general name that has no true content. Philosophy of religion deals above all with the development and understanding of what God is, and through it one makes a beginning of comprehension of what God is." [29] Thus our consciousness of God is immediate, intuitive.

Hence, it is only in the subjective experience, interpreted by philosophy of religion, that we know God as completely revealed. What knowledge of Him then has Hegel gained? God is the only reality, or substance, as Hegel calls it. Things have no independent existence, for all depend on Him: "they have their being of a different degree, strength, size, and content, but the being of all these things is not self-existent. . . . When we ascribe being to different things, it is only a borrowed being, only an appearance of being, not the absolutely self-existent being that God is. God in His Universality, this Universal in whom there are no limits, finiteness, or difference, is the absolute and sole existence, and whatever exists has its roots, its existence, in this Sole Existence." [30]

Following the dialectical mode so basic to his system, Hegel posits its working even within the divine Unity. The universe is evolved or created by God by means of positing it against Himself through self-differentiation. Thus the finite, manifold world of things is created by the infinite and absolute, and by this means God comes to self-consciousness. The world is thus the antithesis of the divine thesis. But this is not the last and permanent stage of existence. In the end the process of self-differentiation comes to an end in transcending itself in a synthesis in which all created things return into the original divine unity. Thus God without the world is not God. And further, He *must* act as He has acted, because it is the law of the dialectical process, of which even God is part. Thus He is not absolutely free.

Hegel denies that this is pantheism; he calls it the concept of substantiality. Pantheism, such as Spinoza's, identifies God with all things. But there is no diversity or manifoldness in God. "God is the sole existent, is absolutely unchanging within Himself, and there is no diversity in His substance." [31] "In the difference of God from the world, and particularly from men, consists the difference between good and evil." [32] However, in God there is no evil; He is altogether good. But in that case He is not the substance of *all* things, as Hegel has so

[29] *Ibid.*, p. 104.
[30] *Ibid.*, pp. 105-106.
[31] *Ibid.*, p. 109.
[32] *Ibid.*, p. 112.

persistently claimed. This is a basic contradiction, which can be resolved only by admitting either that evil does not exist, or if it does—and if God is the substance of *all* things—then evil exists in God as well.

The distinctly Christian comprehension of God is the trinitarian, even though the theologians of that day ignored or denied it. Hegel flatters himself by supposing that he succeeded in illuminating this dogma to a degree never before attained. This dogma lends itself with peculiar facility to Hegel's dialectic, and for that reason he has made it central to his view of Christianity. The essential nature of God is a Trinity, which however does not consist in three *parts*, or individual personal beings, but is a Unity in a threefold manifestation (one *ousia* in three *hypostases*); the Father remains eternally self-identical and In-finite; but the Son is the finite expression of the Infinite, the self-mani-festation of God, for without God's self-revelation no knowledge of Him is possible. In the Spirit, then, the Father and the Son, the In-finite and the Finite, are reunited along with the world which returns to God whence it originally had derived its being. Man thus realizes in the Spirit the essential unity of the divine and human natures, and realizes the ultimate aim of his finite being—which is union with the divine. God then is the absolute Unity in Whom all contradictions and differences—self and non-self, subject and object, finite and infinite—are annulled and reconciled. God is thus an absolutely self-conscious Spirit, immanent in the life of all creation, the ground of all unity in the world, but transcendent in respect to the purpose which the universe in its material and human phases progressively realizes. Thus there is nothing irrational in the trinitarian doctrine. But despite the breath-taking grandeur of this concept, it is not difficult to realize that it is not derived from the revelation of God in Jesus Christ, nor is it based on the trinitarian dogma of traditional historical theology of the fourth century, but is essentially a pantheistic concept much closer to the Hindu idea of the identity of God and man than to orthodox Christianity.

Before we leave this fascinating high-flown speculation, so flattering to man's ego by reason of the identification of the divine and the human, let us look at the reverse side of this concept. It was, among others, Nicolas Berdyaev, who pointed out this aspect of the Hegelian teaching and clearly indicated its baleful consequences. He writes:

> True; the divine self-consciousness and self-knowledge are realized in and through man. But what comfort is that to me? The teaching that the Deity comes to self-consciousness in man, and that the World Spirit attains its height through philosophy which is man's work, may

appear very gratifying to man's pride and elevating to his dignity. But that is to affirm that human independence exists not at all, and man is but a function of the World Spirit, of the World Reason, of the Deity: he is but an instrument, a means, a way toward the realization of goals which are not human at all.[33]

This is then a denial of the fundamental Christian conviction that man is a free moral agent. Hegel did not realize this implication of his own view that men—good and bad alike—are but a fleeting momentary manifestation of the divine, for otherwise he should have understood that the conclusion that Berdyaev has drawn is not only valid, but inevitable. The best that Hegel could say was that man is free in so far as he harmonizes his will with the divine, for he realizes himself only through a conscious self-identification with God. He thus becomes an organ of the divine will. Or to put it in other words, when a man lives the life he was meant by God to live, he is free. However, this is contradictory to Hegel's basic position that man is only a manifestation of the divine Idea; for in that case how can Hegel speak of man as having sufficiently independent individuality to "harmonize" his will with the divine? No wonder that this conception has led to the modern denial of man's moral responsibility, and in Marxism to his subjection to the social mass governed by nonmoral economic "laws." It is this conception of "freedom" that prevails under the communist rule: one is "free" to do what the regime orders!

As for the other principal doctrines of Christianity, they too are interpreted so as to lose their historic meaning. The Incarnation is said to symbolize the oneness of God and man. Salvation no longer is to be thought of in terms of redemption—there is nothing human spirit can be redeemed from, since it is the finite manifestation of the Infinite Spirit—but again in terms of identity of the divine-human. Accordingly, Jesus Christ is not a savior in the sense of historic Christology, nor the God-man of the Chalcedonian formula. His "uniqueness"—a term Hegel greatly dislikes, and with good reason, for to him no one historical event is more revelatory of God than another—consisted in the fact that He discerned the great truth of the divine-human identity. But this perception was bound to become known anyway—if not through Jesus Christ, then surely at least through Herr Professor Hegel. Thus the revelation of God through Jesus Christ is certainly not the

---

[33] Nikolai Berdyaev, *O naznachenie chelovyeka* (Paris: YMCA Press, 1931), pp. 13-14. By permission. Cf. also the translation of this work, *Destiny of Man* (New York: Charles Scribner's Sons, 1937), pp. 15-16; and Matthew Spinka, *Nicolas Berdyaev—Captive of Freedom* (Philadelphia: The Westminster Press, 1950), pp. 68-70.

central fact of human history; it is at best a low form of revelation, since being historical, it is necessarily an imperfect form of the truth that in its highest and purest form is known only metaphysically. "Christology affirms simply that God comes to be Spirit, and this can take place only in finite spirit, in man; in whom there arises the consciousness of the Absolute, and who then is likewise the Absolute's consciousness of itself." [34]

Consequently, sin is at worst only a failure on man's part to realize his own identity with the divine. In fact, even this statement is inadequate, because it is difficult to see how on Hegel's premises there can exist in man sufficient independence of his inner spiritual life to produce sin as defined above. For man does not possess a different mind from the Absolute, since the latter is identical with the sum total of all finite minds. Hence, as Emanuel Rádl, at one time professor of philosophy at the Charles University of Prague writes in his *History of Philosophy*, there exists according to Hegel no moral responsibility before God or man. Everything is subject to the same fate—whether it be Napoleon or a moth burned in a candle flame. All spiritual qualities of men are but phantoms, like rays on the surface of the river, powerless to effect its flow.[35]

Logically, then, even the worst crimes must in some sense be understood as comprehended in some rational scheme—even though we human beings cannot fathom it. Thus it is a true Hegelian precept that *Tout comprendre c'est tout pardonner.* He admired even Napoleon, whom he saw in Jena, despite the fact that the Emperor dealt roughly with the fate of Germany.

Among the particularly influential applications of Hegelian dialectics is his philosophy of history: this teaches that human history is but a gradual development of the Absolute Idea as applied to nations rather than to individuals. Thus history is the scene of divine self-revelation. Its beginnings precede the human phase in the cosmic order, where the Absolute is still in its deep slumber of unconsciousness. For as has already been mentioned, the Absolute comes to self-consciousness only in man. Having been thus awakened, the Spirit becomes aware of its goal, which is the perfect human society. Hegel spoke of a mysterious "cunning of reason" in history which overrules the wills of men and through which the Absolute controls the direction of the historical course. This is Hegel's idea of divine Providence, which utilizes even

---

[34] Quoted in Mackintosh, *The Types of Theology*, p. 110.
[35] Emanuel Rádl, *Dějiny filosofie* (Praha: Jan Laichter, 1933), II, p. 388. My translation.

evil designs and passions of men to its own purposes. Caesar and Napoleon did not consciously seek to do God's will; and yet God over-ruled their selfish aims for His own ends. Every culture, civilization, and era, is only a phase of the divine thought. The goal of human history—the ultimate meaning of the unfolding Idea—is as yet un-revealed. At present we see only the partially spelled out word of the past historical course, and may perhaps attempt to guess its ultimate significance. But every such attempt is fraught with uncertainty; the final meaning may be love, but it may just as well be a lie; it is hard to tell, if one knows only the first letter of the word!

". . . Since philosophy," he writes in the Preface to his *Philosophy of Right*, "is the exploration of the rational, it is for that very reason the apprehension of the present and the actual, not the erection of a beyond, supposed to exist God knows where, or rather which exists, as we can perfectly well say where, namely in the error of a one-sided, empty, ratiocination." [36]

This being so, philosophy deals with the actual embodiment of the historical process as it takes form in the state, which Hegel designates as

> . . . the actuality of the ethical Idea. It is ethical mind *qua* the substantial will manifest and revealed to itself, knowing and thinking itself, accomplishing what it knows and in so far as it knows it. . . . The state is absolutely rational inasmuch as it is the actuality of the substantial will which it possesses in the particular self-consciousness once that consciousness has been raised to consciousness of its univer-sality. Thus substantial unity is an absolute unmoved end in itself, in which freedom comes into its supreme right. On the other hand this final end has supreme right against the individual, whose supreme duty is to be a member of the state.[37]

This concept, which ascribes to the individual citizen "freedom" only in subserving the will of the state—an idea that has been adopted and developed to its ultimate conclusion by the totalitarian fascist and communist regimes—is further explicated in Hegel's *Philosophy of History*, where he writes that the state is

> that form of reality in which the individual has and enjoys his free-dom; but on condition of his recognizing, believing in and willing that which is common to the Whole. And this must not be understood

[36] *Hegel's Philosophy of Right*, T. M. Knox, tr., (Oxford: The Clarendon Press, 1942), p. 10. By permission.
[37] *Ibid.*, pp. 155-56.

as if the subjective will of the social unit attained its gratification and enjoyment through that common Will; as if this were a means provided for its benefits; as if the individual, in his relations to other individuals, thus limited his freedom, in order that this universal limitation—the mutual constraint of all—might secure a small space of liberty for each. Rather, we affirm, are Law, Morality, Government and they alone, the positive reality and completion of Freedom.[38]

No wonder that Hegel regarded the Prussian state as the highest attainment of the world history up to his time! But one imagines that he would not feel very happy about the development his views have taken in the modern Soviet regime!

Nevertheless, it is obvious that Hegel's influence on the subsequent period has been enormous—both positively and negatively. Some Christian theologians have responded favorably to his ideas, while others vigorously attacked the whole "system." At any rate, there is no denying the enormous impact of Hegel's ideas upon the final phase of the humanist era; most of the elements of the decadence of that phase are already present, in principle or in a fairly developed stage, in his system.

## Vladimir S. Solovev, the Philosopher of All-Unity

Another thoroughly monistic idealist is the Russian philosopher-poet-mystic, Vladimir S. Solovev. He is often regarded as the greatest Russian philosopher of the nineteenth century. He was born in Moscow in 1835, the son of Sergei M. Solovev, professor of history at the Moscow University and author of an immense work on *The History of Russia* (29 vols.). His mother came of a distinguished line; among her ancestors was the remarkable Ukrainian religious thinker and mystic, Gregory Skovoroda (1722-1794).

Young Vladimir was a precocious child, mentally gifted, spiritually sensitive. When he was nine years old, he had a vision in which he saw, during the celebration of the Eucharist, a beautiful woman bathed in golden azure. Much later he wrote that on that instant "his love of earthly things vanished." Described more prosaically, one might say

[38] G. W. F. Hegel, *Lectures on the Philosophy of History*, J. Sibree, tr. (London: George Bell and Sons, Ltd., 1905), pp. 39-40. By permission.

that he showed himself a Christian Platonist even at that early stage. He later interpreted the vision as that of the divine Sophia, i.e., the world soul, or God's active agent in the realization of His purpose in creation. Was it a small boy's overwrought imagination? Later in life, after he had the vision twice more, he did not think so. He wrote in his poem, "Three Meetings": "Thrice hast thou shown thyself to me face to face. No pallid thought fashioned thy living form." He recognized in this the vision of the transfigured universe. His philosophical system of all-unity (*èn kai pan*—all things as essentially one) was the outgrowth of these three visions. As such, they permanently affected the thinking of some of the members of the movement, especially Sergius Bulgakov, the outstanding theologian of the party.

The period from 1877 to 1880 was very fruitful. Solovev published some of his best philosophico-theological works. These were his *The Philosophic Foundations of Integral Knowledge, Treatise on Godmanhood*, and *The Critique of Abstract Principles* (his doctoral dissertation). These three works comprise almost all his metaphysical and religious ideas. Then followed a period (1882-89) which brought him much ostracism and heartache: he became interested and deeply involved in utopian schemes of reunion of Christendom. This activity places him in the honorable position of a pioneer in ecumenical attempts, although his scheme involved only the Eastern Orthodox (in fact, only the Russian Orthodox) and the Roman Catholic communions. He regarded Protestantism as part of Western Christendom that would follow the Roman Church into the union. Moreover, the reunion was to serve as a necessary preliminary step toward his grandiose but naive dream of a "free theocracy." This he conceived as a combination of the papal and Russian tsarist authorities.

Theocracy was the theme of his great work entitled *The History and Future of Theocracy*, in which he places the blame for the great Schism of 1054 on the Orthodox East, and recognizes in the papacy the bearer of rightful ecclesiastical authority. It brought him into personal contact with the Croatian canon, Father F. Rački (1884), and through this Roman Catholic priest with Bishop Strossmayer of Diakovo (1886). The good bishop was an outstanding and enthusiastic exponent of Slavic aspirations. But the extremely naive and impractical plan worked out between Solovev and the bishop assumed the form of an organic but free union between the papacy and Russian tsarism: the former was to become the ecclesiastical center of world Christianity, while the tsar, as the heir of the Byzantine imperial powers, was to furnish external protection to the newly formed *orbis Christianorum*. Solovev expressed willingness to recognize the pope not only as "the successor of Peter and as the Western patriarch" (although the East would remain autonomous), but also "as the supreme judge in matters of religion." [39] He repeated this statement in his book, *La Russie et l'Eglise Universelle*, which he published in Paris (1889). Nevertheless, he made this profession "as a member of the true and venerable Eastern or Graeco-Russian Orthodox Church," [40] and he reserved for Eastern Orthodoxy complete administrative autonomy and the free use of the Eastern rite; and for the Russian tsar a dominant position in the ecumenical Church. In matters of dogma, Solovev argued that only the doctrinal decisions of the ecumenical Councils are binding upon the members of the Eastern Orthodox churches, and these decisions contain nothing contrary to the Roman Catholic doctrinal teachings. [41] He accepted, however, the dogmas of the immaculate conception of the Virgin (1864) and of papal infallibility (1870). Moreover, he arrived at the remarkable conclusion that the Schism of 1054 was not *de jure* but merely *de facto;* consequently, the churches are really not divided, but remain spiritually one, for no ecumenical council of the Eastern churches since the Schism has passed a definite judgment on the matter. This is, of course, true, if for no other reason than that no general council had been held in the East since 787. [42] But when Pope Leo XIII learned of the plan, he remarked: "A beautiful idea but, short of a miracle, impossible to carry out." [43]

It must be understood that Solovev regarded himself, by way of anticipation of the proposed reunion of the two communions, as a member of ecumenical Christendom. This has often been looked upon as an incredibly self-contradictory position. But Solovev did not so regard it. In fact, the whole significance of his endeavor lay exactly in this prophetic, anticipatory consciousness on his part that he was a member of the Ecumenical Church of the future. Thus he wished to embody in his own personal case the conditions under which the two communions were to be united; for neither group was to submit to the other, but both were to continue their autonomous existence in the ecumenical unity. As Berdyaev interprets Solovev's position, he

[39] D. Stremooukhoff, *Vladimir Solovev et son oeuvre messianique* (Paris: YMCA Press, 1935), p. 196. By permission.

[40] Vladimir Solovev, *Russia and the Universal Church* (London: Geoffrey Bles, Ltd., 1948), p. 34.

[41] K. Mochulsky, *Vladimir Solovev* (Paris: YMCA Press, 1936), p. 168. By permission.

[42] Stremooukhoff, *op. cit.*, p. 196.

[43] S. L. Frank, ed., *A Solovyov Anthology* (New York: Charles Scribner's Sons, 1950), p. 19.

wanted to be both a Roman Catholic and an Orthodox at the same time. He wanted to belong to the Oecumenical Church in which there would be fullness of a sort which does not yet exist either in Roman Catholicism or in Orthodoxy taken in their isolation and self-assertion. . . . This means that Solovev was a supra-confessionalist; he believed in the possibility of a new era in the history of Christianity.[44]

Solovev himself wrote (1892): "I am as far from the limitations of the Latins as of the Byzantines. . . . The religion of the Holy Spirit which I profess is broader and at the same time more inclusive than all particular religions." [45]

When the new Procurator of the Holy Governing Synod, Constantine Podyedonostsev, banned the publication of Solovev's book on free theocracy and forbade him all publicist activity of whatever sort as harmful to the spiritual interests of the Russian Church, Solovev left Russia once again and went to Paris. His indignation against his own Church was so intense that the books he published during this period reached a pitch of pro-Catholic apologetics that made plausible the claim of Roman Catholic writers that he was a convert to their Church in the formal sense of that word. The most important of these works is his book entitled *Russia and the Universal Church*[46] in which he expounds his unionistic project in great detail and most resolutely espouses the Roman Catholic side in the matter.

However, upon his return to Russia in 1891, Solovev abandoned the reunification efforts and devoted himself for the remaining nine years of his life to the working out of his religious philosophy. To this period belongs his great system of ethics, *The Justification of the Good* (1897). But the last stage of his thinking is characterized by a gloomily apocalyptic mood in which his sense of the power of evil is clearly expressed. The world lies in evil, and Antichrist is at hand. This is the theme of his last work, *Three Conversations on War, Progress, and the End of History*. It includes as the final chapter "A Short Story of Antichrist" in which he repudiates most of his previous utopian thinking, particularly his theocratic utopia of a Christian state and his concept of the reunion of Christendom. Florovsky writes that "in 'The Story of Antichrist' Solovev repudiates the illusions and seductions of

[44] Nicolas Berdyaev, *The Russian Idea* (New York: The Macmillan Co., 1948), p. 178.

[45] Quoted in V. V. Zenkovsky, *Istoriya russkoy filosofii* (Paris: YMCA Press, 1950), II, p. 19. By permission.

[46] Vladimir Solovev, *La Russie et l'Eglise universelle* (Paris, 5th ed., 1922); in Russian it was published in Moscow, 1911. The English translation was published in London in 1948 by Geoffrey Bles, Ltd.

his whole life and condemns them with all his might. 'I wrote it in order to express finally my view of the Church question. . . .' " [47] Moreover, it is remarkable that in this final story he recognizes Protestantism as a separate Christian communion.

Many writers esteem this work of Solovev as his greatest. Berdyaev understandably dissents from this judgment, since his own eschatological views are very different. Nevertheless, the book is a remarkable production. Solovev delineates in it the final conflict between the three Christian communions and the ultimately secularized twenty-first century.

> It was an era of the final bankruptcy of the materialistic theory. The notion of the universe as a system of dancing atoms, and of life as the result of mechanical accumulation of the slightest changes in materia, no longer satisfied a single reasoning intellect. Mankind had outgrown that stage of philosophical infancy. On the other side, it became equally evident that it had long outgrown the infantile capacity for a naive, unconscious faith.[48]

It is in this kind of world that Antichrist appears, in the guise of the emperor of a unified world empire. He is a benevolent, highly cultured ruler of a welfare state who introduces every sort of social reform: he abolishes war, establishes universal peace, and eliminates class struggle and racial antagonisms. In a word, he aims at realizing a paradise on earth *in his own name*. He even goes so far as to attempt to unite Christian churches into one ecumenical body. With that in view, he convenes a world conference of Christendom at Jerusalem. There he offers the Christians all kinds of inducements on the condition that they recognize him as the Church's "sole protector and defender." It is now that Pope Peter II, Elder John of the Russian Orthodox, and Professor Ernst Pauli of the Protestants, recognize the emperor as Antichrist. For although the majority of the faithful of all communions enthusiastically accept the emperor's offer and laud him for his generosity, the three leaders, deserted by their own followers, denounce—most significantly through the mouth of Elder John—the emperor as Antichrist. Thereupon, Peter excommunicates him and is for that daring deed put to death. Elder John likewise dies. Professor Pauli, left alone, leads the remnant of the faithful into the wilderness of Jordan. There both Peter and John are miraculously resurrected and all three

---

[47] Georgy Florovsky, *Puti russkago bogosloviya* (Paris: YMCA Press, 1937), p. 466. By permission.

[48] Vladimir Solovyof, *War and Christianity* (New York: G. P. Putnam's Sons, 1915), p. 187; also in Frank, *op. cit.*, pp. 229 ff.

leaders by mutual recognition unite their communions into one ecumenical Church. But this reunion of the churches comes at the end of the present aeon, for immediately thereafter occurs the second coming of Christ. The apocalyptic millennium has begun.

Solevev did not survive this prophetic vision of the *eschaton* very long. He died, utterly exhausted, in 1900, after becoming reconciled with his Russian Church and receiving communion at the hands of a Russian Orthodox priest. He was then only forty-seven.

We may now turn to the consideration of Solovev's chief contributions to the development of the doctrinal system of the Russian Renascence. The central idea of his religious world view is the all-embracing unity of the living cosmos permeated by the divine Sophia. The idea of All-Unity is an attempt to synthesize theology, philosophy, and science in one all-inclusive world view. Solevev concluded that Western philosophy has failed because in its rationalism (from Descartes through Kant to Hegel) it identified reality with thought, while in its empiricism (from Bacon, through Hume to Mill) it identified reality with the states of human consciousness. He correctly discerned that this logically led to pantheism or atheistic materialism. He conceived his task as expressing Christianity in the form consonant with modern philosophy and science—a universal synthesis of all three. Unfortunately, he never succeeded in integrating into a harmonious system his two principal ideas: that of the Absolute as the "All-Unity" which yet differentiates from itself its own "other," the cosmos; and the idea of the Godmanhood, the transformation of the human into the divine-human.

The Absolute is the ultimate ground of all being—divine, cosmic, and human; thus it constitutes all-unity. It is identical in Solovev's concept with the Godhead; as such, it exceeds all rational comprehension. Godhead is thus the sole existing One, and also the manifold All—the ἐν καί πᾶν. God is the Absolute that *is*, while the cosmos—His other— is the Absolute that is *becoming*. There exist, therefore, two aspects within the Absolute: one self-existent unity free from all determinism, and the other self-differentiated from this unity, and hence characterized by multiplicity, manifesting itself in the cosmos. Both have existed within the Absolute eternally; but the latter assumed its form within time. This notion is clearly of Platonic derivation—his "world of ideas." Solovev therefore never writes clearly in terms of creation, for it implies calling into being a concrete entity *ex nihilo*. The concept of the "other Absolute" Solovev derives from Schelling and his "philosophy of identity." It is difficult to differentiate Solovev's concept of All-unity from Spinozan and Schellingian pantheism, although he resolutely repudiates any such charge. But either the "second" Absolute is actually absolute, in which case it cannot be said to be "becoming," and then all difference between the two kinds of Absolute disappears; or it is "becoming," in which case it is not Absolute; and, by deriving its being from the true Absolute, it cannot be said to be an aspect of the Absolute. If this latter is not pantheism then Solovev is talking about a distinction without a difference.[49] Lossky comes to the same conclusion when he repudiates Solovev's concept of the two Absolutes:

> The world's being is something existing entirely outside God's essence; consequently, God is not pan-unity. . . . The problem of connection between God and the world is solved consistently only by the Christian doctrine of God creating the world out of nothing: according to this doctrine God created the world, both in form and in substance, as something entirely new, different from Himself, without using for this creation any material either in Himself or outside.[50]

Returning now to Solovev's system, in a true Platonic fashion he sees in the objective cosmos only an inadequate and distorted reflection of the eternal pattern of the "other" Absolute. And yet the connection between the two, tenuous though it may be, still exists. It may best be seen in man, for he partakes of both the physical and the spiritual natures. But the evil in the empirical world is a reflection of the evil in the metaphysical, spiritual world. Evil exists in the spiritual world by reason of the rebellious self-affirmation of some spirits who aspired to be equal to God: "Ye shall be as Gods!" Accordingly, the world—physical and partly spiritual—is in rebellion against God. It must therefore be restored to communion with God. This is particularly true of human beings, but applies to the cosmos as well; as Paul expressed it: "We know that the whole creation has been groaning in travail until now; and not only the creation, but we ourselves, who have the first fruits of the Spirit, groan inwardly as we wait for the adoption as sons, the redemption of our bodies." [51]

The divine agent of this process whereby the cosmos and mankind are to be brought back into communion with God is the Sophia—the

---

[49] Cf. Zenkovsky, *op. cit.*, where a similar judgment is expressed.

[50] N. O. Lossky, *History of Russian Philosophy* (New York: International Universities Press, Inc., 1951), p. 128. By permission.

[51] Romans 8:22-23. From the *Revised Standard Version of the Holy Bible*. Copyright 1946, 1952 by Division of Christian Education, National Council of Churches. Reprinted by permission.

divine Wisdom. This is another distinctive feature of Solovev's religious philosophy. As in Plato's conception the visible world is permeated—although imperfectly—by the ideal, so in Solovev's concept the physical manifold world is unified by the Sophia—the living World Soul. Thus the cosmos has a personality—that of the Eternal Feminine. But the divine Sophia is not God. Any such confusion of the "creaturely, biological-human characteristics with the suprahuman realm is the greatest abomination . . . The true apprehension of the eternal feminine has nothing in common with such a silliness and abomination . . ."[52] The World Soul comprises both the divine and the material principles. It could actually refuse to do God's will and to fall away from God by asserting itself in God's stead. This it actually had done.[53] The world therefore needs redemption.

Nevertheless, Sophia is ultimately to achieve unity in all things. Berdyaev writes of Solovev's concept as the intuition of

> an all-embracing unity. He had a vision of integrality, the all-embracing unity of the world, of the divine cosmos, in which there is no separation of the parts from the whole, no enmity and discord, in which there is nothing abstract and self-assertive. It was a vision of Beauty; it was an intellectual and erotic intuition; it was a quest for the transfiguration of the world, for the Kingdom of God . . . there was hidden an ardent love for beauty of the divine cosmos, to which he gives the name of Sophia.[54]

More specifically, Sophia is the name given to the ideal humankind as revealed in Jesus Christ. For Christ is the revelation not only of God, but of perfect man as well. Thus He is both the Logos and Sophia.[55] He alone has realized in Himself the unity toward which all mankind is to strive—the Godmanhood. He perfectly combined in His person the two natures and two wills—the divine Logos or Christ and the perfect human-Sophia. This is the third principal concept of Solovev —the Godmanhood, not limited to Jesus Christ alone (in Whom it was actually realized) but the ultimate goal of all mankind. Thus the divine goal toward which all creation tends is not something hidden, but has already been revealed in the divine-human personality of Jesus Christ. This is Solovev's most genuinely Christian idea, less dependent on the Platonic-Schellingian sources from which so many of his other ideas spring. One is reminded of the glorious insight of

---

[52] Quoted in Mochulsky, *op. cit.*, p. 70.
[53] Zenkovsky, *op. cit.*, p. 47.
[54] Berdyaev, *op. cit.*, p. 168.
[55] Peter P. Zouboff, tr., Vladimir Solovev, *Lectures on Godmanhood* (New York: International Universities Press, Inc., 1944), p. 169. By permission.

Paul in the epistle to the Ephesians: "For he has made known to us in all wisdom and insight the mystery of his will, according to his purpose, which he set forth in Christ as a plan for the fullness of time, to unite all things in him, things in heaven and things on earth.[56]

As for Solovev's concept of man, he teaches that God's need of him has existed within the Godhead eternally; for being Love, He desired a free and consciously voluntary response to His love. As existing in God eternally, this ideal man is not to be identified with the human beings in their physical existence. Nevertheless, "every human being is essentially and actually rooted, and takes part, in the universal or absolute man." [57] In God's own time, this absolute man took on temporal existence as a human being, having been endowed with the "image" and "likeness" of God by receiving freedom. Hence, man is capable of a response to God's love and his highest happiness consists in communion with God. But likewise, just because he possesses freedom, he may affirm himself "apart from God, outside of God." He consequently "falls away or separates himself from God in his consciousness in the same manner as the world soul originally seceded from Him in all her being." [58] This is man's "Fall." By asserting himself, he destroys himself, chooses the path of rebellion. His earthly life then stands midway between two poles: he may either choose to be restored to communion with God, or become enslaved to his material nature and his own passions.

Salvation then is a voluntary return of man to communion with God, a spiritual transformation of the merely human into the divine-human. This then is Godmanhood—theanthropy. It is a concept traditional in Eastern Orthodoxy under the term of "deification." Berdyaev, who shared Solovev's concept, writes of it:

> The idea of God-manhood means the overcoming of the self-sufficiency of man, in humanism, and at the same time the affirmation of the activity of man, of his highest dignity, of the divine in man. The interpretation of Christianity as the religion of God-manhood is radically opposed to the juridical interpretation of the relation between God and man, and the juridical theory of redemption which is widespread in theology both Catholic and Protestant.[59]

Thus the great philosopher of the Russian Renascence does not think of salvation in terms of some environmental change—economic, cultural,

[56] Ephesians 1:9-10.
[57] Zouboff, *op. cit.*, p. 178.
[58] *Ibid.*, p. 199.
[59] Berdyaev, *op. cit.*, p. 173.

or even sacramental—but only in terms of transformed personalities.

It follows then that the task of the Church in Christianizing society "is to regenerate and sanctify the common life and permeate and transform it by the divine life. That is, first of all God's work; but it cannot be accomplished without us. Our life cannot be regenerated without our cooperation. Thus religion is a divine-human affair." [60]

In order to create a Christian culture—a task to which Solovev devoted all the best years of his active life—all human activity must be transformed by the divine. He thought at first that it could be accomplished within history by his concept of free theocracy, preceded by the reunion of Christendom. But in his ultimate view he despaired of the task as being within the confines of history. The Kingdom of God cannot be realized except beyond history, beyond time, in eternity.

In conclusion, we may raise the question whether Solovev accomplished the task he set out to do, namely, to integrate religion, philosophy, and science into a new form acceptable to modern man. A recent German writer answers enthusiastically in the affirmative. Egbert Munzer, a Roman Catholic jurist, entitled his book *Solovyev, Prophet of Russian-Western Unity*. He writes:

> Solovyev is the most Western of Russian thinkers or, to be more precise, the most supranational, for he transmuted a deep love for his own people into a world-embracing charity, rare in our age of nationalism and petty particularisms. He was truly catholic. He lived in a world where there was 'neither Jew nor Gentile.' He was equally free from that shallow cosmopolitanism which mistakes rootlessness for intellectual strength, worldliness for detachment, and spinelessness for objectivity. The internationalism of the socialists and the believers in positive science made no more than a passing impression on him. He plumbed the greater depths where the secondary differences of the phenomenal world are integrated again in the noumenal reality of God, whom he loved with all the ardour of a great soul. This is why he is slowly becoming the treasured possession of thinkers throughout the whole world . . .[61]

There are others, particularly among the Russian religious thinkers, who have been greatly influenced by Solovev—men like Florensky, and Bulgakov, but he does not lack determined critics either, such as Zenkovsky, Florovsky, and, partly, Lossky. Despite the cogent and largely justified analysis and repudiation of Western philosophy, and

---

[60] Solovev, *Collected Works*, III, p. 270.

[61] Egbert Munzer, *Solovyev—Prophet of Russian-Western Unity* (New York: Philosophical Library, Inc., 1956), pp. 2-3. By permission.

the demand for a new synthesis of Christian culture, it cannot be gain-said that Solovev operated with concepts that are not at present dominant or are altogether obsolete. Moreover, the proportion in which the three of his principal ideas are combined is also of primary significance—namely, which is dominant, theology or philosophy? His conception of Christianity—derived from peripheral mystical sources such as Boehme, Baader, and even from the Jewish Cabbala—has proved unacceptable both to the Russian Orthodox and the Roman Catholics. His philosophical system, so largely derived from Platonic-Spinozan-Schellingite sources, certainly cannot be said to be representa-tive of the prevalent philosophical thinking of today or even of his day. And as for science, he really did not deal with the subject suf-ficiently extensively, although his notion of the monads (a Leibnitzian term not used in Leibnitz' sense, although denoting a living universe of physical entities) comes close to the basic principle of the new physics that asserts that atoms are centers of energy. If the integration of these component parts of Christian culture is desirable—and it cer-tainly is—then it is a task that remains to be accomplished. Solovev cannot be said to have successfully completed what he had set out to do.

In fact, it may well be considered whether he himself had not come to that conclusion before he died. His last work reflects a mood of pessimism as to the current world situation, a repudiation of his former sanguine hopes of theocracy and ecumenism, and an apocalyptic ex-pectation of an imminent second coming of Christ, such as makes doubtful all his previous thinking. He felt the approach of doom and the end of the age. Did he not include in the sinister figure of Anti-christ a radical repudiation of his views concerning Christian culture? No definite answer to these intimations can be given, since Solovev died before he could afford us any. His life work certainly was not without most valuable insights, both philosophical and religious; but the task of creating a synthesis of a worthy Christian culture still remains to be attained.

# 7

# Revolt Against Hegelianism

## Søren Kierkegaard and the Existential Theology

Søren Kierkegaard (1813-1855) has only recently achieved recognition on a world-wide scale. He is more properly our contemporary, one born before his time. Even the circumstances of his birth made him an exceptional person—a characteristic he retained throughout his life. He was the youngest son of a wealthy woolen merchant in Copenhagen. His father thought that in his youth, as a desperately poor shepherd boy, he had committed an act of rebellion against God which the elder Kierkegaard ever after had regarded as the unpardonable sin. Hence, he lived the rest of his life in deep and chronic melancholy bordering on hopeless despair. Because of his close intimacy with, and ascendence over, his youngest son, the latter shared his father's somber, gloomy view of life. It warped his spirit permanently. Some years before his death, the elder Kierkegaard revealed his guilty secret to his son, who reacted to it violently, since he had always held his father in adoring love. Søren lost faith not only in his father but in God as well. During this period, according to his own testimony, he lived in riotous profligacy.

But shortly before his father's death he became reconciled to him and at the same time experienced a religious conversion.

At the University, he was particularly attracted by the study of Socrates, and next to him Hegel. Following his "conversion," he decided to study for the Lutheran ministry. In 1839, at the age of twenty-six, he fell in love with and became engaged to a sixteen-year-old damsel, Regina Olsen. His love was ardently returned. But within two years he abruptly broke his engagement without explanation. Naturally, she was puzzled and offended, and in resentment she married her previous suitor. Søren's reasons had to do with his father's guilt and his own previous profligacy and melancholy; moreover, his exceedingly rigorous views of marriage required that he have no secrets from his future wife—and he felt that he could not properly communicate to her his father's secret. As he wrote in his *Journal* for 1843:

> But if I had had to explain myself then I would have had to initiate her into terrible things, my relation to my father, his melancholy, the eternal darkness that broods deep within, my going astray, pleasures and excesses which in the eyes of God are not perhaps so terrible, for it was dread that drove me to excess, and where was I to look for something to hold on to when I knew, or suspected that the one man I revered for his power and strength had wavered.[1]

He attempted to explain his reasons for the act in his early books, although he adopted so "indirect" a method that it is to be doubted whether he succeeded either with Regina or the world. This melancholy caused him to feel isolated from his fellows, a "solitary," and was a source of his lifelong suffering.

Kierkegaard conceived his task in relation to contemporary Christendom to be similar to Socrates'—that of "midwifery." Or, to put it in another way, he played the Socratic role of a Protestant "gadfly." His literary style is artistically superb. He penned passages which rank with the greatest of nineteenth century literature. His writings are divided almost from the beginning into those representing his deliberately "indirect" method and those written under his name. The former were mostly published under a variety of pseudonyms, such as Victor Eremita, Frater Taciturnus, Hilarious Bookbinder, Johannes Climacus, and Anti-Climacus. This very device should warn us against identifying too closely the views expressed by his pseudonymous char-

---

[1] *The Journals of Søren Kierkegaard*, Alexander Dru, ed. and tr. (London: Oxford University Press, Ltd., 1938), p. 122. By permission.

acters with his own opinions. But at the same time, he wrote a number of *Discourses* under his own name in which he expressed his personal views directly. After 1848, when he experienced a "second conversion," he abandoned the indirect method and addressed himself both to a sharp critique of the Danish Lutheran Church and Christendom in general, and to an effort to convey a positive message aimed at the needed reform.

His first books, *Either/Or* (1843), *Repetition* (1843), *Fear and Trembling* (1843), *Philosophical Fragments* (1844), *The Concept of Dread* (1844), *Stages on Life's Way* (1845) and the *Concluding Unscientific Postscript* (1846) are devoted either to his masterly description of "life's stages"—esthetic, ethical, and religious—or to his *bête-noir*, the Hegelian system. Esthetes live for the enjoyment of beauty, for the satisfaction of bodily, intellectual, or esthetic appetites and passions. The "Seducer's Diary" in *Either/Or* is the best example of this attitude toward life, and is written in an exquisite and truly esthetic manner excellently suited to the theme. The various aspects of the esthete's life are characterized as hedonism and eudaemonism; such a man betrays no ethical or religious concerns, even though he does not lack intelligence and a highly developed appreciation of beauty. But the esthete lives for the momentary and passing enjoyment; he is an exponent of "art for art's sake." Furthermore, the esthetic life is a butterfly existence; it does not take life seriously, and disdains to commit itself to any responsibility. It ultimately leads to a sense of emptiness and futility, and thus to despair, for it is essentially superficial, unsatisfying, and trivial.

> My life is absolutely meaningless. When I consider the different periods into which it falls, it seems like the word *Schnur* in the dictionary, which means in the first place a string, in the second a daughter-in-law. The only thing lacking is that the word *Schnur* should mean in the third place a camel, and in the fourth, a dust-brush.[2]

The esthete who is fortunate and perceptive enough to realize the true character of his life must become thoroughly disgusted with it. In such a moment of illumination he comes to the realization that such a life is devoid of any lasting satisfaction.

This realization leads to the second stage of life, the ethical. It is

---

[2] S. Kierkegaard, *Either/Or*, David F. Swenson and Lillian Marvin Swenson, trs. (Princeton: Princeton University Press, 1944), I, p. 29. By permission.

best represented in the figure of Judge William in his advice to the young esthete: "What then must you do? I have only one answer: despair. . . . So then choose despair, for even despair is a choice; for one can doubt without choosing to, but one cannot despair without choosing." [3] In this stage Kierkegaard is obviously dealing with the Kantian concept of the ethical as the highest category, and of duty for duty's sake. Nevertheless, it does not destroy the esthetic; it only dethrones it. Henceforth, it does not dominate, it only subserves. But the transition from one stage to the other is made not on the basis of some philosophical conviction prompted by objective consideration; it is an act of will, a desperate leap whereby one hurls himself from one stage to the other. This is the theme of his book *Philosophical Fragments.* Mere philosophizing never leads to decision. Like Hamlet, one never acts on the basis of objective observation of philosophical *pro* and *con;* he saves himself only by a leap into the dark. This then is faith which excludes scientific certainty; for if we had certain knowledge, we would not need faith.[4]

The ethical task consists in subjecting the individual to the universal. "The ethical as such is the universal, it applies to everyone . . ." [5] To assert oneself against the universal is sin. The failure to direct oneself in accordance with the demands of the universal ethic is to fail in developing one's personality: "The most important thing is not to cultivate one's mind, but to mature one's personality." [6]

The third stage is the religious. But before we come to consider it, it will be well to turn to Kierkegaard's lifelong involvement in a struggle with the then reigning philosophy of Hegel. One of his keenest insights is his basic conviction that religion is not essentially an intellectual perception of the rationality of the universal scheme, but something essentially different. For that reason he assails "the System"—as he ironically calls Hegelianism—with all the caustic wit and mordant logic of which he is capable,—and of them he was supremely capable! Most of his overstatements and exaggerations may be understood only in relation to his over-strong denial of the essence of Hegelianism. For the "Herr Professor," and particularly all the "Privat-docents" (Hegel's admiring followers), although condescendingly acknowledging histori-

[3] *Ibid.,* II, pp. 175, 177.
[4] S. Kierkegaard, *Philosophical Fragments,* David F. Swenson, tr. (Princeton: Princeton University Press, 1936), pp. 29-36, particularly p. 35. By permission.
[5] S. Kierkegaard, *Fear and Trembling,* Walter Lowrie, tr. (Princeton: Princeton University Press, 1941), p. 79. By permission.
[6] *Either/Or,* II, p. 137.

cal Christianity, have "changed all that," like Moliere's "physician in spite of himself." They have substituted rational knowledge for Christian faith.

They had no need to believe because they thought they knew. Kierkegaard objects to the rationalistic method wherein a philosopher plays the role of a detached observer, an objective spectator, whose chief concern is intellectual cognition. He writes:

> The objective faith—it is as if Christianity also had been promulgated as a little system, if not quite so good as the Hegelian; it is as if Christ—aye, I speak without offense—it is as if Christ were a professor, and as if the Apostles had formed a little scientific society. Verily, if it was once difficult to become a Christian . . . it has now become so easy that the only ambition which stirs any competition is that of becoming a speculative philosopher. And yet the speculative philosopher is perhaps at the farthest possible remove from Christianity . . ." [7]

In opposition to this objective method of the philosopher and the scientist, Kierkegaard posits his "passionate" attitude toward the meaning of life. It has to do not with speculation about the meaning of the cosmos, but rather with an anxious personal concern about one's own fate and destiny in the face of inevitable death. The question is not even What is Christianity? but rather, "How am I to become a Christian?" [8] The individual is himself involved in the subject matter of his study; he is not sitting on a reviewing stand watching the world go by. Nor can God be known as an object, one of the objects studied by scientists. He is, rather, a subject. He is not a thing, but Spirit. Hence, the methods used by science—necessarily restricted to material objects —or of philosophy—particularly such as restricts itself to rationalism— do not apply to God, Who is not an object and Who infinitely exceeds all rational comprehension. Accordingly, the historic ontological "proofs" of the existence of God are unconvincing unless one already believes in God on some other ground.

> I merely develop the ideality I have presupposed, and because of my confidence in *this* I make so bold as to defy all objections, . . . ; but what else is this but to presuppose that God exists, so that I really begin by virtue of confidence in him?" [9]

[7] S. Kierkegaard, *Concluding Unscientific Postscript*, David F. Swenson and Walter Lowrie, trs. (Princeton: Princeton University Press, 1944), p. 193. By permission.
[8] *Ibid.*, p. 545.
[9] *Fragments*, p. 33.

This, then, leads us to Kierkegaard's "existentialism." He uses the term "existence" as contrary to the concept of "being." The difference between these two terms consists in the fact that human beings alone possess consciousness. A thing or an animal "is" but does not "exist," because it lacks the distinguishing human trait of self-consciousness. Kierkegaard, as well as the subsequent existentialists, regards the confusion between a thing and a person as a fundamental fallacy. But for Kierkegaard, the mere fact of self-consciousness is not enough; unless he is conscious of his eternal destiny, he does not "exist." "Christianity proposes to endow the individual with an eternal happiness, a good which is not distributed wholesale, but only to one individual at a time." [10] "True Christianity as it exists in living subjects, or as living selves become themselves by becoming true Christians, is a becoming, not being. It is a becoming eternal. It is a becoming true—becoming a being with only one aim and that an absolute one." [11] Thus understood, the term cannot be applied to God, Who is eternal and infinite, and has never needed to become so. Existentialism then emphasizes the realization of the Christian objectives in personal experience, by means of personal decisions, and not a communication of knowledge. It is directed against all attempts at objective or rationalistic Christianity (e.g., of Kant or Hegel), and is essentially subjective, individual. "The task of becoming subjective, then, may be presumed to be the highest task . . ." [12]

We have thus at last reached Kierkegaard's treatment of religion, particularly of Christianity. We may distinguish here two aspects of his thought: his radical critique of the existing form of Christianity, particularly that of the Danish Lutheran Church, and his own concept of true Christianity. As for "the monstrous illusion we call Christendom," he concludes that it is the salt which had wholly lost its savor; *i.e.*, it has completely accommodated itself to the worldly standards. To deny Christianity or to take it seriously "is regarded as equally scandalous." He writes about the case of a man doubting that he is a Christian:

> Or if he happened to be married, his wife would say to him: 'Dear husband of mine, how can you get such notions into your head? How can you doubt that you are a Christian? Are you not a Dane,

[10] *Postscript*, p. 116.
[11] Richard Niebuhr, "Søren Kierkegaard," in Carl Michalson, ed. *Christianity and the Existentialists* (New York: Charles Scribner's Sons, 1956), p. 40. By permission.
[12] *Postscript*, p. 146.

and does not geography say that the Lutheran form of the Christian religion is the ruling religion in Denmark? For you are surely not a Jew, nor are you a Mohammedan; what then can you be if not a Christian? It is a thousand years since paganism was driven out of Denmark, so I know you are not a pagan. Do you not perform your duties at the office like a conscientious civil servant; are you not a good citizen of a Christian nation, a Lutheran Christian state? So then of course you must be a Christian! [13]

Kierkegaard did not always employ irony in denouncing the secularized concept of Christianity. Toward the end of his life he reached the stage of vitriolic attacks upon the religious deadness of the Danish Church, not sparing the primate himself. He advised men "by refusing any longer . . . to participate in the public worship as now conducted . . . you will have one less crime upon your conscience, and that a heavy one; for you will no longer take part in making a mockery of God." [14] On his deathbed, he refused the ministrations of a Lutheran pastor.

On the positive side, Kierkegaard first of all demands a personal decision, a resolute and complete break with everything pertaining to one's own will and the acceptance in faith of God's will. This he calls an act of "infinite resignation" (i.e., repentance), an act of will. He is particularly fond of citing the example of Abraham in his willingness to sacrifice Isaac in obedience to what he understood to be God's will. As an act of will it is within man's own power. This element of personal decision is an outstanding feature of existentialism. "In resignation I make renunciation of everything, this movement I make by myself . . ." [15] But this "dying to the world" must be supplemented by faith, which is not an act of will but God's gift of grace. But neither the resignation nor faith is the result of reflection, but essentially a leap of resolute will into darkness.

Among the most important of Kierkegaard's ideas is his distinction between Religiousness A and Religiousness B. The first of these may be understood as involving no "absurdity," but rather what Aquinas designated by the term "natural theology." It comprises such aspects of religious knowledge as may be understood on the basis of sense-perceptions and reason. Accordingly, such religion is to be found both among Christians and non-Christians.

> The knowledge of God within 'Religiousness A' is a knowledge of God in His immanence. For, by any natural capacity, man can know

---

[13] *Ibid.*, p. 49.
[14] Quoted by David F. Swenson in *Fragments*, p. xxviii.
[15] *Fear and Trembling*, p. 69.

nothing of God in His unlikeness to man, that is, in His transcendence. In this realm 'there is and can be no consciousness of the qualitative difference between God and man, and between eternity and time. This comes through the realization of the tragic cleft within man's own existence by which there arises the existential pathos which forces a man to the brink of "Religiousness B." ' [16]

Religiousness B, or Christianity proper, is the heart of Kierkegaard's position. It roughly corresponds to Aquinas' "revealed" religion, except for the basic difference that it is not only above natural reason, but completely contrary to it. Being beyond the possibility of human understanding, it is paradoxical, incomprehensible to reason, and therefore impossible of apprehension.

> What now is the absurd? The absurd is that the eternal truth has come into being in time, that God has come into being, has been born, has grown up, and so forth, precisely like any other individual human being, quite indistinguishable from other individuals.[17]

Thus the basic tenet of Christianity—the Incarnation of Christ in Jesus—can never be rationally proved or comprehended; in fact, it is wholly self-contradictory, involving the concept of an infinite God revealing Himself in a finite man. It must be accepted by faith and believed against reason. The same applies to the trinitarian and the two-natures-of-Christ dogmas, which are the necessary consequences of the Incarnation.

But the chief of these paradoxes of Christianity concerns God Himself; for in His transcendence He is qualitatively different from man. He is eternal, man is finite; He is holy, man is a sinner; He is Being, man is becoming. Man then is "absolutely unlike" God,[18] who is thus "wholly other" in relation to him:

> But the absolute difference between God and man consists precisely in this, that man is a particular existing being (which is just as much true of the most gifted human being as it is of the most stupid), whose essential task cannot be to think *sub specie aeterni*, since as long as he exists he is, though eternal, essentially an existing individual, whose essential task it is to concentrate upon inwardness in existing; while God is infinite and eternal.[19]

---

[16] H. V. Martin, *The Wings of Faith* (London: Lutterworth Press, 1950), pp. 53, 54. By permission.

[17] *Postscript*, p. 188.

[18] *Fragments*, p. 37.

[19] *Postscript*, p. 195.

Any attempt to comprehend the Godhead by means of our limited human reason is as absurd as for a child to try to scoop up the ocean in his sandpail. This then is the radical rejection of the virtual Hegelian pantheism, the assertion that man is an infinitesimal momentary manifestation of the Absolute Idea. It is to repudiate this identification of God and man that Kierkegaard asserts the opposite extreme, *i.e.*, that God is "absolutely unlike" man and man is infinitely and qualitatively different from God.

Since it is only by faith that a Christian receives this revelation of an otherwise incomprehensible God, this faith is directed to Jesus Christ, Who is the revelation of this *Deus absconditus*. Moreover, this faith has for its object Christ Himself, not His teaching.

> This is what Kierkegaard means when he insists that Christianity is not a communication of knowledge, but an existence-communication. It answers not to man's reason but to man's existence. . . . Christ is the eternal Truth, not in the sense that He taught the truth, nor in the sense that He expressed the truth in His character or in the deeds of His daily life; but He is the truth in Himself, that is, in His very nature as God-man.[20]

The tremendous emphasis Kierkegaard places on faith naturally suggests repudiation of knowledge. Faith is "an assurance of things hoped for," a synthesis of paradox and belief, rather than an assurance derived from knowledge. Kierkegaard has been likened to a modern Tertullian and the latter's emphasis on the phrase ascribed to him, *credo quia absurdum*. "What has Jerusalem to do with Athens?" Kierkegaard indeed has done more to stress the impossibility of knowledge and understanding in the realm of the basic Christian tenets than any other modern, with the exception of young Barth, who had been at the time under the compelling influence of Kierkegaard, and who has since repudiated this extreme position. Kierkegaard's favorite simile is that a Christian driven to depend on faith rather than knowledge is like a man swimming over seventy thousand fathoms of water. And yet "faith *must* not *rest content* with unintelligibility." [21] For as Hugh Martin remarks, "the highest understanding is to know that there are some things understanding cannot grasp." [22] Moreover, it is well to remind ourselves that reason is unable to understand even the physical universe or the nature of matter, but restricts itself to the scientific study of how matter acts.

[20] Martin, *op. cit.*, pp. 61, 60.
[21] *Postscript*, p. 540.
[22] Martin, *op. cit.*, p. 75.

In conclusion, although I gladly admit the great services of Kierke-gaard in combatting absolute rationalism (Hegelian and any other), formalism, and secularism, I feel constrained to point out that his opposition to these extremes took an equally extreme form. It was a distortion of Christianity as serious as the ones he fought against. This is particularly true of his insistence on the absolute unlikeness between God and man. If God is "wholly other," and is qualitatively different from man, then the belief that man was created in the divine image is undermined and untenable. Either man had never been so created, or he has completely lost this divine image. This is the most radical form of the "total depravity" tenet such as one can hardly find in the entire history of Christian thought. Moreover, it is likewise completely contrary to our Lord's teaching as found in the Gospels, or indeed the whole New Testament. Surely the revelation of God in Jesus Christ does not lead us to believe that He is wholly unknowable and incomprehensible, or that faith is "absurd!" And the revelation in Christ ought to be given greater weight than the thought of Kierkegaard. Thus in his protest against the Hegelian identification of God and man, Kierkegaard has gone to the opposite extreme of asserting God's absolute transcendence. If God dwells in the light unapproachable— and He does—He also chooses to dwell in the human heart.

In venturing an adverse judgment upon some of Kierkegaard's tenets, I am glad to avail myself of Mackintosh's summary:

> Yet his [Kierkegaard's] effects have been purchased at a price too great for the faith engendered by Jesus Christ. The conclusion is unavoidable that, in his efforts to alter the balance of contemporary religious thought, Kierkegaard induces new distortions of belief so violent and perverse as gravely to imperil our hold on the New Testament conception of God and of the life His children are called to lead. Thus . . . his individualism is of so extreme a type as largely to disqualify him from understanding actual religion.[23]

But just in this connection it should be remembered that Kierkegaard himself strenuously insisted that he was "an exception," and thus warned against making his personal understanding of what it is "to become a Christian" a norm for all. Hence, there can be no such thing as "a Kierkegaardian movement," and those who created it forgot that to become a disciple of "an exception" is to nullify the exception. Kierkegaard made himself a Don Quixote in his utter devotion to his ideal. The devotion is incumbent on all Christians; but the manner of applying it is not.

---

[23] H. R. Mackintosh, *Types of Modern Theology*, p. 257.

## *Albrecht Ritschl, the Father of the Social Gospel*

Another theologian who was stirred to a lifelong literary conflict with the conclusions of Hegelian, particularly the Left-wing Hegelian, tenets, but in a manner vastly different from that of Kierkegaard, is Albrecht Benjamin Ritschl (1822-1889). It was particularly the Hegelian philosophy of history, as applied by the Tübingen school —especially by Ferdinand Christian Baur—to the critique of early Christianity, which saw in the thesis-antithesis formula the very key to the interpretation of the real and imagined conflicts of that period, that aroused Ritschl's ire. The most important—and lasting in its effects—was this school's supposed contrast between the teachings of Jesus and Paul, or the concepts of the historical Jesus and the metaphysical Christ; Baur proclaimed Paul the virtual creator of the theology of the divine Christ which gained complete sway over the historic Christian Church. It was this tendency of substituting the "historic" Jesus for the "mythical" Christ that stirred Ritschl to enter the theological arena girded for a decisive fight. He went for his starting point to the Schleiermacherian emphasis on religious experience, although he developed the concept far beyond the stage at which the older theologian had left it. He emphasized the historical and ethical character of Christianity as against the metaphysical, and placed Jesus Christ as the revelation of God in history at the center of his system.

Ritschl was born in Berlin, the son of the Lutheran bishop of Pomerania. At home he was brought up pietistically, which is perhaps the reason for his subsequent radical revolt against this tendency. He received his education mainly at Bonn and Tübingen; at the latter place, as has been noted, he fell under the sway of Ferdinand Christian Baur, and later became his principal opponent. In 1852 he became profess extraordinarius at Bonn, and seven years later attained the status of fu.. professor. In 1864 he was called to teach systematic theology at Göttingen, where he remained for the rest of his life. The great work in which he formulated his theological point of view is *The Christian Doctrine of Justification and Reconciliation*, published in 1874. Brunner regards it as "the second milestone in the theological history of the last century." [24] In this work Ritschl inverts the usual order of theological sequence, normally beginning with a consideration of God and leading on to man and his redemption from sin. He starts with the conception of justification of man as sinner and leads on to the doctrine concerning God as its presupposition. Nevertheless, around the doctrines of justification and reconciliation as facts of religious experience —and be it noted that reconciliation *follows* justification, and is not the basis of the latter—he builds all other doctrines. He adopts this order on the principle of proceeding from the known to the unknown— from the Christian experience of salvation from sin to the derived knowledge about God, Who is essentially unknowable unless revealed in Jesus Christ. Within the empirical realm, religion may be studied as scientifically as the natural sciences, for one deals there with ascertainable, experienced facts. Thus religion is a function of a moral being, concerned with the life of moral freedom. It has to do with life rather than theory, with the historical facts regarding God's revelation in Christ rather than with metaphysical speculation, and with ethics rather than with mystical states of the soul. Adopting the Lotzean epistemology, he postulates as the functions of the mind making value-judgments and causal judgments, or in other words religious and theoretical knowledge. And although the two are connected with each other, the value-judgments are more basic for all knowledge, and absolutely basic for religious knowledge. "Every cognition of a religious sort is a direct judgment of value." [25] These value-judgments (or better, worth-judgments—*Werturteile*—for "value" refers to price rating, "worth" to moral excellence), rest on the grounds of their beneficial significance for us, and are thus independent of the objective value of the thing under consideration; a memento of someone dear to us—a parent or friend—may be priceless to us, although possessing no commercial value whatever. Ritschl writes:

> Scientific knowledge is accompanied or guided by a judgment affirming the worth of impartial knowledge gained by observation. In Christianity, religious knowledge consists in independent value-judgments, inasmuch as it deals with the relation between the blessedness which is assured by God and sought by man, and the whole of

[24] From *The Mediator* by Emil Brunner. Copyright 1947 by W. L. Jenkins. The Westminster Press. Used by permission. Barth, with his characteristic opposition to Brunner, denies the latter's estimate. Cf. Barth's *Protestant Thought*, p. 390.
[25] Albrecht Ritschl, *The Christian Doctrine of Justification and Reconciliation*, H. R. Mackintosh and A. B. Macaulay, trs. (Edinburgh: T. & T. Clark, 1902), p. 398. By permission.

the world which God has created and rules in harmony with His final end. Scientific knowledge seeks to discover the laws of nature and spirit through observation. . . .[26]

Theology has to do, not with natural objects, but with states and movements of man's spiritual life.[27]

Accordingly, "religion and theoretical knowledge are different functions of the spirit, which, when they deal with the same objects, are not even partially the same, but are divergent throughout." On this basis, there cannot be, or ought not to be, any conflict between religion and science; each has its own sphere of investigation and its own methods of carrying on its work. Both yield valid knowledge, but of different kinds. Ritschl thus withdraws religion into the inner citadel of Christian faith, where it judges what is religiously valid rather than what pertains to the scientific truth. Thus theology, Ritschl affirms, ". . . should not be concerned with any theoretical explanation of the universe. The world only comes within the scope of theology because God has placed human beings in a certain relationship to it, and that with a moral end in view." [28] These final ends Ritschl, evidently inspired by Kant's doctrine of the realm of ends, defines in terms of the Kingdom of God.

Consequently, Ritschl vehemently assails the cosmological, teleological, and ontological "proofs" of the existence of God because they rest essentially upon reason rather than on faith in God as engendered by Christian experience. He thus agrees essentially with Kant (although on different grounds) and repudiates Thomas Aquinas as a rationalist. He condemns even Melanchthon for his "return to Aristotle," and for thus failing to follow Luther's lead. In fact, he would have no truck with any form of "natural theology."

Christianity, then, is true—in fact it is the absolute religion—because

The revelation of God in Jesus, when responded to in active faith, gives man actual freedom and mastery over nature. It redeems him from sinfulness through the divine forgiveness, and implants in him that motive of love which aims at the moral organization of mankind. It gives the blessedness of a sonship to God and of participation in the kingdom of God, which is at once a reality and a task.[29]

[26] *Ibid.*, p. 207.
[27] *Ibid.*, p. 20.
[28] Flew, *The Idea of Perfection*, p. 388.
[29] Eugene W. Lyman, "Ritschl's Theory of Value-Judgments," in *The Journal of Religion*, V (Chicago: The University of Chicago Press, 1925), p. 508. By permission.

In short, Christianity is true because it works. This is theological pragmatism.

Passing on, then, to Ritschl's concept of God—which, be it remembered, is derived from the Christian experience of salvation—he asserts that the only knowledge of God worth having is that of His revelation in Jesus Christ and the experiences of those who have been reconciled with Him through Jesus Christ. God thus known reveals Himself as a personality whose purpose for the world guarantees victory over the evil in the world on the part of those who trust Him. God is love: the objects of this love are of the same spiritual nature as He, for they too are persons. God's love is informed by His constant, purposive, understanding will, aiming at the promotion of the highest good of persons. But he gives them what they need for their highest spiritual maturity, not what they want for their selfish ends. Thus His love is steadfast, demanding reciprocal love on their part. God carries out His purpose unconditionally, against all resistance. The ultimate goal of this relation of the love of God for man and man's for God is the Kingdom of God—the realm of personal ends.

But just because Ritschl judges God from the vantage point of His relation to men, he disclaims any knowledge of the inner relations within the Godhead, such as is postulated by the trinitarian doctrine. The same applies to the doctrine of the two natures in Christ or to His pre-existence. Christ's task and function are limited to the revelation of the purpose of God in the establishment of the Kingdom. Ritschl devotes to Christ a considerable section of his book, which is replete with references to His Godhead, or divinity. But the voluble discussion is not equally illuminating; in fact, he makes the impression of trying to hide his meaning by confusing his reader. I understand him to say that Christ's "divinity" is a value-judgment. He writes:

> But if Christ by what He has done and suffered for my salvation is my Lord, and if, by trusting for my salvation to the power of what He has done for me, I honour Him as my God, then that is a value-judgment of a direct kind.[30]

Is this, or is it not, an acknowledgment of Christ's divinity? I find it hard to answer. On the one hand, Ritschl asserts unequivocally that

---

[30] *Justification and Reconciliation*, p. 398; cf. also p. 465, where Ritschl asserts that "in His own order He is unique," but only from the standpoint of God's kingdom.

"Christ is the Bearer of the final revelation of God." [31] But if that is so, surely there can be no question that the God thus revealed is divine. That is mere tautology. Why then is there any hesitation on Ritschl's part about saying so? Is it perhaps that God is also a value-judgment? I confess that I am puzzled by it.

The second principal focus of Ritschl's interpretation of Christianity is his concept of the Kingdom of God. As we have already seen, the will of God toward the establishment of the Kingdom found its perfect revelation and realization in Christ. The work of Christ is conceived in terms of "redeeming" men, and the progressive incorporation of them into the Kingdom of God, of which He is the founder. The redemption is not a matter of a miraculous change in the soul of man—thus eliminating the taint of the original and the acquired sins residing there—but a moral change of character. This personal transformation is not an end in itself, but the means for the transformation of the world.

The instrument of this transforming process is the society of spiritually changed and ethically dominated men—the Church, of which Christ is both the Founder and the Lord. Ritschl thus concludes,

> Christianity, then, is the monotheistic, completely spiritual, and ethical religion, which, based on the life of its Author as Redeemer and as Founder of the Kingdom of God, consists in the freedom of the children of God, involves the impulse to conduct from the motive of love, aims at the moral organisation of mankind, and grounds blessedness on the relation of sonship to God, as well as on the Kingdom of God. [32]

Accordingly, the individual believer finds salvation only within the Christian community which thus becomes "the body" of its Lord, Jesus Christ. The Church is the *present* agent of the redeeming work inaugurated by Christ. Ritschl interprets the idea of "reconciliation" or "atonement" as purely subjective: it is the change of man's idea of God from the false conception of Him as Judge to the true conception of Him as Love. Thus the immediate end of salvation is the individual believer's freedom from sin; but the final end is the Kingdom of God— the "beloved community."

The aim of the Christian Church is two-fold: the "individual" salvation is balanced by the "social gospel." No one is redeemed merely for his private enjoyment or benefit; the privilege conferred on him by God's free grace implies corresponding responsibility. It is not an end

[31] *Ibid.*, p. 388.
[32] *Ibid.*, p. 13.

in itself, but a means toward a larger end. But neither can the "beloved community" be built without transformed individuals, or by any means, cultural, economic, or political, save those of spiritual transformation. And although Ritschl is rightly regarded as the father of the "social gospel," he is not to be held responsible for the misuse of the term as implying other than the spiritual connotation.

The importance of Ritschl's emphases for the modern apprehension of Christianity is so obvious as to need no labored exposition. In the first place, it has led to a clearer understanding of the historical character of Christianity. A whole galaxy of scholars henceforth have devoted themselves to the study of the origins and early history of the Church, among whom men like Adolf von Harnack and Shirley Jackson Case occupy an honored position. Harnack unfortunately is too generally judged from the single small volume originally taken down in shorthand from his popular lectures. His much more massive and solid contributions to the study of church history are thus not sufficiently taken into account. In the second place, the emphasis on the social implications of the gospel found such a host of eager exponents during the first half of the century, as to give the predominant social character to the whole era, particularly in America. This is not to say that Ritschl's interpretation is not overly conditioned by the theological situation of his day or his own personal limitations; nor does it imply that the exponents of the modern social gospel, in their enthusiasm for the new aspects of truth, did not jeopardize other equally important truths or weaken, not to say abandon, some basic Christian convictions.

# 8

# The Eclipse of Christianity

## Ludwig A. Feuerbach, the Philosopher of Humanist Atheism

If Kant's dualism had been subverted by his monistic epigoni, Hegel's idealism had suffered a similar fate at the hands of his materialistic followers. They formed the school of "left wing Hegelians." In general they remained faithful to their master's monism, but instead of regarding the ultimate nature of reality as that of mind or spirit, they substituted for it matter. This had far-reaching consequences for science and philosophy, but particularly for religion. For assuming that the stuff of reality is material, they soon drew the conclusion that God as a spiritual entity does not exist. And since to deny God leads to the denial of man, they made the further deduction that man is only a psychosomatic organism without any spiritual nature whatever. We have reached the familiar situation of modern secularism with its inherent atheism, which more than anything else testifies that the era of humanism has reached an end. For the principal characteristic of secularism is just this denial of the spiritual nature of man. We shall illustrate the various aspects of this period in the systems of thought of such men as Feuerbach, Marx, Comte, and Nietzsche.

First of all, then, let us turn our attention to Ludwig Feuerbach (1804-1872). He first studied theology at Heidelberg, but later (1824) changed to philosophy at Berlin under Hegel. In 1828 he began to teach philosophy at the University of Erlangen, but was not successful at this career. He abandoned it for that of a private scholar and a free-lance writer. This was made possible by his marriage to a moderately well-to-do wife, upon whose income he lived in modest comfort for the rest of his life.

His lifelong interest was religion, or rather a radical attack upon its historic form in an attempt to substitute for it his own "*ersatz*" of religious anthropology. He was influential in so far as his views—in a somewhat modified form—have passed on through others, particularly through Karl Marx, to become extremely important in the complex of the present-day secularism. His principal works comprise *Das Wesen des Christentum* (1841), translated by George Eliot under the title *The Essence of Christianity* and republished recently by H. Richard Niebuhr.[1] His two other books, *The Philosophy of the Future* (1843) and *The Essence of Religion* (1851) are likewise to be noted. For our purpose, the first-named work is the most important. Its thesis is that God is the projection into infinity of our own self. And despite Feuerbach's denial of his dependence on Hegel, his own thesis is but an inversion of the Hegelian assertion that the Absolute finds its fullest self-objectification in man. Feuerbach simply transposed these terms. In fact, as Karl Barth points out, even for Schleiermacher theology was essentially anthropology—the awareness of the subjective feeling of dependence. Accordingly, Feuerbach's philosophy as well as "theology" are anthropocentric, humanistic, and materialistic. For him the true *ens realissimum* is man; thus authentic being is not to be found in the noumenal realm of Kant, or the Absolute Idea of Hegel: it is in man considered as a material entity. He asserts that thought is engendered by the senses: ". . . it has relation to its object first through the senses, *i.e.*, passively, before defining it in thought." [2] Thus senses *produce* thought, which is only a function of matter. Man is therefore basically a physical—not even psychosomatic—organism. It leads him to assert that "man is what he eats." Religion then, as has already been mentioned, is the projection of man's highest thoughts into transcendent dimensions. Accordingly,

---

[1] Ludwig Feuerbach, *The Essence of Christianity*, George Eliot, tr., (New York: 1857, and New York: Harper & Brothers, 1957). I used the 1857 ed. Otherwise, by permission.

[2] *Ibid.*, p. 6; new ed. p. xxxv.

> . . . I show that the true sense of Theology is Anthropology, that there is no distinction between the *predicates* of the divine and human nature, and, consequently, no distinction between the divine and human *subject*.[3]

> God is man, man is God; it is not I, but religion that denies the God who is *not* man, but only an *ens rationis*, since it makes God become man, and then constitutes this God, not distinguished from man, having a human form, human feelings and human thoughts, the object of its worship and veneration. I have only found the key to the cipher of the Christian religion, only extricated its true meaning from the web of contradictions and delusions called theology.[4]

God, then, is the noblest work of man—a view which has been adopted by many "emancipated" individuals, particularly among those inspired by humanistic motivation. Berdyaev calls the view the "mangodhood" in contrast to "Godmanhood." Dostoevsky has depicted the type in many of his characters, particularly in Ivan Karamazov. Ivan concluded with Feuerbach that morality is autonomous, not dependent upon faith in God.

Having then convinced himself of the truth of his pleasing discovery that God is man, and having stoutly identified this view with the true interpretation of Christianity, Feuerbach proceeds to elucidate his view. He finds the proof of it in the Christian doctrine of Incarnation, which teaches that God has revealed himself by assuming in Jesus Christ the human nature. "The Incarnation is nothing else than the practical, material manifestation of the human nature of God. . . . Man was already in God, was already God himself, before God became man, i.e., showed himself as man." [5]

> . . . I prove that the son of God is in religion a real son, the Son of God in the same sense in which man is the son of man. . . .[6]

> The Father and Son in the Trinity are therefor father and son not in a figurative sense, but in a strictly literal sense. The Father is a real father in relation to the Son, the Son is a real son in relation to the Father, or to God as Father. The essential personal distinction consists only in this, that the one begets, the other is begotten.[7]

The Virgin Mother is then necessary for the manifestation of the Son in human flesh, since "she conceives without man the Son whom

---

[3] *Ibid.*, p. 7; new ed., xxxvii.
[4] *Ibid.*, p. 6; new ed., xxxvi.
[5] *Ibid.*, p. 77; new ed., p. 50.
[6] *Ibid.*, p. 8; new ed., xxxvii.
[7] *Ibid.*, p. 100; new ed., p. 69.

the Father begets without woman." [8] This bit of flummery is hardly in keeping with Feuerbach's naturalism. This bizarre, if not blasphemous, Christology, comprising even the "Virgin Birth," serves Feuerbach as an excuse for ascribing to Christ all the virtues and excellences aspired to by men. One wonders, since God is man or at most only a projection of human aspirations, how the physical relation between the Father, the Son, and the Mother is to be understood!

But despite his reiterated and emphatic assertion that theology is really anthropology and God is man, and that any idea of God existing apart from and independently of the cosmos—an idea Feuerbach regards as mere *Wunchwesen*, wishful thinking—he vehemently denies that his system is atheistic. Indeed, he denounces atheism in the strongest terms. Since man is God, the denial of God is the denial of man, of humanism. He apparently identifies anthropocentrism with the only true religion. He is an enthusiastic asserter of "Yes" to man and to life in general, and is sincerely, even passionately, concerned with human values as he understands them. He writes:

> Hence he alone is the true atheist to whom the predicates of the Divine Being—for example, love, wisdom, justice—are nothing; not he to whom merely the subject of these predicates is nothing. And in no wise is the negation of the subject necessarily also a negation of the predicates considered in themselves. These have an intrinsic, independent reality; they force their recognition upon man by their very nature; they are self-evident truths to him; they prove, they attest themselves. [9]

Nevertheless, there is a basic contradiction in all his humanism: if God does not exist independently of man, or, in other words, if the cosmos is devoid of such qualities as love, wisdom, and justice that are regarded by Christians as of the very essence of God, where did man, who is after all a product of the cosmos, derive these qualities? Is not this arguing that something can be derived from nothing? Or that a river may rise above its source? Feuerbach's reasoning is infected by the fatal error of all humanist atheism—the endowing of man with attributes which are denied to the rest of the universe. He failed to see that to deny God as a self-existent entity is to deny man as well.

But it must not be thought that the identification of man with God applies to any individual human being as such. No! Feuerbach ascribes it to the relation existing between men, or to humanity as a whole.

---

[8] *Ibid.*, p. 102; new ed., p. 71.
[9] *Ibid.*, p. 43; new ed., p. 21.

Again, since there is no humanity in the abstract, only that which consists of the aggregate of individuals, the totality cannot possess qualities which the parts lack. Nevertheless, Feuerbach writes: "The necessary turning-point of history is therefore the open confession, that the consciousness of God is nothing else than the consciousness of the species." [10] All historic, positive religions have evolved as "the traditions of the primitive self-consciousness." They were, therefore, necessary stages in human moral and cultural development. They are not to be regarded as aberrations, but as stages of growth. Their errors are the inevitable products of immaturity as well as positive perversions. It follows, therefore, that religion is to be equated with an attitude of reverence toward the human race.

Accordingly, since *"Homo homini Deus est,"* the proper relation among men must be that of love. "Love to man must be no derivative love; it must be original. If human nature is the highest nature to man, then practically also the highest and first law must be the love of man to man." [11] But as has already been pointed out, such an ethic assumes that love—which to a Christian has its source in God—exists in a universe in which God does not exist. This kind of fallacy was pointed out to the Russian nihilists in Vladimir Solovev's pithy aphorism: "Man is descended from a monkey; *therefore,* let us love one another."

And finally, it may be of interest to note how desperately Feuerbach has striven to apply his principles to all the major tenets of historic Christianity by his *reductio ad absurdum* of the sacraments of baptism and the Lord's Supper. He, of course, denies to them all sacramental significance. But why then does he retain them at all? Although it would have been natural for him merely to declare them to be superstitions—magical rites derived from pagan antecedents—and thus dispose of them altogether, he not only chooses to include them in his system but actually ascribes to them considerable importance. To be sure, bereft of all sacramental significance baptism is reduced by him to the beneficial custom of bathing, and the Lord's Supper to the laudable function of eating and drinking! In fact, Feuerbach waxes lyrical in his apostrophe to water!

> How many saints have had recourse to the natural qualities of water in order to overcome the assaults of the devil! [One wonders whether he means some supernatural devil or only a natural devil.] . . . . To purify oneself, to bathe, is the first, though the lowest of virtues. . . . The man rising from the water is a new, a regenerate man.[12]

[10] *Ibid.,* p. 340; new ed., p. 270.
[11] *Ibid.,* p. 341; new ed., p. 271.
[12] *Ibid.,* p. 346; new ed. pp. 275-76.

In other words, cleanliness *is* holiness. Feuerbach himself in jest referred to this bizarre concept of baptism as the "pneumatic hydrotherapy." The Lord's Supper is understood in the same stark naturalistic sense: "eating and drinking is, in fact, in itself a religious act; at least, ought to be so. . . . Therefore, let bread be sacred for us, let wine be sacred, and also let water be sacred! Amen." [13]

This "*ersatz*" religion of atheistic humanism of Feuerbach, despite his claim to philosophical impeccability and logical cogency, is untenable. Eduard von Hartmann, himself no friend or defender of religion, has pointed out Feuerbach's fallacy of basing his identification of God with projected human desire by asserting that just because men wish for something, this does not *prove* that it does not actually exist. The real problem is to ascertain its existence irrespective of whether or not we wish it. If all we wish for did not exist, this world would be not only frustrating, but essentially irrational.[14] Accordingly, Feuerbach's system of thought would not demand an extended treatment on our part, were it not for the powerful influence which it has exerted upon his contemporaries and the later humanist and secularist thinkers. Actually, his book became the bible of the left wing Hegelians and had a powerful effect upon the Russian nihilists. Both Engels and Marx wrote of its "liberating influence" and the sense of freedom it gave them.[15] And although Marx later attacked Feuerbach in the same venomous way in which he turned against Hegel, yet Feuerbach may safely be accounted as the legitimate or illegitimate father of *this aspect* of Marxism.

Feuerbach's influence upon the Russian leaders of nihilism was even greater. Chernyshevsky, who may be regarded as the chief protagonist of the movement, was a thoroughgoing Feuerbachian. When the tsarist government exiled him to Siberia and deprived him of all books, Chernyshevsky continued to gain disciples among his fellow exiles by reciting Feuerbach, whom he knew almost by heart. The same may be asserted about that fiery apostle of "total destruction," Bakunin, who was thoroughly imbued with Feuerbach's principles, although he applied them differently.

It was in his disciples, therefore, that Feuerbach's importance lies. And views closely similar to his own may easily be found among the

[13] *Ibid.*, p. 347; new ed. pp. 277-78.
[14] Cf. Mackintosh, *Types of Theology*, p. 128.
[15] Cf. Otto Rühle, *Karl Marx, his Life and Work* (Garden City, N.Y.: Doubleday & Company, 1943), pp. 32-33.

contemporaneous exponents of non-theistic humanism, although their true parentage is generally not acknowledged even to themselves.

## Karl Marx and Dialectical Materialism

Among those whose secularizing influence upon the modern age has been the greatest was Karl Marx, a son of a Westphalian lawyer of Jewish ancestry—*not* of proletarian origin. He was born in Trier in 1818. For many generations, many of his male ancestry on both sides had been rabbis. His father, Hirschel, was a liberal Prussian patriot, who for prudential reasons submitted to baptism when Karl was six years old, and changed his name to Heinrich. He had postponed this step until after his mother's death; but religiously it meant little, if anything, to him.

Little Karl was a precocious child. At the age of twelve he was matriculated at the Trier gymnasium, and five years later he entered the University of Bonn to study law. But the year he spent there was not successful, apparently because he lacked his father's servility. On the contrary, he was intolerant of any slight upon himself on account of his Jewish origins. Nevertheless, he won the affections of the prettiest girl of the town, Jenny von Westphalen, a companion of his sister. Although her parents were against the match—the Westphalens were of the nobility—years afterward Karl married his Jenny just the same.

In 1836 Karl became a student in the already famous University of Berlin, where the great luminaries of the period—Hegel, Schleiermacher, and von Humboldt—taught, although the two first named were already dead. Karl studied law, but he soon fell under the spell of the regnant Hegelianism. Because of his proficiency, he was admitted into the circle of advanced left wing Hegelians, called the Doctors' Club. Marx's opinions rapidly changed under their influence. The members of the Club, who regarded themselves as the vanguard of cultural progress, eagerly embraced the views of David Strauss, Bruno Bauer, and particularly Ludwig Feuerbach—men who subverted Hegel's teaching from idealism to materialism. However, Marx finally received his doctor's degree at the University of Jena (1841)—Berlin proved too stringently conservative for him.

The young doctor looked about him for a suitable career, and finally chose journalism. He joined the staff of the recently founded (1842) daily paper, *Rheinische Zeitung*, of which he later became the editor-in-chief. A liberal paper, it constantly had to fight the strict censorship of the conservative government—a suitable task for the editor's natural pugnacity. And although his articles were acclaimed brilliant, he became dissatisfied with them because he realized his lack of grounding in sociology and economics. Accordingly, when the Prussian king, Frederick William III, either instigated or issued an order for the suppression of the paper (1843), Marx was genuinely glad to be rid of his onerous duties. He said of the event that by it he was "set free" by the government to do what he had desired to do anyway: to go to France and study socialism at first hand. But before leaving Germany, he married his beloved Jenny.

In Paris he joined the group of radical fellow-Germans and collaborated with them in the publication of the *Deutsch-Französische Jahrbücher*. He published in it numerous articles, one of which (1843) sets forth his attitude toward religion. Starting from Feuerbach, he declares his own increasingly anti-Hegelian position. In this article is found that notorious slogan, "Religion is the opium of the people." [16] He advocates the abolition of religion on the ground that "The people cannot be really happy until it has been deprived of illusory happiness by the abolition of religion. . . . Thus the criticism of heaven is transformed into a criticism of earth, the criticism of religion into a criticism of law, the criticism of theology into a criticism of politics." [17] He even adumbrates his later famous "class struggle" concept by asserting that the necessary political revolution is the work of the proletariat. Revolution depends upon the proletariat attaining to general dominion and then liberating the rest of society.

It was of the greatest importance that during the Paris period Marx met Friedrich Engels, with whom he remained in intimate relation, both in literary and financial respects, for the rest of his life. Engels was the son of a Barmen textile manufacturer, representing his father's firm abroad. Another contact made by Marx was with Pierre Joseph Proudhon. The latter was a self-educated printer, who developed a socialist system adapted and further developed by Marx. Also among his acquaintances was the fiery Russian nihilist, Michael Bakunin, in whom Marx found his principal rival for the control of the First International.

When the *Deutsch-Französische Jahrbücher* were forbidden by the French government—under pressure from Prussia—five of the contributors, Marx among them, were expelled from France. He then moved to Brussels. It was here that he threw himself into the organization of a

---

[16] *Ibid.*, p. 57.
[17] *Ibid.*, pp. 57-58.

revolutionary movement called the German Working Men's Association. He at last asserted his own principles of revolutionary work by violently repudiating Proudhon's views as "sentimental," and "utopian," and by breaking with even his own collaborator, Wilhelm Weitling. He also entered into polemics with Bakunin and broke with the German left wing Hegelians, particularly Feuerbach. Henceforth, his was to be a "scientific" socialism that he later called communism, in order to make the distinction clear. In 1847 a "congress" of the revolutionary groups was held in London which was to organize a formal international Communist League. It adopted a constitution, but also decided to issue a "Manifesto." It was Marx (who did not attend the congress) and Engels, the two *bourgeois* intellectuals, who produced this famous declaration of the principles of society's ultimate conquest by the proletarians. The thesis concludes with the motto copied from an earlier publication, "Proletarians of all countries, unite!" and comprises such measures as the expropriation of all landed property, a graded income tax, abolition of inheritance, centralization of economy in the state, creation of labor armies, and assumption of control over education.[18]

The year 1848 was a year of revolution. Marx and other communists assumed that it was the predicted and hoped for proletarian uprising. He therefore hastened back to Germany, and assumed the editorship of the *Neue Rheinische Zeitung*, a paper that for vitriolic criticism and pitiless mockery of anything less than a proletarian revolution on communist principles had no equal. By this time Marx realized that a democratic victory over the forces of absolutism was a *bourgeois*, not a proletarian, victory. Nevertheless, when the first issue appeared in June, all chances of success for the communist cause were lost; the proletarians had joined the liberal *bourgeoisie* in support of the Frankfurt parliament. Marx denounced them savagely as the *Lumpenproletariat*—the riff-raff. The peasantry were not included in his conception of a proletarian revolution, and were denounced as "troglodytes," not even conscious of their own real interests. Marx fulminated against the parliament, calling it a "talking shop" and a "council of old women." This radicalism provoked such intense wrath among the democratic leaders of the nation that appeals were made to the Ministry of Justice to intervene. Stockholders owning shares in the *Zeitung* withdrew, and Marx was forced to secure his own financial support. In the end the

---

[18] Karl Marx and Friedrich Engels, *The Communist Manifesto* (New York: International Publishers Co., Inc., 1948), p. 30.

paper was prohibited, and Marx was given twenty-four hours to leave the country.

After a month's stay in Paris, when a police sergeant served a notice on him that he *et son dame* must leave within twenty-four hours, he went to London. This was to be his home for the rest of his life. At first the situation of the Marx family was desperate; without means, often ailing (he suffered from his liver, boils, and carbuncles), and his children gravely ill, he could not have survived had it not been for Engels' generous support. This condition of chronic, dire poverty lasted almost to the end. He eked out for a time a slender income by becoming the European correspondent for the *New York Tribune*, edited then by Horace Greeley. It was Fourierist in economics. But the earliest articles he contributed—at five dollars per—were actually written by Engels.[19] The latter spoke contemptuously of the paper as "this rag." Later Marx himself wrote articles that still make interesting reading. He, for instance, denounced England for not restraining Russia from advancing into the Balkans.

However, his main interest and occupation centered in his revolutionary activity. He organized the Workers Educational Society and frequently lectured to its members. He quarrelled with everyone who had the temerity to dispute his opinions or leadership. But curiously, the organization of the International Workingmen's Association—the first of the "Internationals"—was not in any real sense his creation; he was at most a drafted collaborator. Nevertheless, he soon gained dominant control of its German contingent centered in England.[20] As for the other national groups, they had leaders of their own with whom Marx carried on an incessant guerrilla warfare. He was especially bitter towards Ferdinand Lasalle, the leader of the German section, despite the fact that he—Marx—could not lead the movement, since he was permanently barred from returning to his native land. He made venomous attacks upon Lasalle, calling him the "Jewish Nigger." He assumed the same hostile attitude toward Bakunin and wrote a scurrilous and slanderous pamphlet against him. The Russian anarchist replied in kind. The inability of Marx to share leadership with others led to neverending bickering among the intellectual elite and greatly hurt the movement as a whole. Finally, at the Hague congress of 1872, the Marxist and Bakuninist factions fought a battle royal for supremacy—and what

[19] E. H. Carr, *Karl Marx* (London: J. M. Dent and Sons, Ltd., 1938), p. 114. By permission.

[20] Cf. *Ibid.*, pp. 181 ff.

a battle it was! Bakunin was expelled from membership mainly on the basis of Marx's charges, which Carr terms "not merely stupid but fundamentally dishonest. . . . At the Hague congress he [Marx] had annihilated his adversaries; but by the same stroke he had committed political suicide." [21]

The leadership of the badly disorganized International then passed to the American section, but by 1876 it had succumbed altogether.

Marx's undoubted superiority of intellectual powers among the leaders of the international communist movement—that proved so profoundly influential in our modern world—is acknowledged mainly in regard to his ponderous *magnum opus, Das Kapital*. The first volume of this "bible of the working class" was published in Hamburg in 1867 and was the only one which appeared during his lifetime (he died in 1883). The second and third volumes were edited by Engels from the notes left by Marx, and were not published until 1885 and 1894 respectively. Since this is presumably the *fons et origo* of communism—although the present Soviet-Chinese dominated movement exhibits such basic divergences from it as to be in a real sense fundamentally different —we must now turn our attention to its analysis.

Marx defines his system as "dialectical materialism," claiming that it alone is "scientific." As such, communism is a dogma, not a mere theory. Despite all his denials, he remains recognizably related to the left wing Hegelians, substituting matter for the Absolute Idea, but otherwise following the terms of the Hegelian dialectic. By applying the concept of thesis, antithesis, and synthesis to the field of economics, he operates with capitalism as the thesis that *produces* its opposite, proletarianism; i.e., capitalism distils its own poisons by creating a class which will presumably "liquidate it." As in orthodox Hegelianism, thesis and antithesis are in a state of tension, opposition, struggle. This integral state is of its very essence. Accordingly, "class war" is something inevitable and necessary to the relation between capitalism and communism; it does not depend on "wishful thinking;" it is in the nature of things—a scientific law. The resulting conflict eventuates in a synthesis—the "classless society"—but the development stops there. At this point Marx abandoned Hegel's scheme.

But how can matter—inert matter—be said to possess the dynamism ascribed to it, necessary for a revolutionary philosophy? This is where the adjective "dialectical" acquires meaning. Marx ascribes to matter a dynamic quality that is anything but material. Consistent materialism, being passive, would be wholly opposed to a revolutionary

[21] *Ibid.,* p. 257.

élan, and thus would negate the very *raison d'être* of revolution. But communism is dynamic, active, truly revolutionary. Accordingly, the term "dialectical" stands for something exceedingly real: namely, for a dynamic force which Marx defines as "economic"—whatever myth-ical entity that may be! This he regards as a natural law as certain and dependable in its workings as that of gravitation. For if existing condi-tions were produced *in toto* by mechanical causes, how absurd to suppose that any human being could change them! A revolutionary philosophy must be active, dynamic, and therefore non-mechanical. Accordingly, communism, although it claims to be basically materialis-tic, is really crypto-spiritual. That is the meaning of the adjective "dialectical."

It follows, therefore, from the very nature of dialectical materi-alism that economic forces are the primary factors of man's environ-ment; man is what they make him. Hence, he has no free will, for he is not a spiritual being. As Marx wrote in the introduction to *Capital:*

> But here individuals are dealt with only in so far as they are the personifications of economic categories, embodiments of particular class-relations and class-interests. My stand-point, from which the evolution of the economic formation of society is viewed as a process of natural history, can less than any other make the individual re-sponsible for relations whose creature he socially remains, however much he may subjectively raise himself above them.[22]

This is the theory termed "economic determinism." But why not apply it to the capitalists as well? Or does Marx do it? If so, he should hold them as guiltless, as impotent in the grip of the economic forces, as are the proletarians.

Historical materialism is but an extension of the same thought. The term signifies that each period of history assumes the sort of super-structure (*Oberbau*) that its economic substructure (*Unterbau*) de-termines. Thus capitalistic economy, which is distinguished from the previous economies by the fact that a minority has seized control over the means of production (machinery) and thus has succeeded in forcing those who do not own machinery to work for them, produces social relations of its own, i.e., enables the minority to live by the labor of the majority. This in the Marxist scheme of things is the veritable Fall of Man. In the *Communist Manifesto*, Marx writes: "The history of all hitherto existing societies is the history of the class struggle." The capitalistic form of society differs from all previous ones in the fact that it is the last of such exploiting societies.

---

[22] Karl Marx, *Capital, a Critique of Political Economy* (New York: The Modern Library, copyright 1906), p. 15. By permission.

Hence, transitions from one phase of social development to another are not the result of free decisions of men, or of the emergence of new concepts of justice or truth, but solely of the change of the productive forces; these in turn may be determined by new inventions. When such a new economic pattern appears and comes into conflict with the existing social pattern, a social revolution will inevitably result. Thus, for instance, when an agricultural economy is supplanted by a manufacturing or a commercial one, the whole cultural "superstructure" of that country changes accordingly.

Such being the case, then, the entire structure of society is created by, or based on, the economic substructure. In the *Communist Manifesto* Marx writes:

> What does the history of ideas prove, if not that mental production changes concomitantly with material production? In every epoch, the ruling ideas have been the ideas of the ruling class. . . . Law, morality, and religion have become to him [the proletarian] so many bourgeois prejudices, behind which bourgeois interests lurk in ambush.[23]

Accordingly, all culture and science, as well as religion, are formed by the power of the material and economic conditions of their time.[24] As such, they are merely an appearance, an "epiphenomenon," and not fundamental reality. But if this be true, how can men change the world? As soon can they divert the earth from its orbit, or abolish the law of gravitation!

Disregarding the obvious implications of this view, from which it necessarily follows that the capitalist society is just as much created by the necessity of its substructure as is the communist, Marx passionately denounced the blatant injustices of the former. Of what does this injustice consist? This leads to the second main element in Marxism, its political economy, the most important part of which is the theory of value. How is the value of a given product or commodity determined?

The theory itself is not original with Marx; it was held by Adam Smith and Ricardo. This, "the most perverse of paradoxes," as Carr calls it,[25] deals with the "exchange-value," not "use-value." It is the value to the buyer or seller, not to the consumer. And the word "commodity" is arbitrarily applied to "the products of labor," and not, e.g., to a virgin forest, an unworked mine, or fishing rights. The

---

[23] *The Communist Manifesto*, pp. 50, 39-40.
[24] Cf. Rühle, *op. cit.*, p. 316.
[25] Carr, *op. cit.*, p. 261; cf. the whole section, pp. 258-72.

word "labor" is likewise qualified: it does not mean that the value of a commodity depends on the amount of time which it takes to produce it, for then the product of an unskilled or slow workman would be more valuable than the one produced by a skilled laborer. Consequently, Marx defines "labor" as "simple average labor," although he nowhere gives a precise definition of the meaning of the term. And finally, Marx practically nullifies all that he has said by further stating that in the last resort the value depends on the condition of the market.

But why is it necessary for Marx to adopt this rigmarole? One can understand the puzzle only in the light of what Marx derives from this abracadabra—namely, the *theory of surplus value*. This latter notion is supremely important to him, for it constitutes the ground for his condemnation of the capitalist system as necessarily unjust and wrong. For the point he makes is not that an individual capitalist here and there is unjust, but that the whole system is unjust.

He then concludes: since the "value" of a given commodity is produced solely by labor, but since the laborer does not receive as wages the full value of his work, there accrues a profit to the employer. This profit results solely from the employer's compelling the worker to keep on producing beyond the stage when the value of his labor equals the amount of his wages. Suppose a worker receives three shillings which he actually earns in six hours; the employer then compels him to work twelve hours and thus to produce commodities valued at six shillings. He pays the worker three shillings and pockets the other three. These latter three shillings are called by Marx the "surplus labor value," and constitute the exploitation practiced by the capitalists upon the workers. This "injustice" will then continue as long as the capitalist economic order continues; when, in the communist order, production will be solely for consumption, the "surplus value" will become meaningless. As Carr remarks, in speaking of the "surplus value":

> . . . by this clever manipulation of terminology [Marx] created the impression of something illegitimate and fraudulent. But now that the labour theory of value has long been abandoned by all competent economists, the theory of surplus value . . . has become equally untenable. . . . The real strength of the Marxist position lies elsewhere. . . . It is perfectly legitimate to believe that the worker does not secure a 'fair' proportion of the product of his labour. . . . But these are moral judgments, and have nothing to do with the theory of surplus value propounded by Marx as an economic law.[26]

[26] *Ibid.,* pp. 268-69.

The third component part of communism is the theory of the state. *The Communist Manifesto* declares that the "executive of the modern state is but a committee for managing the common affairs of the whole bourgeoisie." Engels in his *Anti-Dühring* amplifies this verdict by adding that the state is the necessary product of the class struggle, and as such it will "wither away" when the classless society is attained.

These opinions of Marx and Engels have proved embarrassing later on. For communism, once it established itself, became a totalitarian state—a superstate. Marx had obviously wholly ignored all other aspects and functions of the state but those that bear a class character; but there is need in any society—capitalist or communist—of prevention of crime, of public services, such as postal authority, etc. What Marx-Engels should have said is that the communist state will subserve the interests of the communist society; but instead, they speak of abolishing the state altogether, or of its "withering away," blessed be the phrase! For they think in too exclusive a fashion of the state as a superstructure of the capitalist society which protects itself by means of the army, its legal system, police, and other coercive means. The democratic state is therefore a contradiction in terms, as the rule of the people cannot exist while the society is divided by the class struggle. The real power is always in the hands of the dominant class, while the workers have only the empty privilege, as Lenin wrote, of choosing people to misrepresent them. Hence, the only true "people's democracy" is based on an *economic* equality (since the economic forces are the only creative forces) and it is absurd to establish a parliamentary regime if the people do not possess economic liberties first. Accordingly, Marx, in 1872, suggested the only amendment he ever proposed to the *Communist Manifesto:* namely, that the "existing state machine" must be smashed, destroyed, and not merely taken over and utilized by the new dominant class.

Nor was Marx's thinking as to what constitutes the proletarian class crystal clear; living in England as he did, he identified the proletariat with the *industrial* workers—the group which in course of time developed the labor unions; he excluded from it both the *Lumpenproletariat* (the class-unconscious workers) and the peasantry. Both he and Engels had nothing but contempt for the latter. It was Lenin who later effected the appearance of an alliance between the workers and peasants (the hammer and sickle) that formed the fighting force of the Russian Revolution. But even then the industrial worker has such absolute predominance in the alliance as to nullify any effective power of the peasants.

Since capitalists and proletarians are necessarily opposed to each other, "class struggle" is the natural and inevitable result of the tension between them. This also follows the rule of the Hegelian dialectic. Marx did not invent the struggle; he only underscored it. What he did invent is the notion that the proletarian class is *messianic* by its very nature, i.e., that it does not share in the original sin of the acquisitive society.

Victory in this struggle, according to Marx, is in no doubt; it must inevitably go to the proletariat. This certainty rests on the calculation that the capitalist order has the seeds of its destruction within itself. It is of its very essence that because of competition this class will grow ever smaller in numbers, while the proletarian class will consequently grow ever larger. Thus ultimately the latter group by its vast numerical superiority will be able to secure victory over its exploiters. Such victory could be won at the ballot box in a democratic society. But it would be absurd to expect the possessors of wealth and power to give up their unjust privileges voluntarily; hence the final conflict must necessarily be violent.

Once victory is won, the new society must be created under the "dictatorship of the proletariat." This phrase, which appears only once in the writings of Marx, namely, in his *Critique of the Gotha Programme* (1875), was later concretely elaborated by Lenin and Stalin. Marx had been so intent on the overthrow of the old order that he had but a vague notion concerning the building of the new. He had envisioned the dictatorship as a comparatively short, temporary interlude. During it, the small remainder of the avowed class "enemies" were to be liquidated, and the proletarian masses were to be trained for and integrated in the new order. However, the Russian leaders of the Revolution have converted this theory into a practically permanent dictatorship of the party over the proletariat. Moreover, the communist stage of society would not be reached immediately; rather, it would be preceded by the socialist period, during which the rule of "from each according to his ability, to each according to his deserts," would prevail. It is only afterwards that the ultimate goal of the "classless society" would be reached, when the rule of "from each according to his ability, to each according to his need" would at last obtain. In no communist-dominated country has this stage been reached. At this point Marx parted company with Hegel, for the dialectical process of thesis versus antithesis, producing its synthesis in perpetuity, ceased; beyond the "classless society" there is no further development. It is the millennium of the Christian hopes, the utopia which he so despised in Proudhon and others. It is the *"ne plus ultra"* of world history. This concept is the heroic act of sheer faith, an act of utterly uncritical, incredibly fatuous credulity. As a "scientific" postulate it is wholly unprovable and really absurd; for it assumes as certainty that the substitution of one economic system for another will of itself make men so good that they will govern themselves in peace, justice, and equity! And yet this glittering promise, based on an utterly false assumption, lures vast numbers of the wretchedly poor and the hopelessly indigent the world over—the promise of a permanently peaceful and affluent society!

It is not within the scope of this short study of Marxist communism to include here the developments since the Russian Revolution of 1917. The changes in Marxist theory introduced by Lenin and his successors, as well as other communist leaders, have been so radical and fundamental as themselves to disprove the "scientific" character of Marxism, despite the lip-service paid to it by its pretending disciples. Nevertheless, the impact of Marx's thought upon the modern world is so truly epochal and world-shaking that it would take a separate fairly large treatise to trace it in all its ramifications. The outstanding authority on Marxism, E. H. Carr, concludes his study of such an impact by words which need serious pondering by all non-communists:

> Seen therefore in the broadest historical perspective, the impact of the Soviet Union on the western world symbolizes the end of that period of history which began in the 16th and 17th centuries and was marked by the world-wide ascendancy of western Europe and in particular of the English-speaking peoples. . . . But like other great historical movements, it owed its success not merely to its own power and to the enthusiasm which it generated among its disciples, but to the inner crumbling of the order against which it was directed. The impact of the Soviet Union has fallen on a western world where much of the framework of individualism was already in decay, where faith in the self-sufficiency of individual reason had been sapped by the critique of relativism, where the democratic community was in urgent need of reinforcement against the forces of disintegration latent in individualism. . . .[27]

Religion, particularly Christianity, is conspicuously included in the complex of western culture under this attack. The ultimate aim, despite the temporary accommodation granted for prudential reasons by the communist rulers to religious communions, is the destruction of all religion as the survival of superstitions of a less enlightened past,[28] its

---

[27] E. H. Carr, *The Soviet Impact on the Western World* (New York: The Macmillan Co., 1947), p. 112. By permission.

[28] I have attempted to describe the religious conditions under the Soviet regime in three works, the latest of which is *The Church in Soviet Russia* (New York: Oxford University Press, Inc., 1956).

place to be taken by science. In this the Comtean positivism finds its most effective realization.

Furthermore, a former Marxist and one who to the end of his life was appreciative of some aspects of Marx's system, Nicolas Berdyaev, summarized his judgment of Marx's denial of humanism as follows:

> Marx . . . demonstrates the collective disintegration of humanism and man's image. . . . Marx denies the value of the human individuality and personality, and of the Christian doctrine of the soul and its undeniable significance. For him man is but an instrument, paving the way for the advent of non-human or superhuman principles in whose name he declares war on humanist morality. . . . Marx is the child, too, of human self-affirmation, of man's presumption and rebellion against God, of his affirmation that the human will is the highest of all.[29]

This, to my way of thinking, is the principal ground for the rejection of Marx's system.

## Auguste Comte, the Founder of Positivism

Related to, but different from the Feuerbachian anthropology, is the positivistic sociology and scientism of Auguste Comte (1798-1857). He was born in Montpellier, the eldest son of a merchant and his devout wife. The latter dedicated her first-born to the service of the Church. The precocious child grew up in fervent piety, which, however, he lost, to his mother's intense grief, while he was a pupil in the Polytechnic School of Paris. The sixteen-year-old student of mathematics also absorbed the republican spirit of the institution, which set him against the Napoleonic regime. This resulted in his being ignored for a government appointment, and reduced him to virtual penury. After staying with his parents for a while, he returned to Paris, where he eked out a living by giving lessons; but his principal occupation was an intense study of science, political economy, and economics. He was particularly indebted to Condorcet, and later for a time was influenced by St. Simon. Under their inspiration he undertook the lofty task of planning the reorganization of society. With this aim in view, he

[29] Nicolas Berdyaev, *The Meaning of History* (London: Geoffrey Bles, Ltd., 1936), pp. 158-59. By permission.

produced, between 1830 and 1842, the six volumes of the *Course of Positive Philosophy* (the word "Course" being later changed to "System"), upon which his fame rests. He had married in 1822, a woman of twenty who had been of the *demimonde*. In this act he had been moved by compassion for her, hoping to restore her to a respectable life; but shortly afterwards she left him for her former lover. This plunged him into a mental depression causing him to be hospitalized. When he recovered, he resumed his studies. They brought him increasing fame. In 1844, when he was forty-six, he met the sister of one of his pupils, Madame Clotilde de Vaux, who, despite her convent education, was one of the "emancipated" young women of the time. Her husband, having embezzled some government funds, abandoned her. Comte fell madly in love and proposed marriage to her (of course, the common-law marriage, since no other was possible). But she refused, although henceforth until her early death, she remained his ardent disciple. Thereafter, he revered her memory as that of "St. Clotilde." He died surrounded by his disciples, after the manner of Socrates.

Comte's system centers about two principal ideas: one is "the law of the three stages"; the other is the "subordination of the head to the heart," i.e., the utilization of all means toward the welfare of humanity. The development of human society exhibits three phases: the theological, the metaphysical, and the positive. This assumption itself presupposes the essentially Christian view of history, beginning in creation and aiming at a certain goal toward which all development tends: without that presupposition the "three stages" of history would make no sense. All these stages are necessary for the particular historical era which produced them and which dominated each of them. When humankind attained sufficient cultural development for the next stage, it left behind its former mode of thought and like a chambered nautilus built for itself "more stately mansions." Accordingly, the primitive savage started with fetishism, proceeded on to polytheism until in the civilized state he reached the final theological stage of monotheism. But during this entire era the phenomena of nature were explained by the supernatural, or divine, agency. Angels and devils, mysterious forces identified with the spirit world, peopled man's universe at this earlier stage; during its last phase, the monotheistic period—reached in the Jewish, Christian, and Moslem periods—the ultimate explanation was God.

In the second stage—the metaphysical—natural laws took the place of God. Man sought the causes of natural events impinging upon his life in laws outside himself, and safety in submitting himself to their inexorable sway. This is an intermediate stage, in which the human mind has not yet rid itself entirely of its inadequate grasp of reality, but substitutes one supernatural explanation for another. Instead of the old gods, it is the "nature of things" that is invoked—the search for ultimate principles. All this only prepares the way for science.

The third and final stage will have been reached when man no longer seeks for theological or metaphysical causes, but is content with "pure facts." This method alone yields tested scientific knowledge—positivism. The sole endeavor of the future scientist shall be the discovery and interrelation of facts in order to utilize them toward an ever more satisfying life for human society. Thus Comte repeats, although in a modified form, the basic principle of Hume in repudiating metaphysics and theology, although he is even closer to Lessing's theory, developed in his *Education of the Human Race* (1780) and illustrating the cultural development of mankind by the successive stages of childhood, youth, and manhood. Comte guards himself against the charge of unoriginality by asserting that for twenty years he has purposely abstained from reading Vico, Kant, Herder, and Hegel, for the sake of "cerebral hygiene," so as not to contaminate his thought by foreign ideas! But Hegel's philosophy of history bears great similarity to Comte's, although the basic difference consists in the character of the successive stages of historical evolution: for Hegel they are the temporal unfolding of the Absolute Spirit, while for Comte they are all relative, their "truth" transcended by the next stage. In other words, no "truth" is ever absolute; all is relative to the current conditions.

There are, according to Comte, only six sciences: mathematics, astronomy, physics, chemistry, biology, and "social physics." It is the last-named that he regards as the queen of sciences, and to it he devotes most attention. It is his emphasis on the "scientific study of society" that has earned him the title of "the father of sociology." By means of it he has aimed to reconstruct moral, religious, and political systems of humankind. According to him, man is a psychosomatic organism possessing, besides his physical nature, intelligence and moral (even religious) sense, but developing fully *only* in society. Apart from society, man is not man. Comte therefore soon concluded that the previous course of philosophical and political development had gone radically astray in placing the individual at the center of its attention and forgetting the all-important social influences upon the individual's conditioning of his entire personality. Accordingly, he subordinated the individual to society, particularly in the political sphere. He was no "democrat," but favored the aristocratic rule of society. His last political motto, Order and Progress, was interpreted by him conservatively; he was against "attempting political reconstruction before spiritual," and concluded that "politically what is wanted is Dictatorship, with liberty of speech and discussion." [30] He took a decidedly dim view of the Dutch, English, and American revolutions, which he labeled "Protestant revolutions." Perhaps his most bizarre political proposal is "the Great Western Republic, formed of the Five Advanced Nations, the French, Italian, Spanish, British, and German," to which much of his work *A General View of Positivism*, published in 1848—the same year in which Marx's *Communist Manifesto* made its appearance—is devoted. [31] In the light of the present-day situation, the prognostication of Comte makes curious reading indeed!

Nevertheless, our predominant interest centers upon his second principal objective, the utilization of the total impact of positive philosophy upon the welfare of humanity—what he called "the subordination of the head to the heart." Despite all his protestation that the theological stage is a thing of the past, Comte's system really rests on religious presuppositions and aims supremely at a religious goal. But his critique of the former religious system centers upon the belief in God; in his own religious system he substitutes the whole of humanity in God's place. Accordingly, just as did Feuerbach, he repudiates any suggestion of atheism. He writes to his most famous disciple, John Stuart Mill (1845) that such a description does not apply to them, since they believe in the Great Being, Humanity, and therefore cannot be called atheists. [32]

But it is not enough to exclude God from men's minds: such a negative procedure results in a mere vacuum. He knew, as Nietzsche knew, that "only what is replaced is destroyed." Accordingly, Comte, essentially an agnostic, created a positivist religion, "religion of humanity," with the motto "*Réorganiser, sans Dieu ni roi, par le culte systematique de l'humanité.*" [33] He was so confident of the speedy victory of his religious system that in a letter of 1851 he predicted that before 1860 he would preach the true religion of positivism in the Notre Dame Cathedral! [34] Basic to the concept of Comte's religion is the ethic of love. The chief commandments of Christianity—love God and your neighbor—he reduces to only one, *Live for humanity*. He writes:

> Love, then, is our principle; Order our basis; and Progress our end. Such . . . is the essential character of the system of life which

[30] Auguste Comte, *A General View of Positivism*, J. H. Bridges, tr. (Stanford, California: Academic Reprints, n.d.), pp. 124, 127 (headings of sections).

[31] *Ibid.*, pp. 92 ff.

[32] Quoted in Henri de Lubac, S.J., *Le Drame de l'Humanisme Athée* (Paris: Edition Spée, 1950), p. 165.

[33] Quoted on the title page of *A General View of Positivism*.

[34] Karl Löwith, *Meaning in History* (Chicago: The University of Chicago Press, 1949), p. 90.

Positivism offers for the definite acceptance of society; a system which regulates the whole course of our private and public existence, by bringing Feeling, Reason, and Activity into permanent harmony.[35]

Accordingly, ". . . the Heart, the Intellect, and the Character mutually strengthen and develop one another, because each is systematically directed to the mode of action for which it is by nature adapted." [36] But be it well noted that the worship is directed toward humanity as a whole, not to an individual. In fact, Comte did not have a very high opinion of men individually; he extols the Great Being, the ideal humanity, but even in this regard he places the French nation first, the Western cultural community next, and only then the rest of the world population. Nevertheless, he excludes from this totality criminals, both high and low. Among the former kind he names Nero, Robespierre, and Napoleon. Only those who were in some sense "benefactors" of mankind are to be included in "humanity." It is in this "Great Being" that the positivists "live, move, and have their being." In fact, it is in this "survival in humanity" that his concept of immortality consists: it is nothing more substantial than being remembered by the posterity. The best expression of this idea is found in the words of George Eliot, who, by the way, was, along with her husband, Frederic Harrison, among the most influential of Comte's English disciples. Her poem, "Oh, May I Join the Choir Invisible," reduces immortality to the inspiration that one's own life may exert upon future generations, urging "man's search to vaster issues."

But Comte knew that the cultivation of such a total devotion to the grand task he envisaged requires discipline. He therefore actually created an elaborate organization closely modelled on the Roman Catholic Church, whose system he greatly admired, in contrast to Protestantism which he regarded as "anarchistic." This then is a religious communion without God, and Roman Catholicism without Christianity. The elaborate cult, private and public, propounded for the purpose of training men in humanistic piety comprises not only the dogmatic tenets, but also elaborate ritualistic symbolism, ceremonies, and practices. The private cult centers upon women in order to encourage the sense of family unity. The public cult has for its object the adoration of Humanity. There are to be three devotional exercises lasting two hours, nine sacraments, temples and a priesthood. Comte read the *Imitation of Christ* daily, substituting the word "humanity"

---

[35] *A General View of Positivism*, p. 355.
[36] *Ibid.*, p. 358.

for "God." He drew up a Positivist Calender, consecrating each month to some field of achievement; there were to be eighty-four of them yearly, each intended to celebrate some worthy "benefactor" of mankind. It included not only scientists and thinkers, but founders of religions, such as Confucius and Mohammed; yet Jesus was conspicuously omitted, although the Apostle Paul was included. Paul is said to have "corrected" the work of Jesus. Comte lavishes such epithets as "great," "admirable," and "incomparable" on him and asserts that Paul depended more on Greek thought than on that of Jesus.[37] Even Madame de Vaux has a place in the Calendar ("Saint Clotilde") as the symbol of Humanity, and Comte addresses to her language usually reserved by devout believers for Christ or the Virgin.

Furthermore, the new religion was to be served by a class of priests, paid by the state, who were to be "servants of humanity" rather than "slaves of God." They were to be highly educated, not only in the religion of humanity, but in philosophy and science generally. Even the medical practice was assigned exclusively to this priesthood.

> The primary condition of their authority is exclusion from political power, as a guarantee that theory and practice shall be systematically kept apart. . . . By entirely renouncing wealth and worldly position, and that not as individuals merely, but as a body, the priests of Humanity will occupy a position of unparalleled dignity. . . . All functions, then, that co-operate in the elevation of man will be regenerated by the Positive priesthood. Science, Poetry, Morality, will be devoted to the study, the praise, and the love of Humanity . . .[38]

Membership in the temples of humanity is to be organized on voluntaristic principles, but those who join are to be subjected to rigorous discipline in order to attain a high degree of moral attainment. The goal of this training is the substitution of altruism for egoism in all social relations. In this endeavor of transforming humankind by a moral regeneration Comte expected the hitherto effective religious forces to join him. He particularly entertained high hopes that the Jesuits would be won for his project. He regarded the Jesuit Order as the real power within Roman Catholicism. In 1862 he went so far as to consider issuing "An Appeal to the Ignatians" (he disliked the name of Jesus so much as to avoid using it for the Jesuits), calling upon their general to proclaim himself the spiritual head of the Roman Catholic Church and to reduce the pope to a simple prince-bishop of Rome! The general

---

[37] Auguste Comte, *Système de politique positive* (Paris: 5th ed., 1929), III, pp. 409 ff.

[38] *A General View of Positivism*, pp. 367-68.

was then to make Paris the headquarters of this "holy alliance" between *his* Church and the Positivist world association.[39]

A criticism of this bizarre system may be restricted to a few basic tenets: first of all, the denial of the existence of God, using the word in its long-established connotation, necessarily disposes of all talk of the "divinity of humanity." Man is but a creature of his cosmic environment; if there is nothing divine in the cosmos, there can be nothing divine in human society. *Ex nihilo nihil est.* This is actually the conclusion of some of Comte's most outstanding disciples, such as John Stuart Mill, who bewails bitterly "the melancholy decadence of a great intellect." Emile Littré, the most eminent French positivist, declares that positivism

> demands an atheistic conclusion and does not warrant the serious entertainment of any substitute cults. Sentiment, devotion, love are after all cerebral-physiological processes; we may investigate them, but they should not direct our thinking to mystical fancies. There is nothing mystical about love and altruism, nor anything degrading in selfishness. These two have their roots in basic instincts of the organism.[40]

Nevertheless, Comte has had an enormous influence upon our modern culture. His scientism and relativism have become substitutes for religion among vast numbers of educated people. Our secularist culture is simply saturated with these concepts, although they are not always traced back to Comte.

The "religion of humanity" also has become a most popular substitute for Christianity. Many idealistically motivated people of generous impulses in the service to humanity have embraced it. They are to be found not only in the ranks of social workers, but also largely in radical social movements. They are inspired by a genuine zeal for justice, racial equality, social and economic fairness, hatred of war, and an ardent desire to rebuild the world generally. They love man but have no use for God.

And lastly, one may discern in the humanistic interpretation of

[39] de Lubac, *op. cit.*, p. 218. Cf. *Système de politique positive*, III, p. 553, where Comte writes: "It consisted in attempts of Jesuitism to regenerate the papacy, whose spiritual office became truly vacant since its temporal transformation. . . . Profoundly convinced of that connection, the eminent founder of Jesuitism exerted himself to institute, under a modest title, a true pope beside the Roman prince—a free chief of a new clergy capable of overcoming Protestantism in reorganizing Catholicism." (My translation).

[40] Quoted in Tsanoff, *The Moral Ideals*, p. 482; cf. John Stuart Mill, *Auguste Comte and Positivism* (London, 1882), p. 199.

Christianity itself one of the subterranean influences of Comte. Some extreme "social gospellers" knowingly or unwittingly model their own social betterment programs on essentially humanistic ideas, derived from the welter of motivations in which the Comtean influence is still recognizable.


## Friedrich Nietzsche and the Ethic of the Superman


Friedrich Nietzsche (1844-1900), who, during his lifetime, was practically ignored, so that his books had to be privately published and found exceedingly few readers, has found in the course of time a large and enthusiastic following. His influence has steadily increased, although it has not reached the dizzy heights of which he had dreamed (for he did not pretend to modesty) when he had predicted that one day university chairs for the interpretation of Zarathustra would be established all over the world! Nevertheless, he is a mighty prophet of our secularist age, and as such his thought must be taken seriously.

He was born in a Lutheran parsonage: "I am a descendant of whole generations of Christian clergymen," he wrote of himself. Originally, he asserted, the family was Polish: "And yet my ancestors were Polish noblemen." [41] He despised Germans so fanatically that occasionally he prided himself on his supposed Polish antecedents. But although the family tradition destined him for the ministerial office, he lost faith in God in his early twenties (in 1865) and thereupon chose classical philology as his subject of study. The chief influences shaping his early thinking emanated from Schopenhauer and Wagner, although Feuerbach, despite Nietzsche's denial of his debt to him, also contributed mightily to young Nietzsche's atheistic convictions. He accepted the nonexistence of God as an indisputable and indubitable fact; hence, his repudiation of all theistic presuppositions, particularly the Christian, was radical. Karl Löwith calls him "not so much the last disciple of the pagan god Dionysos as the first radical apostate of Christ." [42] But despite this denial, Nietzsche held that the idea of God,

---

[41] "Ecce Homo" in *The Philosophy of Nietzsche* (New York: Random House, Inc., *Modern Library*, 1937), p. 8. By permission.

[42] Karl Löwith, "Nietzsche's Doctrine of Eternal Recurrence," in *Journal of the History of Ideas*, June 1945, p. 284. By permission.

so assiduously cultivated during almost two millennia of Christian history, is firmly rooted in the minds of most people, even those who live as practical atheists. To secure release from the thralldom of this idea, it is best not to argue against it or try to disprove or ignore it, but to uproot it boldly and resolutely by a heroic act of will. It is "our own preference that decides against Christianity—not arguments." [43] Thus if God is to die within us, we must kill Him; we must become "the assassins of God."

This, then, is the first task: to secure our liberation from the idea of God; for faith in God, according to Nietzsche, debases and enslaves. Man must win his release from such an ignoble subjection—he must free himself. He writes:

> I am quite unfamiliar with the feeling of 'sinfulness'. . . . 'God,' 'the immortality of the soul,' 'salvation,' a 'beyond,'—these are mere notions, to which I paid no attention, on which I never wasted any time, even as a child. . . . I am quite unacquainted with atheism as a result, and still less as an event: with me it is instinctive.[44]

Furthermore, like Feuerbach, he substitutes man for God as the object of reverence, but with the difference that he refuses to indulge in Feuerbach's terminology and knows that his anthropology is not theology; and further, that instead of reverencing the divine in humanity, he elevates the Superman in its place.

But let no one imagine that the freedom man thus secures relieves him from moral requirements, although these requirements are natural. Not at all. Just because man confronts the universe alone and cannot look to God either for an explanation of the forces of nature, or for a teleological significance of human life—nor can he place his burdens and responsibilities on God—he must seek help in himself. For there is none other in all the world. To assume this attitude of heroic self-reliance is a herculean task; for one must first of all convince oneself that although there is absolutely no meaning in the universe, human life need not be altogether meaningless and futile. And although there exist no absolute values, man may still seek and attain relative values. To succumb to the assumption of the absolute meaninglessness of human life is nihilism. Then indeed life would be "a tale told by an idiot, full of sound and fury, signifying nothing." Against such a conclusion—the creed of Bazarov in Turgenev's *Fathers and Sons*—Nie-

---

[43] Henri de Lubac, S.J., *The Drama of Atheist Humanism.* Copyright 1950. (New York: Sheed & Ward, Inc.), p. 22 By permission.
[44] "Ecce Homo," pp. 23-24.

tzsche fought furiously, doggedly, without respite—although in my judgment vainly. If there is no God—the sum total of all real meanings in the cosmos—there can be no meaning in human life that is only a product of the forces of the world. But Nietzsche *had* to believe in something, for no man lives without faith—not even Bazarov, who at least believed in his scientific experiments with frogs! The only difference is to be found in what one believes. Nietzsche then strove to find a relative meaning in the world, in life, in the joy of living. He said Yes to the world. He accepted the universe.

But the assumption that God is dead was for Nietzsche only the starting point. He was among the first to realize clearly and definitely that the loss of faith in God necessarily involves the invalidating of the ethics and the moral concepts originally derived from and resting upon the basic tenets of Christianity, with which the entire Western civilization was permeated. These tenets were already greatly debased and diluted, but they still functioned, implicitly or explicitly, as standards of conduct and of moral judgment. Hence, the task was to uproot the entire spiritual order of the existing society and to substitute for it a new system of values based on nature (although not on the evolutionary hypotheses of Darwin and Lamarck, for he called the adherents of these theories "the learned cattle"). This was Nietzsche's conception of "transvaluation of all values." For this clearness of vision, the logic of deduction, he is to be commended. There are too many people who do not realize that Christian ethic cannot survive if Christian faith is surrendered as its basis. Nietzsche knew better; he knew that secularism succeeds Christian humanism as surely as that cut flowers will wilt.

The new ethical system, then, was to be diametrically opposed to the ethic of Christianity, which he regarded as the negation of this world and a rejection of it for some imaginary, nonexistent "other" world. Nietzsche believed only in this world; for him there was no other. The source of all life, of all that exists, is the will to power, that same driving force which Schopenhauer recognized as the ultimate source of all. On the other hand, Nietzsche thought that Christianity inculcated a life-denying morality based on the repudiation of the world, on love, on humility, on the denial of this driving force of self-assertion, on meekness, on suffering, on pity for the weak—in one phrase, on the beatitudes of the Sermon on the Mount. To Nietzsche, this was a crime against life; is was sentimentality, weakness, sheer mawkishness; it was degrading, cowardly, slavish. It resulted in the monkish flight from the world, in coddling the degenerate and the weak. It was, in a phrase, "slave morality" as opposed to the "master morality."

Hence, he called himself "the first Immoralist" and directed his life-long struggle not so much against the faith in God as against the ethic derived from the Christian faith. He writes:

> What do God and faith in God matter in our day? God is no more than a faded word today—not even a concept. . . . War against the Christian ideal, against the doctrine which makes beatitude and salvation the aim of life, against the supremacy of the poor in spirit, the pure in heart, the suffering, the failures. . . . When and where was there ever a man worthy of the name who resembled that Christian ideal? [45]

> First I deny the type of man who formerly passed as the highest—the *good,* the *benevolent,* the *charitable;* and on the other hand, I deny that kind of morality which has become recognized and dominant as morality-in-itself, the morality of decadence, or, to use a cruder term, Christian morality.[46]

The new man who is to replace the current Christian type is dominated by a life-affirming ethic, by the Will-to-Power. He must say Yes to this world. Accordingly, Nietzsche rightly realizes that beside Christianity his principal enemy is nihilism. For this outlook on life is wholly negative and purposeless. It sees no values in life; hence, it assumes a disdainful, superior, hyper-critical mien, but itself is cold and empty.

In a fierce opposition to this supercilious pose, and in a conscious opposition to the Schopenhauerian rejection of life as evil (although he followed this earliest of his teachers in affirming the Will-to-Power), Nietzsche's thought is life-affirming, positive. It combines on the one hand the cult of Dionysus, the god of orgiastic, self-affirming, riotous life—the very contrast to the Crucified One—with the exaltation of the "higher man," the Superman, the ideal of whom he created in Zarathustra. About his supreme creation, *Thus Spake Zarathustra,* Nietzsche remarks: "This is *my* experience of inspiration. I have no doubt that I should have to go back millenniums to find another who could say to me: "It is mine also!" [47] He further rhapsodizes over his own production by affirming,

> This work is utterly unique. Let us leave the poets out of consideration: it may be that nothing has yet been produced out of such a

---

[45] Quoted in de Lubac, *op. cit.,* pp. 63-64.
[46] "Ecce Homo," p. 136.
[47] *Ibid.,* p. 101.

super-abundance of strength . . . The fact that a Goethe or a Shakespeare would not have been able to breathe for a moment in this terrific atmosphere of passion and elevation; the fact that compared with Zarathustra, Dante is no more than a believer, and not one who *creates* truth for the first time—a world-ruling spirit, a *Destiny;* the fact that the Vedic poets were priests and not even fit to unfasten Zarathustra's sandal—all this is of no great importance; it gives no idea of the distance, of the azure solitude, wherein this work dwells.[48]

In the ideal image of Zarathustra Nietzsche affirms the "heroic" virtues he found exemplified among the ancient Greeks. Greek affirmation of sheer physical beauty, power, and genius excites his unbounded admiration. Accordingly, Zarathustra commands a morality of hardness and strength, a life of creativity and power. The hero submits to no restraint of his Will-to-Power; he is the master, imposing his dominance on the ignoble herd of ordinary men. Civilization, therefore, must be transformed in accordance with this aristocratic, Napoleonic principle of ruthless power that knows no guilt or restraint: the traditional moral values must be transformed. The process requires surgery, not pills. For

virtues are functions of survival in the struggle for existence and reflect the position and the tactics of those who entertain them. What man values is an index to what he is. . . . The noble, the dominant, self-reliant and creative, regards himself as a determiner of values, not subject to obligations. Courage, high-mindedness, self-possessed sobriety, clear insight, justice, straightforward candor, are his virtues. He despises cowardice, meanness, lying. . . . He is the great friend and the great enemy.[49]

The personification of this ideal, Zarathustra, asserts: "Say Nay in the face of all that makes for weakness and exhaustion. . . . Say Yea in the face of all that makes for strength, that preserves strength and justifies the feeling of strength." One hears in it the very accents of secularist titanism, of the Napoleonic complex. Nietzsche himself likens his Superman to Caesar Borgia, for his Superman possesses not virtue in the current, despised sense of the word, but the Renaissance *virtù*. Hitler and Mussolini, although they would undoubtedly have been rejected by Nietzsche as vulgar pretenders, were nevertheless inspired by a very similar concept of conduct. This then is the secularist gospel of mangodhood as against the Christian Godmanhood. But it is *not* humanism nor personalism; in fact, it is a total denial of the

[48] *Ibid.*, pp. 104-05.
[49] Tsanoff, *op. cit.*, p. 518.

humanist view of life, particularly of Christian humanism, if by those terms we mean that the human personality is either potentially or actually the highest value in the world. For Nietzsche had nothing but the deepest contempt, yea even loathing, for the ordinary man, the "herd-man." ". . . I never address myself to the masses," he writes: "man is to him [Zarathustra] something inchoate, raw material, an ugly stone in need of the sculptor." [50]

But since the Superman (and let us note that Nietzsche always speaks of him in the singular, never in the plural) does not exist except in Nietzsche's imagination, how will the "higher man" come into being and attain mastery over the contemptible masses? Can the ordinary man be transformed into the Superman by the analogy of a sculptor shaping a rough stone? It appears not. Nietzsche in fact despairs of the present age and ardently wishes for its total destruction. His hope lies in the collapse of the decadent old order. "I predict a new age of tragedy: the highest art of life-affirmation, tragedy, will be reborn when mankind is conscious, but *without any feeling of suffering*, that it has behind it the hardest but most necessary of wars . . ." [51] He further prophesies a "second Buddhism" for Europe: the economic order will produce plenty, security, and mediocrity for all; political democracy will level all men to one uniform "equality," and men will grow petty, soft, self-indulgent, and pacific. The result will be "a kind of European Chinadom, with a meek, Buddhist-Christian faith, and in practice prudently epicurean, as the Chinaman is—reduced men." [52] And then the "new barbarian," virile, ruthless, warlike, driven by thirst for power, will swoop upon these weak and defenseless herd-men like a wolf upon a sheepfold and put an end to this decadent civilization. During the "dark ages" that will then follow the weaklings will be weeded out; the strong, virile, life-affirming will seize control. Therein lies Nietzsche's hope for the new world of "higher men."

Nevertheless, even this stage of development, during which the rule of the "survival of the fittest" (or the "fightiest") would obtain, is not final. Nietzsche's ultimate hope lies in the ancient Greek idea of the recurrent cyclical nature of the world, ever waning but ever renewing itself. This idea had been supplanted by the Christian view of history—a lineal progression toward a God-appointed final goal, "the far-off event toward which all creation tends." Nietzsche reaffirmed

---

[50] "Ecce Homo," pp. 133, 112.

[51] *Ibid.*, pp. 69-70.

[52] Quoted in G. A. Morgan, Jr., *What Nietzsche Means* (Cambridge, Mass.: Harvard University Press, 1941), p. 355. By permission.

the Greek concept and developed it into his basic world view of Eternal Recurrence. Karl Löwith contrasts these views:

> Is the ultimate standard and pattern of our existence the classical view of the world as an eternal cosmos, revolving in periodic cycles, or is it the Christian view of the world as a unique creation out of nothing, called forth by the omnipotence of a non-natural God? Is the ultimate being a divine cosmos, recurrent like a circle in itself, or a personal God, revealing himself not primarily in nature but in and to humanity under the sign of the cross? [53]

Nietzsche chooses the classical view, even thus manifesting his rejection of Christianity. He regards it as an antidote to nihilism, futilitarianism, meaninglessness of life. Henceforth he can look for redemption from the current decadence and to a return to the "joyful wisdom" of his adored Greeks. Through the mouth of Zarathustra he ecstatically chants his hymn of joy, "I love thee, O Eternity!" [54] Seven times is this liturgical chant repeated. When the blessed consummation shall come, he does not know. But when it arrives, it will last a thousand years.

So after all, this radical denier of Christianity, this self-styled Antichrist and "the first Immoralist," had to resort to faith, even though it was faith in an outworn and long-discarded theory of Eternal Recurrence. But why the ecstasy? If the Dionysian-Appollonian life of the Greeks is to be restored in the next cycle of recurrence, so is Christianity and the decadence of Nietzsche's own abhorred nineteenth century—and so is Nietzsche himself! And if this deduction appears fantastic and unbelievable, let me quote Morgan, who appears to favor the view:

> If the universe ever reaches a total state exactly identical with a previous state, the principle of determinism implies that the whole process must then repeat exactly the same course previously followed between the two states, so that every event recurs identically in every detail, and so on to all eternity. As previously argued, a finite universe must sooner or later repeat itself; therefore, it is in fact always repeating itself, always has, always will. [55]

Thus we reach what appears to me a "*reductio ad absurdum.*" One may adapt concerning Nietzsche Festus' remark to Paul: "O Friedrich,

[53] Löwith, *Meaning in History*, p. 215.
[54] "Thus Spake Zarathustra" in *The Philosophy of Nietzsche*, pp. 233-36.
[55] Morgan, *op. cit.*, p. 288.

thy great learning has made thee mad!" If only it were so! But has not our secularist age absorbed much of Nietzsche's "joyful wisdom" and proclaimed it as its own?

Nevertheless, Nietzsche's influence upon the end of our humanist era is so overwhelming as to warn us against too facile a dismissal of him. Berdyaev, who was himself deeply influenced by him (although by way of opposition), expressed the following weighty judgment of him:

> After Nietzsche, humanism is no longer possible. He had laid bare all its contradictions. And thus European humanism, the immediate reign of humanity pure and simple, meets its death on the peak of spiritual culture. . . . The humanist ideal is no longer tenable, and its culture is repudiated or set aside. . . . He regretted the exhaustion of its forces which he felt in himself. . . . For, although Nietzsche had reached the extreme height of daring in his passionate and rebellious affirmation of the creative individuality, the human image in him grows dim and faint. In its place we are given the mysterious and poignant image of the Superman . . . holding out the possibility of an anti-Christian, atheistic and satanical religion.[56]

[56] Berdyaev, *The Meaning of History*, pp. 157-58.

# 9

# Prophets of Christian Humanism

## Feodor M. Dostoevsky, the Novelist of Good and Evil

Perhaps the first reaction some readers may have to the inclusion of Dostoevsky among the philosophers and theologians will be one of amazement: "Is Saul (Dostoevsky) also among the prophets?" Indeed he is. In fact, unless his religious view of life is comprehended, there can be no understanding of his fairly large literary lifework. And the failure to understand his religious message on the part of many secularists accounts for their misjudging him so grievously by regarding him merely as a psychologist. Many hold that he is but an expert in abnormal psychology because of his own psychopathic neurotic state. He was indeed abnormal—as his epileptic seizures indicate. But he utilized even his neuroses for a deeper insight into human motivations; he knew life in the raw, and dealt with it with grim realism. But he also knew of redemption from the deepest degradation—and that is the principal difference between him and the contemporary authors of the "realistic" school.

Feodor M. Dostoevsky (1821-81) was the son of a fairly well-to-do doctor in the hospital for the poor. His ancestors were gentry who had originally come from Lithuania. Feodor's grandfather was a priest in the Ukraine. Andreyevich Mikhail was a stern, choleric man, whose drunken rages led him to deeds of cruelty; the children were frightened of him. Yet, Feodor's childhood was comparatively happy. After the death of his mother (1837), a gentle soul, his father retired to a small estate consisting of two villages near Tula. He became even more gloomy and severe in his drunken fits (he serves as the model for the debauchee Feodor Pavlovich in the novel *The Brothers Karamazov*) and ended by being murdered by his serfs two years later (1839).

Feodor, an intelligent and studious youth—an introvert and melancholic who suffered with epilepsy ever since his childhood—was sent by his father to study at the College of Military Engineering, to prepare for a career in which he had no interest. He was an omnivorous reader ever since childhood; he read everything he could lay his hands on, and thus acquired a taste for literature. He knew not only the Russian authors—Pushkin, Lermontov, and Gogol—but even the outstanding foreign writers—Corneille, Balzac, George Sand, Victor Hugo, Lord Byron, and Charles Dickens. But he also was familiar with the Bible. He spent six years at the school in St. Petersburg, and obtained his commission in 1844. But his army duties bored him; he gave most of his time to reading and to attempts at writing. Three years later he resigned from the army to devote himself altogether to a literary career. He wrote his first novel, *Poor Folk*, under the influence of Gogol and submitted the manuscript to Nekrasov and Grigorovich. Both of them were enchanted by the story; they rushed to his lodgings at 4 o'clock in the morning and "almost crying began to embrace him." [1] Then in turn they asked that arbiter of literary taste, Belinsky, to pass judgment upon the work of the hitherto unknown young author. The latter, too, was enthusiastic about this hyper-sentimental story and proclaimed the author a genius (thus confirming Dostoevsky's own secret opinion). Even before the novel was published (1846) he became famous, being shamelessly lionized in Petersburg *salons* by the sensation-hungry ladies. This sudden fame proved harmful to him. But his next several productions were so severely criticized that he regained the appropriate mental balance.

Having become a recognized literary phenomenon, Dostoevsky joined a secret coterie of liberal young "revolutionaries"—he himself being one of the most advanced among them—the so-called Petra-

[1] K. Mochulsky, *Dostoevsky, zhizn i tvorchestvo* (Paris: YMCA Press, 1947), p. 34. By permission.

shevsky circle. He read St. Simon and Proudhon and adopted views similar to theirs. He even followed Belinsky into adopting Feuerbach's atheism. And although Belinsky's contemptuous remarks about Christ offended him, he yet "passionately accepted all his teaching" which Mochulsky characterizes as "atheistic communism." [2] God had no place in Dostoevsky's writings of that period. He, furthermore, fell under the influence of the rich, aristocratic Nikolai Speshnev, a radical who was one of the first to be acquainted with Marx's *Communist Manifesto*. This man, who possessed a demonic attraction for Dostoevsky, served later as the novelist's model for the equally demonic figure of Nikolai Vsevolodovich Stavrogin, the hero of *The Demons* (softened in the English translation to *The Possessed*).

All such meetings as the Petrashevsky circle having been strictly forbidden during the reign of the reactionary Tsar Nicholas I (1825-55), a gathering of this group was broken into by the police and thirty of its members, along with Petrashevsky, were arrested (1849). Dostoevsky was taken into custody at night in his own lodgings.[3] Twenty-one of these unfortunates, Dostoevsky included, were sentenced to death. On December 22, 1849, the execution by a firing squad was to take place. The condemned were taken out to the Semenovsky Square and all preparations for the execution were proceeded with. But before the order "Fire!" was given, they were informed that the Tsar had graciously spared their lives, commuting the sentence to exile in Siberia. Dostoevsky never forgot those moments when he had faced imminent death and eternity; he described them in several of his books, especially in *The Idiot*. He was sent in chains to Siberia for four years at hard labor. On the way there he was given a copy of the New Testament by a compassionate woman—a gift that henceforth he treasured and which produced a fundamental change in his thinking. For during his imprisonment he "judged himself" and experienced what he himself designated as "the resurrection from the dead." He wrote to the woman who had given him the copy of the New Testament:

> I am a child of unbelief and doubt even now and (as I well know) I shall be to the grave. What fearful suffering this desire to believe has caused me and still causes me as it increases in strength in my soul as the contrary proofs multiply! However, God sends me at other times many minutes during which I am entirely at peace: . . . and during such minutes I have composed for myself a confession of faith

---

[2] *Ibid.*, p. 99.
[3] Cf. *ibid.*, p. 110, where this version of the events is given on the basis of Dostoevsky's own description. It differs from other current accounts.

. . . ; this is it: to believe that there is nothing more beautiful, more profound, more sympathetic, more reasonable, more manly and perfect than Christ, and not only nothing like Him exists, but I say to myself with jealous love, that it even cannot exist. And even more: if someone were to prove to me that Christ is not the truth, I would rather remain with Christ than with the truth.[4]

This was the conversion, the spiritual transformation of Dostoevsky, which he experienced in that fearful Siberian prison. Henceforth, despite many moral lapses and tormenting doubts, he remained faithful and loyal to Christ. He still believed much of what men like Belinsky taught; but he chose Christ.

He served his sentence at a prison camp in Omsk, sharing his life with murderers, robbers, and other criminals, for there was at the time no separation of the political from the criminal prisoners. He describes his experience in *The House of the Dead*. It is during these long and tortuous four years that he learned to know the innermost soul of the Russian people, even the most degraded and brutalized. After his release, he enlisted in a Siberian foot regiment as a private, for he was not as yet allowed to return to European Russia. During the five years he spent at Semipalatinsk where the regiment was quartered, he met the public prosecutor, Baron Wrangel, who found in Dostoevsky the only educated man with whom he could converse on cultural themes. The two became fast friends, relieving each other's loneliness and hunger for companionship. But more fateful was Dostoevsky's acquaintance with the wife of a minor customs official, Maria Dmitrievna Isayeva. He fell madly in love with her. Her husband, a hopeless drunkard, made life unbearable for her; but when he conveniently drank himself to death, Dostoevsky was at last free to marry her. She was a hysterical, neurotic, irresponsible woman, who at the time of her marriage to Dostoevsky had a penniless teacher for a lover, whom she was said to support for years afterwards. Moreover, she had a son by her first marriage—a worthless young puppy—whom Dostoevsky had to support. If he needed a post-graduate course in very abnormal psychology, he certainly had it in this unfortunate marriage! One meets similar situations in many of his novels: they are not imaginary but descriptive of his own experience.

In March, 1859, he was at last allowed to return home. He resumed his literary career and tried to restore his reputation. His brother, Mikhail, joined him in starting a periodical of a liberal and populist character. In it he issued three of his novels. But two years later the

[4] *Ibid.*, p. 125.

government forbade the publication on account of an offending article. Later, the brothers started another periodical, but the venture ended in financial failure. His brother died, and Feodor voluntarily assumed his debts as well as the support of his family. With his own finances in disorder and with the additional burdens thus assumed, Feodor found himself insolvent. In order to avoid the debtors' prison, he was forced to leave Russia for Western Europe.

From 1865 to 1871 he lived abroad for the third time, supporting himself by writing for various magazines in Russia. But the editors took advantage of his desperate situation by paying him the lowest rate of remuneration, although he was already recognized as one of the outstanding authors. Moreover, his own unconquerable passion for gambling, at which he almost invariably lost what he could ill afford to venture, often plunged him into destitution. During this tragic period of his life he wrote most of his novels without even seeing the proofs; consequently, their artistic quality suffered.

Even during the previous visits to Western Europe he had arrived at the conclusion that the essential character of its civilization was bourgeois. This he discerned as a symptom of decadence. He was thoroughly disillusioned with it, and henceforth, in the true spirit of Slavophilism, he expected salvation to come from Russia, particularly from the peasantry. Educated Russians were entirely imbued with atheistic Western ideas. He writes about them later in *The Brothers Karamazov*, where he expresses his judgment in the words of Elder Zosima:

> God will save Russia [through the peasants] . . . It is different with the upper classes. They, following science, want to base justice on reason alone, but not with Christ . . . and they have already proclaimed that there is no crime, that there is no sin.[5]

He longed to return home, for Europe represented for him only "a precious graveyard." At last in 1871 he was able to return to Russia, having been freed from the debt, a release to which his second wife, Anna Grigoryevna, contributed the major share by her steadying influence. The remaining eleven years of his life were the happiest; he won increasing fame as a writer and his family life was incomparably more peaceful than during his first marriage. It was during this period and that immediately preceding his return that his greatest works were published: *Crime and Punishment* (1866), *The Idiot* (1868-69), *The*

---

[5] F. M. Dostoevsky, *The Brothers Karamazov* (New York: Grosset & Dunlap), p. 350.

*Possessed* (1871-72), and finally *The Brothers Karamazov* (just prior to his death and left unfinished). He died in 1882, acclaimed as among the most famous contemporary Russian authors—and they were among the most brilliant in Europe.

Dostoevsky's religious message is "experiential," for as a rule he echoes in his characters his own life and thoughts. This applies to both the good and the bad "heroes." Leon Shestov characterized him as "Kierkegaard's double." Dostoevsky is an existentialist in the sense that for him ideas are never abstract, but are personalized in his characters. One hardly ever learns how these people swarming in his pages make a living; that is unimportant. But they are acutely, passionately concerned with "the damned questions" of their existence. As Ivan Karamazov states it: "We in our green youth have to settle the eternal questions first of all." It is truly astonishing with what clearness he has analyzed and diagnosed the conditions of his time, even though the symptoms of the cultural and spiritual malaise were not as yet fully developed. He transcended the merely objective and factual and penetrated to the core of its spiritual meaning. Instead of being merely a psychologist, as he is so often looked upon by imperceptive critics, he is, as he himself asserted, "a realist in the higher sense: that is to say, I indicate all the depths of the human soul." He reacted violently against the dominant secularism of the day which in Russia of the sixties took the form of the nihilism of such men as Chernyshevsky and Pisarev, but which in Western Europe was characterized by the materialism of Feuerbach, scientism of Comte, pessimism of Schopenhauer, and lastly by the atheism of Nietzsche.

Dostoevsky first of all protested vehemently against the materialistic denial of the spiritual aspect of human personality, reducing man to a mere psychosomatic organism. Man, even in his most degraded condition, still possesses will, self-determination, freedom of choice, no matter how limited. He is not predominantly a rational being, or a momentary manifestation of an Absolute Idea, or a helpless victim of the economic or other outward environmental forces. He is free within limits, and therefore morally responsible. To Dostoevsky, this is the supreme fact about man—his free will, and his abuse of it. For the fatal gift of moral freedom is commonly and universally wrongly used. To assert oneself, to will selfishly, is to destroy oneself. This is the cause of human tragedy, both individual and historical. But at any rate, man has the possibility of choosing; he is not "a key on a piano keyboard," a cog in a machine.

This thesis underlies Dostoevsky's *Letters from the Underworld*.[6] It is a rather gruesome story revolving around a most unpleasant character—a spiteful, malicious recluse nursing a bitter grudge against the world because of undoubted wrongs he suffered. He retires into his hole of living quarters (be it noted that the Russian title, *Zapiski iz podpolya*, actually designates the space under the floor of the cellar, thus suggesting the dwelling place of cockroaches and rats), whence he spits out his impotent rage. The man is by no means a likeable or respectable character: he is ill and full of spleen, as he himself says. And worst of all, he has no desire to be cured. This is Dostoevsky's way of saying that a confirmed sinner cannot be saved, because he does not want to be saved. It reminds one of Jesus's searching question to the sick man at the Bethesda pool: "Wilt thou be whole?" But despite the undoubted degradation of the man in Dostoevsky's novel, he still possesses free will, even though he exercises it to his own destruction. His denunciation of society rings true. He, for instance, discusses the theory that humankind is governed by reason and self-advantage—an obvious reference to the rationalists and utilitarians, such as Chernyshevsky and the nihilists—and that science will one day order human life so beneficently that man would

> . . . immediately stop to do mischief and immediately become good and kindly, because being enlightened and understanding his present advantages, he would clearly discern his own individual advantage in the good . . . and he would necessarily begin to do good. . . . This is not enough: then, you say, science itself will instruct man . . . that he possesses neither will nor caprice of his own and has never done, and that he is nothing more than something on the order of the keys of the grand piano or the handle of a hand organ. And above all— there are in the world the laws of nature: so that everything man does is done altogether not in accordance with his want, but by itself, according to the laws of nature. . . . All human actions, by themselves, will then be computed according to those laws, mathematically, on the order of the tables of logarithms, up to the 180,000th degree, and entered into a calendar. . . . Then—well in one word, then will arrive the bird Kagan! . . . But man is stupid, phenomenally stupid! . . . I would not wonder, for instance, if suddenly from one or another place of this future general intelligence there arose some gentleman with an unpleasant—or better to say—a degenerate and cynical physiognomy who, setting his hands akimbo, would say to us all: "How now, gentlemen? How about kicking with our foot all that intelligence at once into dust, with the exclusive aim of sending all those logarithms to the devil and that we may live again according to our stupid will?

[6] F. M. Dostoevsky, *Letters from the Underworld* (Everyman's Library, New York: E. P. Dutton & Co., Inc., 1913).

In short, because man always and everywhere, no matter where he may be, loves to act as he pleases, and not at all as reason and advantages order him." [7]

Man, then, is not primarily rational and is not guided by his highest economic advantage—as Chernyshevsky asserted in his celebrated novel, *What is to be Done*,[8] which became the nihilists' bible—but is essentially irrational, a creature of will and caprice. This is the tragedy of man.

Having thus asserted his fundamental conviction that man is basically governed by "his stupid sweet will," Dostoevsky proceeds to elaborate this thesis in all his subsequent writings. He distinguishes primarily between those who assert themselves selfishly, even viciously—the "dark souls"—and those who use their free will in the way God desires them to use it—by subordinating their will to the divine. These are the "bearers of light." To assert oneself is to destroy oneself; the way of salvation lies only in a voluntary surrender of oneself to God. This essentially Christian insight affords us an understanding of Dostoevsky's deep-seated conviction that human moral freedom, being generally wrongly used, is a fearful responsibility and a tragic aspect of human nature. Its chronic abuse is the cause of man's misery and the source of humankind's woes and evils. This is the Fall of man—his self-centeredness, self-assertion (what Nietzsche called the Will-to-Power) and what Christian theology has always designated as the original sin. It results in suffering and terrible evils, both individual and social. And the tragic thing about it is that it is self-caused: man has chosen evil of his own volition, not because of some impersonal fate or environmental conditions—certainly not because of God's fiat!

Dostoevsky depicts his conflict with the nihilists—with their thesis that rational man is above the law and ought to live according to his advantage—in concrete life situations of his characters. Among the first to be considered let us choose Rodyon Raskolnikov in *Crime and Punishment*. A law student, the son of a poor widow, he lives in a St. Petersburg garret in utter poverty. Sick and starving, having pawned his last valuables, he is in danger of not being able to finish his university course and thus losing the benefit of all the sacrifices of his mother and sister as well as his own strenuous efforts. He is desperate. In a pub he overhears some students arguing over the fashionable doctrine whether a man of superior endowments, possessing the necessary will power, is not superior to the moral code of ordinary "herd-men." It strengthens

---

[7] F. M. Dostoevsky, *Zapiski iz podolya* (Berlin: "Mysl," 1922), pp. 22, 26-28. My translation.

[8] Significantly, it was reprinted by the Soviet publishing office in 1947.

in him the conviction that he is a superman and therefore above the normal moral requirements. He goes to the old money lender with whom he pawned his last possessions and kills her with an axe. Having stuffed his pockets at random with a few pawned articles, he intends to rush away; but in the doorway he meets the old pawnbroker's subnormal sister. He kills her as well. His first crime has led to an unpremeditated second one. He reaches home in high fever, and for weeks lies in bed, delirious. His crime is not traced to him, but to an innocent young fellow, a painter working in the house where the crime occurred, who is arrested instead.

Raskolnikov could have gone free had not his conscience, awakened by the young prostitute, Sonya, forced him to confess. He is sentenced to a Siberian imprisonment, to which Sonya follows him. He finds that he is not a superman. Had he been one of the superior breed, he would not be troubled even had he murdered numberless victims, as did Napoleon or other celebrated "heroes." For a really superior man there is no such thing as "conscience," and therefore no moral difference between right and wrong. Did he really repent his crime? No! What he raged at was his weakness in *not* being a superman, and that "he had been unsuccessful and had confessed it." [9] Raskolnikov is not one of the "light bearers." Perhaps Dostoevsky wanted to say no more than that there is such a thing as conscience. At any rate he suggests that Raskolnikov's sufferings and Sonya's love have brought him to the point where his moral transformation could begin. "But that is the beginning of another story—the story of the gradual renewal of a man, the story of his gradual regeneration . . . but our present story is ended." [10]

Even more to the point is the characterization of Ivan Karamazov and Nikolai Stavrogin in the two novels, *The Brothers Karamazov* and *The Possessed*, respectively. For they illustrate not only the thesis that to assert oneself is to destroy oneself, but also (particularly in the case of Stavrogin) that the destruction extends to others—even innocent persons—as well. Evil is like the ever expanding concentric rings on the surface of water when a pebble is thrown in. Ivan Karamazov is modelled on the figure of Belinsky, although with considerable differences. As has already been mentioned, Dostoevsky greatly admired the latter prior to his Siberian imprisonment. But Ivan also represents the Westernists among the educated classes of Russia. He is the ex-

[9] F. M. Dostoevsky, *Crime and Punishment* (New York: The Modern Library, n.d.), p. 526.
[10] *Ibid.*, p. 532.

ponent of a certain type of practical atheism: he does not so much reject God as he does God's world, the evil in that world. His views as to God are not at all self-consistent; he is essentially an agnostic. When his father, Feodor Pavlovich, asks him whether God exists, he asserts "No, there is no God." He likewise denies immortality and the existence of the devil.[11] But later, in his conversation with his youngest brother, Alyosha, he changes his tune; then he asserts almost in the same breath that "man has actually invented God"; and a little later that ". . . I can't expect to understand about God. . . . I have a Euclidian earthly mind . . ." And thereupon he launches into what amounts to a confession of belief in God:

> And so I accepted God and am glad to, and what's more, I accept His wisdom, His purpose—which are utterly beyond our ken; I believe in the underlying order and the meaning of life; I believe in the eternal harmony in which they say we shall one day be blended. . . . Yet, would you believe it, in the final result I don't accept this world of God's, and, although I know it exists, I don't accept it at all. . . .[12]

> Besides, too high a price is asked for harmony; it's beyond our means to pay so much to enter on it. And so I hasten to give back my entrance ticket. . . . It's not God that I don't accept, Alyosha, only I most respectfully return Him the ticket.[13]

Thus Ivan symbolizes those confused and fuzzy liberal thinkers who, although verbally asserting their belief in God, live practically as if He did not exist. Ivan cannot accept the fact of evil and blames God for not eliminating it from His scheme of existence; he refuses to pay the price of redemption, since "too high a price is asked" for it. Suffering, understood in Ivan's way, embitters and drives men to resentment against, or even repudiation of, God. Only when accepted as a means of redemption—in Alyosha's way—does it purify and ennoble. But Ivan does not love men and cannot understand how anyone can love his neighbor; for he is a stranger to the Christian concept of loving men in their sins. He even allows his father to be murdered, although he anticipated the foul deed and deliberately chose to absent himself from home on the night of the murder. Assuming that his brother Mitya would be the murderer, he shrugs off all responsibility with the retort of Cain: "Am I my brother's keeper?" He is likewise estranged

---

[11] *The Brothers Karamazov*, p. 145.
[12] *Ibid.*, pp. 257-58.
[13] *Ibid.*, p. 269.

from the people for whom, in the pride of intellect, he has nothing but contempt; in this he symbolizes the educated upper classes of Russian society, actually separated from the masses—a situation revenging itself upon them during the fearful year of the Revolution! Not only is Ivan guilty of the sins of omission, he is likewise involved in those of commission. For Smerdyakov, the lackey, this illegitimate son of the old sensualist, overhears Ivan asserting that, since there is no God, "everything is lawful," and he is the one who kills the old man. He is not detected, for Mitya is apprehended and sentenced for the crime; but before he hangs himself, Smerdyakov confesses his crime to Ivan, at the same time charging him with responsibility for the deed:

> *You* murdered him. . . . I was only your instrument, your faithful servant. . . . You said 'everything is lawful'. . . . For if there is no everlasting God, there's no such thing as virtue, and there's no need of it. . . . You are like Fyodor Pavlovich, you are more like him than any of his children; you've the same soul as he had.[14]

Thus Smerdyakov (whose name means "the stinking one," for he represents the unwashed, ignorant masses; Ivan himself called him "the raw material for revolution . . . when the time comes") draws the logical conclusion from Ivan's atheism that there is no distinction between good and evil and "everything is lawful," even murder.

Ivan is horrified at Smerdyakov's accusation, but acknowledges its truth. He falls physically and mentally ill and during a spell of brain fever he suffers a hallucination: he experiences a terrifying vision of the devil (in whom he professes to disbelieve)—in reality the objectification of his own perverted, divided self. The devil is of his own making! The skillfully written account is susceptible of being interpreted either as an objective occurrence or a "nightmare." The visitor expresses Ivan's own thoughts and expounds maliciously his own maxims and principles. Ivan at last recognizes that "it's I, *I myself speaking, not you!*" The devil taunts him with Ivan's own remark— "*Le diable n'existe point*"—no one believes in him. He laughs at Ivan's remorse—has he not said that there is no difference between good and evil? Ivan threatens to kill him, but the devil only laughs—Ivan would have to kill himself! He then continues to expound Ivan's own theory regarding the "new" society: What is necessary above all is that humankind destroy the idea of God in themselves—the very requirement made by Nietzsche!

---

[14] *Ibid.*, pp. 704, 706, 714-15.

As soon as men have all of them denied God—and I believe that period . . . will come to pass—the old conception of the universe will fall of itself . . . and, what's more, the old morality, and everything will begin anew. . . . Man will be lifted up with a spirit of divine Titanic pride and the man-god will appear. From hour to hour extending his conquest of nature infinitely by his will and his science, man will feel such lofty joy from hour to hour in doing it that it will make up for his old dreams of the joys of heaven.[15]

Does not this remind one irresistibly of Nietzsche's Superman?

Ivan then wakes up from his dream. What happens to him in the end is not revealed—it remained unwritten because of Dostoevsky's death.

Even more pointedly and poignantly is the thesis that self-affirmation results in self-destruction—and that of not only the guilty individual but of others as well—carried out in the story of Nikolai Stavrogin and Peter Verkhovensky in *The Possessed*. With an uncanny prevision, Dostoevsky dramatically depicts the working of a "cell" of revolutionaries, bent on forcibly imposing a "new" society on the ruins of the old. The story is based on an actual event—the murder of a member of the so-called Nechaev secret society. Verkhovensky is actually modelled on the figure of Nechaev: he envisions an "ideal" transformation of society by means of a violent revolutionary action. But in order to reach the goal, society must be subjected to utter despotic regimentation reminding one of the communist regime. This thesis is elaborated by a member of the group, Shigalev, who, in order to attain the absolute freedom of the future society insists on despotic tyranny. Verkhovensky, the self-appointed architect of this ideal society, must, however, secure a leader for the enterprise. He chooses Stavrogin, an aristocratic intellectual, who keeps himself aloof from the ordinary rank and file. He is like a fake pearl, which looks genuine enough, although it actually is only a cheap imitation of the real thing. As has already been mentioned, this proud and vicious "demonic" character is modelled on the figure of Speshnev, whose radical revolutionary theory young Dostoevsky had accepted. Verkhovensky pleads with Stavrogin: "I need you, you; without you I am nothing. Without you I am a fly, a bottled idea; Columbus without America." [16] Thus even the "Führer" principle is introduced, to anticipate future Hitlers and Stalins! And Stavrogin's fate is involved in

---

[15] *Ibid.*, p. 734.

[16] F. M. Dostoevsky, *The Possessed* (New York: Random House, Inc., 1936), pp. 426-27. By permission.

that of the revolutionary movement, although he himself, a young man who had been pampered by his mother and admired as a paragon by his acquaintances, is actually so depraved by his lust and viciousness that he no longer can feel either love or hate. He is, in the modern phrase of T. S. Eliot "a hollow man" living in wastelands, or in the designation of Camus an utterly depersonalized "stranger."

In a chapter suppressed by Katkov, editor of the magazine in which the story was originally published, Stavrogin, in an interview with Archimandrite Tikhon of the local monastery, confesses his disbelief in God but his absolute faith in demons: "I do believe in the devil, I believe canonically, in a personal devil, not in an allegory, and I don't need confirmation from anybody." [17]

The ideal society that this "demonic" *Führer* is supposed to bring about, is described by Verkhovensky as follows:

> Listen. First of all we'll make an upheaval. . . . Our party does not consist only of those who commit murder and arson, fire off pistols in the traditional fashion, or bite colonels. They are only a hindrance. I don't accept anything without discipline. . . . Listen. I've reckoned them all up: a teacher who laughs with children at their God and at their cradle is on our side. The lawyer who defends an educated murderer because he is more cultured than his victims and could not help murdering them to get money is one of us. The schoolboys who murder a peasant for the sake of sensation are ours. The juries who acquit every criminal are ours. . . . Among officials and literary men we have lots, lots, and they don't know it themselves. . . . The Russian God has already been vanquished by cheap vodka. The peasants are drunk, the mothers are drunk, the children are drunk, the churches are empty. . . . But one or two generations of vice are essential now; monstrous, abject vice by which a man is transformed into a loathsome, cruel, egoistic reptile. That's what we need!" [18]

The little group murders a member who wishes to leave them, and another member who intends to commit suicide, assumes the blame. He is Kirillov, perhaps the only sympathetic, although also pathetic, character in the story. He concludes that since the idea of God is an invention of mankind which is afraid of death, the denial of God's existence is tantamount to the denial of the fear of death. Only a man not afraid to die is free, is man-god. And to prove that he, Kirillov, is man-god, he will voluntarily commit suicide, for only this act can serve as the supreme expression of self-determination. "I am bound to shoot myself because the highest point of my self-will is to kill myself

[17] *Ibid.*, p. 697.
[18] *Ibid.*, pp. 427-28.

with my own hands. . . . I can't understand how an atheist could know that there is no God and not kill himself on the spot." [19] And so the frenzy of self-destruction spreads ever more widely. The whole plot ends, after a frustrated and rather comical attempt at social revolution, with the death of the "leader" Stavrogin, who hangs himself. He who aspired to demonic powers, proves to be insane, weak, and powerless. Evil destroys itself. The devil is a fool. Only Verkhovensky, the scoundrel that he is, escapes, leaving the rest to suffer the consequences of his "grand idea."

Such, then, is Dostoevsky's judgment of the inevitable result of the nihilist ideas of Chernyshevsky and Pisarev, which dominated the sixties. They were imported from Western Europe, and served as archetypes of those of the Bolshevik leaders. In the West they roughly corresponded to the Marxist and Nietzschean principles.

But if the abuse of free will leads to self-destruction, the right, God-intended use of it is the way of redemption from evil. To Dostoevsky, Christianity extols spiritual freedom. The highest value is that of the redeemed human being. Not even God accepts a response to His love unless it is freely and voluntarily given. Forced love is no love but a contradiction in terms. Dostoevsky illustrates this concept of the redemptive function of freedom in a number of his characters, the most outstanding of which are Prince Myshkin in *The Idiot* and Elder Zosima and Alyosha Karamazov in *The Brothers Karamazov*. The former of these, although comprising elements of the author's spiritual autobiography, need not detain us long. For although it was intended to portray a "truly beautiful personality," a "Russian Don Quixote," the attempt was not particularly successful.

The young prince is pictured in the opening of the story as having just returned from Switzerland, where he had been treated for epilepsy and a retarded mental condition. He is an orphan, practically penniless, although soon to inherit millions. The only relative he visits is a general living in St. Petersburg. General Epanchin is not particularly overjoyed at this meeting. In the family circle the prince meets his young cousin, Aglaya, a vivacious and capricious girl inclined to make fun of the awkward youth, and yet strangely attracted by him. In the end they fall in love with each other. Myshkin, despite his "idiocy," radiates a strange personal charm, because of his childlike goodness, humility, and kindness, which make him welcome in society. He brings out the best in people because he believes the best of them. He reminds one strongly of that genuinely Russian concept of a true Christian—humble, voluntarily accepting humiliation, gladly suffering contempt, repaying good for evil. Often he is mentally undeveloped, psychologically abnormal; he is *"yurodivyi"*—a fool for Christ's sake. Such is Prince Myshkin; when a proud young puppy, Ganya, slaps his face in public, the prince's only comment is: "How will he be ashamed of this act!" He is cheated and bullied by others of his friends and even strangers, but freely shares his wealth with them. He is brought into contact with a famous beauty, Nastasya Philippovna, who as a young girl was seduced by a wealthy landowner, who befriended her after her parents' death, had her well educated, but then made her his mistress. Despite her wealth, her reputation is ruined ever after; only Myshkin treats her not as a "fallen" woman, but as an unfortunate one. His "queer" conduct toward Nastasya Philippovna as well as to a whole host of other acquaintances is ascribed to his "idiocy." But it is evident that Dostoevsky meant it to be regarded as essentially Christian. The prince's sympathy, or rather his redemptive compassion for Nastasya Philippovna finally results in love, although he does not cease to love Aglaya as well. But Nastasya Philippovna is also loved by the passionate Rogozhin, who in a fit of jealousy murders her. The conflict within Myshkin's soul over this involvement, dramatically portrayed by Dostoevsky, eventuates in the prince's lapse into his former state of idiocy. As a portrayal of a Christian, Myshkin may have greater meaning to a Russian who still retains something of an appreciation for the type of the "fool for Christ." But to a Western Christian, Myshkin is an unacceptable model, for it suggests that the abnormal psychosis is an essential feature of the religious life. Dostoevsky himself felt that he had not succeeded in carrying out his intent.

Such is not the case with the ideal portrayed by Father Zosima and his young disciple, Alyosha Karamazov. Zosima, modelled on the figure of Father Ambrosy of the Optina Pustyn monastery, is the Elder in the local monastery. Because of his experiences during his previous career, he is able to help the large number of pilgrims who resort to him for aid in their various needs. He had been a roistering officer who, because he had insulted a fellow-officer, was challenged to a duel. But the night before the duel, the memory of his dead brother brought him to realize his sinfulness and to repent. At the duel he allowed his opponent to fire the first shot, and thereupon he threw away his pistol and apologized to the offended man. Since this was regarded as a disgrace upon his military "honor," he resigned from the regiment and retired to the monastery. Dostoevsky portrays in him his conception of the function of the Church—redemptive, purgative of all pride, aiming at the attainment of self-mastery through suffering, but serving the needs of all others in love. Zosima exhorts the fellow monks:

> Love a man even in his sin, for that is the semblance of Divine Love and is the highest love on earth. Love all God's creation, the whole and every grain of sand in it. Love every leaf, every ray of God's light. Love the animals, love the plants, love everything. . . . Loving humility is marvelously strong, the strongest of all things, and there is nothing else like it. . . .
>
> To transform the world, to recreate it afresh, men must turn into another path psychologically. Until you have become really, in actual fact, a brother to everyone, brotherhood will not come to pass. No sort of scientific teaching, no kind of common interest, will ever teach men to share property and privileges with equal consideration for all. . . .
>
> They have science; but in science there is nothing but what is the object of sense. The spiritual world, the higher part of man's being is rejected altogether, dismissed with a sort of triumph, even with hatred. The world has proclaimed the reign of freedom, especially of late, but what do we see in this freedom of theirs? Nothing but slavery and self-destruction.[20]

Alyosha Karamazov, modelled after Vladimir Solovev, had been born in that cesspool of sin which had been his home, escaped it by becoming a novice in the local monastery and a disciple of Elder Zosima. He eagerly imbibed the teaching of his beloved mentor who, before his death, commanded Alyosha to return to "the world" and live there as a "light-bearer" in the midst of its darkness. Zosima said to Alyosha:

> This is what I think of you, you will go forth from these walls, but will live like a monk in the world. You will have many enemies, but even your foes will love you. Life will bring you many misfortunes, but you will find happiness in them, and will bless life . . .[21]

But before he left the monastery, Alyosha experienced an overwhelming sorrow: not only did his beloved Elder die, but his body decayed so quickly as to cause a scandal to the brethren who had expected—according to their superstitous belief—that the body of a saint would not decay. Since Zosima's did decay, he could not have been the saint he had been held to be. Here again Dostoevsky shatters the popular faith of the Russian folk and shows that the real sanctity

---

[20] *The Brothers Karamazov,* pp. 354-55; 335-36; 348; 350.
[21] *Ibid.,* pp. 313-14.

of the soul has no such effect on the body. But Alyosha did not yet know it. He was tempted to rebel against the evil in the world, just as had his atheistic brother, Ivan. Nevertheless, he experienced a profound change when in a dream he heard the voice of Father Zosima. Aroused from his dream, he left the monastery.

> Alyosha stood, gazed, and suddenly threw himself down on the earth. He did not know why he embraced it. He could not have told why he longed so irresistibly to kiss it, to kiss it all. But he kissed it weeping, sobbing and watering it with his tears, and vowed passionately to love it, to love it for ever and ever. 'Water the earth with the tears of your joy and love those tears,' echoed in his soul. . . .
>
> He longed to forgive everyone and for everything, and to beg forgiveness. Oh, not for himself, but for all men, for all and for everything. . . . But with every instant he felt clearly and, as it were, tangibly, that something firm and unshakable as that vault of heaven had entered into his soul. . . . He had fallen on the earth a weak boy, but he rose up a resolute champion, and he knew and felt it suddenly at the very moment of his ecstasy. And never, never, all his life long, could Alyosha forget that minute.[22]

This is the novelist's way of describing the miracle of conversion; it may lack the theologian's technical niceties, but it is a description of a genuine redemptive and transforming experience. Instead of the miracle of an "incorruptible death," there is the miracle of an incorruptible life. For Alyosha thereafter becomes a light-bearer, engaged in concrete redemptive acts of loving service.

Thus, according to Dostoevsky, religion is not to be lived in a holy retirement; it is to be a redemptive force in the world of sin. Had Dostoevsky lived to complete the work, he would have portrayed Alyosha not as a plaster saint, miraculously free from the taint of the Karamazovs (and they symbolize all humanity); indeed, Alyosha himself confesses, "I, too, am a Karamazov." In the world, he marries and becomes engulfed in all manner of iniquity—but not to the end. He repents, abandons his profligacy, returns to the monastery, which he then serves as a reincarnation of Father Zosima.

In Dostoevsky's vision, the salvation of Russia, and by means of Russia of the world, must come from "the monastery"—from the religiously transformed persons. For Dostoevsky loved the Orthodox Church not as it was but as it ought to have been. As Vyacheslav Ivanov concludes:

[22] *Ibid.*, p. 404.

Dostoevsky never went so far as to foretell how all this will be accomplished; but he has predicted what must occur. *The Brothers Karamazov* treats of 'the mission of the Russian monk'; but by monasticism Dostoevsky understands primarily a new, mystical monastic consecration, an asceticism, discipline and readiness to serve the world that will be disclosed by no outward insignia. These anonymous monks and lay brothers will be sent out into the field of humanity, not to weed out the tares, which must, as Christ says, grow up with the corn, but to be as the warmth of the sun and a quickening rain coming in due season.

The whole life of Russia must be permeated by a principle quite different from the principles that have hitherto governed the organization of life. Once it is permeated by this new principle, all forms of coercion and constraint, and of the organized lie, will fall to pieces. . . .[23]

But perhaps the most impressive statement of Dostoevsky's conviction that the way of redemption is the way of freedom, is to be found in that truly inspired piece of the nineteenth century literature—a veritable work of genius—that is imbedded in *The Brothers Karamazov* under the heading "The Grand Inquisitor." Its profundity, its aptness in portraying the root evil of the secularist "gospel" of salvation by compulsion, by bread alone, by scientific "miracles," by political conquest, is unmatched anywhere.

The scene of the legend is laid in medieval Seville; it opens on a splendid auto da fé to which all the population of the city has been gathered in the public square. Suddenly, unobserved, Jesus appears among them. All recognize him and throng about Him, while He extends His hand in blessing. He approaches the cathedral just as a sad little procession is nearing it: mourners carrying an open white coffin, in which lies a seven-year old girl. The mother, encouraged by the crowd, throws herself at His feet, imploring His help. And He, as of old, again speaks His *"Talitha cumi."* The little girl opens her eyes, sits up, and wonderingly looks at the flowers in her hand.

The scene has been observed, from a distance, by the ninety-year old Grand Inquisitor. He frowns and motions his guards with an imperious gesture to take Him. The crowd, cowed, falls back. The guards take their Prisoner and throw Him into the dungeon at the Palace of the Inquisition.

That night the old Inquisitor calls upon his Prisoner and, while the

latter remains completely silent, says: "Why hast Thou come to interfere with us? For Thou knowest that Thou hast come to interfere
with us. But knowest Thou what will happen tomorrow? . . . Tomorrow I shall condemn Thee and burn Thee at the stake as the worst of
heretics."

The old man then charges his Prisoner with the folly of rejecting the
beneficient offers of "the wise and dread spirit" in the wilderness. The
spirit said on that occasion:

> Thou wouldst go into the world with empty hands, offering men
> some kind of freedom which they, in their simplicity and natural
> licentiousness, cannot even comprehend and which they fear and
> dread—for there has never been anything at any time more insuf-
> ferable for man and the human society than freedom! But seest Thou
> these stones in the barren wilderness glowing with heat? Turn them
> into bread and humankind will run after Thee like a flock, grateful
> and obedient, although ever trembling lest Thou withdraw Thy hand
> and Thy bread cease! But Thou didst not desire to deprive man of his
> freedom, and therefore Thou hast rejected the offer; for what kind of
> freedom is it—Thou hast thought to Thyself—where the obedience
> is bought with bread? Thou hast replied that man does not live by
> bread alone. But knowest Thou that in the name of that earthly bread
> the spirit of the earth shall rise up against Thee and shall attack and
> vanquish Thee? And all shall follow him, shouting: 'who is like unto
> this beast? for he has given us fire from heaven!' Knowest Thou that
> ages shall pass and mankind shall proclaim by the lips of its wise men
> and scientists that there is no crime, and consequently no sin; there
> are only the hungry? They shall write on their banners: 'Feed them,
> and then expect virtue of them!' . . . We alone shall feed them in
> Thy name, lying that it is in Thy name! . . . In the end, they shall
> lay their freedom at our feet and shall say to us: 'make us slaves, but
> feed us!'

Passing on to the second "temptation," the old Inquisitor continues:

> Thou didst desire man's free love, that he should freely follow
> Thee, being fascinated and captivated by Thee. Instead of the rigid,
> ancient law, man should decide for himself with free heart what is
> good and what is evil, having only Thy image before him as his
> example. . . . Thou didst hope that man, following Thee, would
> remain satisfied with God alone and need no miracle. But hast Thou
> not known that as soon as man rejects miracle, he rejects, at the same
> time God? For man seeks not so much God as a miracle. . . . We
> have corrected Thy feat, and based it upon *miracle, mystery, and
> authority*. And men rejoiced that they were again led like a flock
> and that at last there was lifted from their hearts that terrible gift
> which had brought them such tortures. . . . Why hast Thou come
> to interfere with us? . . . We are not with Thee, but have gone

over to *him*—that is our mystery! We have left Thee long ago and have gone over to *him*—eight centuries ago! . . .

Why hast Thou rejected the last offer? If Thou hadst accepted the third counsel of the mighty spirit, Thou wouldst have accomplished everything that man seeks on earth: that is, before whom to bow, to whom to entrust his conscience, and how all may unite, finally, in one peaceful, common, and harmonious ant-heap—for the need of universal unity is the third and last torture of men. . . . Hadst Thou accepted the world and Caesar's purple, Thou wouldst have organized a universal rule and wouldst have brought about universal peace. For who can rule men but he who rules their consciences and in whose hands is their bread? We have taken over even the sword of Caesar; and in taking it over, we have ultimately rejected Thee and have gone over to *him*. . . . I repeat, tomorrow Thou shalt see that obedient flock which at the first motion of my hand shall heap glowing coals at Thy stake at which I shall burn Thee, because Thou hast come to interfere with us. For if anyone has ever deserved our stake more than others, it is Thou! Tomorrow I shall burn Thee. *Dixi!*[24]

The Grand Inquisitor stands for all those who attempt to save men by force; they despise common men as stupid and vicious, not really knowing what is good for them. Accordingly they must be constrained for their own good. The Grand Inquisitor stands not only for the authoritarian Church; more fittingly, he is the symbol of the social movements, such as Marxism, proclaiming a forcible imposition of the utopian perfect society by means of "bread alone." He stands for political dreams of social betterment by means of military conquest. But Dostoevsky penetrates beyond these outward self-justifying pretenses of the would-be social saviors to the fact that they are "with him"—the Tempter, the Evil Spirit, and that they have really denied God, even if they profess Him and pretend to work in His name.

This, then, is a brief, and undoubtedly quite inadequate, sketch of Dostoevsky's religious thought. Its central theme is that man, as a spiritual being, is terribly free; he is free to destroy himself as well as save himself by means of freedom. Berdyaev summarizes this aspect by writing:

That tragic judgment of freedom Dostoevsky depicts in the judgment of his heroes: freedom passes into self-will, into rebellious self-affirmation of man. Freedom becomes objectless, empty, and it destroys man. Such objectless and empty is the freedom of Stavrogin and Versilov; the freedom of Svidrigailov and Feodor Pavlovich

[24] From *Nicolas Berdyaev: Captive of Freedom* by Matthew Spinka. Copyright 1950, W. L. Jenkins. The Westminster Press. My translation. By permission.

Karamazov is disintegrating; the freedom of Raskolnikov and Peter Verkhovensky leads to crime; the demonic freedom of Kirillov and Ivan Karamazov destroys man. Freedom as self-will annihilates itself, passes into its opposite, disintegrates and destroys man . . .

On the other hand, freedom rightly used

. . . leads to the way of Godmanhood. In Godmanhood human freedom unites with the divine freedom, the human image with the divine image. By an inward experience, and inward living of freedom is attained the light of that Truth. . . . But Christ is not an external law, an external rule of life. His kingdom is incompatible with the kingdom of this world. And Dostoevsky angrily denounces all deviations of Christianity toward the religion of constraint and force.[25]

## Nicolas Berdyaev, the Philosopher of Personalism

Among those who repudiate our secularist civilization most consistently, comprehensively, and vehemently is the Russian religious philosopher, Nicolas A. Berdyaev (1874-1948).[26] Since his acceptance of the Christian world-view he had been a man in revolt against a world in revolt against God. Having rejected God, our era is now in the process of repudiating man, as far as his spiritual nature is concerned. This is seen in such movements as fascism and communism; for having rejected God, we are now renouncing man.

Berdyaev was born in Kiev of an old aristocratic family, and although in opposition to it, he retained the best features of his aristocratic upbringing throughout his life. His father, a retired officer in the Cavalier Guard, placed him in the Pages' Corpus. But soldiering was not Nicolas' chosen career; he was a serious, studious youth, eager to learn the meaning of life. Thus philosophy was his most congenial study. After graduating from the military school, he entered Kiev University. Previously, he had read philosophy "on his own." At fourteen he had already read Kant, Schopenhauer, and Hegel. He

---

[25] Nikolai Berdyaev, *Mirosozertsamie Dostoevskago* (Praha: YMCA Press, 1923), pp. 73-75. My translation. By permission.

[26] For a fuller account of his life and thought, cf. my book mentioned in footnote 24. For a definitive biography, cf. Donald A. Lowrie, *Rebellious Prophet, a Life of Nicolai Berdyaev* (New York: Harper & Brothers, 1960).

bears witness to the potent influence exerted on him during his later life by the biblical prophets, Job, the Greek tragedies, Cervantes, Shakespeare, Goethe, Byron, Dickens, Balzac, Ibsen, Dostoevsky, Tolstoy and Tyutchev. At the University he fell under the spell of Marx and played a prominent part as leader of the student Marxist circle. He was consequently expelled from the University and exiled for three years to the Vologda province, although during the last year he was allowed to reside at Zhitomir. But he affirms that he never was an orthodox Marxist, nor a materialist or a positivist. He writes in his spiritual autobiography:

> During a certain period of my life I have been an atheist, if one understands by that term an anti-theist, the rejection of the traditional religious notions about God. But I have not been an atheist, if by that term one understands the rejection of the supreme spiritual principle of spiritual values independent of the material world. I have not been a pantheist.[27]

But the deterministic, anti-humanist character of orthodox Marxism, the doctrinaire denial of the ethical nature of man, soon compelled Berdyaev to part company with his fellow-revolutionaries. He had learned from Kant that the highest value in the world is the human personality, and this conviction remained fundamental to his creed throughout his whole life. He had supposed in joining the Marxist circle that the new revolutionary gospel was humanistic. But a closer acquaintance with the movement convinced him of the contrary; he saw with grief that among the Marxists there was no more respect for personality than among the bourgeoisie. It was this that caused him to break with the revolutionaries and gradually turn to, and accept, the essentially Christian interpretation of the meaning of human existence. Dostoevsky's influence contributed mightily to this change, particularly his concept of Christianity as depicted in "The Grand Inquisitor," to which Berdyaev never tires of referring. Nevertheless, he insists in his autobiography that he never experienced a "conversion" as that occurrence is commonly understood: "I did not experience the crisis of conversion perhaps for the reason that my spiritual life consists of crises." [28] His religious goals have been twofold: "the search for meaning and the search for eternity. The search for meaning was my first search for God, while the search for eternity was my first search for

---

[27] Nikolai Berdyaev, *Samopoznanie* (Paris: YMCA Press, 1949), p. 100. By permission. My translation. There exists an English translation, *Dream and Reality*, but it is essentially a paraphrase.
[28] *Ibid.*, p. 89.

salvation." [29] ". . . I am more a *homo mysticus* than a *homo religiosus*." [30] Nevertheless, he remained all his life opposed to the "official" Orthodoxy of the Russian Church, at times even violently criticizing it:

> I never pretended that my religious thought had a churchly character. I sought the truth and experienced as truth that which was revealed to me. The historic Orthodoxy has appeared to me insufficiently ecumenical and limited, almost sectarian. I am not a heretic [he had been so accused] and least of all a sectarian; I am a believing freethinker.[31]

During the First World War he published an article severely denouncing the Holy Governing Synod. He was to be tried in court as a "blasphemer"—a crime punishable by permanent exile to Siberia. But the trial was postponed on account of the War and was never resumed.[32] Because of his individualist interpretation of Christianity, he is not to be regarded as a typical representative of Russian Orthodoxy. That purpose could be served far better by Father Sergius Bulgakov, who likewise had passed from Marxism to Christianity, but became a priest and in the end—as dean of the Orthodox Academy in Paris—the outstanding theologian of his Church. Berdyaev at best represents the free, lay character of Russian religious thought.

When the First World War broke out, and particularly after the victory of the Bolshevik Revolution in October of 1917, Berdyaev found himself violently opposed to the new regime. In a book written during that time, but not published until later when he was already abroad, Berdyaev savagely denounced the secularist and atheistic intellectuals of Russia for the "treason" they had committed against the Russian people that revenged itself upon them in such a ghastly fashion in the Revolution. But he likewise condemned the Revolution. And although he was appointed by the faculty of the University of Moscow to the chair of philosophy, a man of his convictions could not long retain the post. He was twice arrested and jailed, and finally in 1922 was expelled from Russia along with seventy like-minded members of the intelligentsia. At first, he lived in Berlin, but two years later he moved to Paris, where he remained the rest of his life. The books he wrote during this period of exile brought him to the attention of the

[29] *Ibid.*, pp. 89-90.
[30] *Ibid.*, p. 93.
[31] *Ibid.*, p. 199.
[32] *Ibid.*, pp. 219-220.

world. But, as he has recorded in his spiritual autobiography, "I am not satisfied with any of the books I have written, or any word I have spoken." [33]

Berdyaev is the philosopher of freedom *par excellence*. As a Kantian, he learned from his master that human personality is of the highest value, and he spent a lifetime elaborating that thesis. Dostoevsky taught him the religious significance of spiritual freedom, a lesson Berdyaev enforced in all his books. But before he was able to affirm and expound his own religious convictions, he had to establish them philosophically. For he was a religious philosopher, not a theologian. In his estimation, most modern philosophy since Kant has been anti-religious—particularly that of Marx and Nietzsche. They denied the authentic personality of man—Berdyaev's cardinal tenet. Consequently, he repudiated them.

For a long time he also struggled with Kantian epistemology, which had dug an impassable gulf between the phenomenal and the noumenal worlds. But in the end he returned to his first love, Kant, and placed him, along with Plato, on the highest pinnacle of philosophical fame. For Kant as a dualist affirmed the existence of the noumenal, as well as the phenomenal, world, thus placing the spiritual world upon a sure and certain foundation. And although Kant himself did not successfully blaze a path to the apprehension of the spiritual world, he prepared the way for others to do so. Berdyaev writes of him: "Among the philosophers Kant possesses the greatest significance. The philosophy of Kant is philosophy of freedom." [34]

Berdyaev is one of those who, following in the footsteps of Kant, blazed a path to the spiritual realm by his Christian personalism, or existentialism. He defines the latter as ". . . the knowledge of the human existence and the knowledge of the world through the human existence." [35] He classified himself as belonging to that type of philosophy which is nowadays called "existential" (not that of Heidegger and Jaspers, but of Augustine, Pascal, Kierkegaard and Nietzsche).[36] "The principal characteristic of my philosophical type consists above all in *having placed at the basis of philosophy not being, but freedom.* Not one other philosopher has done that, it seems, in such a radical form." [37] For him, then, personality, the existent subject, is primary, while being, the ontological object, is secondary. Being denotes matter, existence stands for the spiritual entities. Accordingly, "existence is not essence, is not substance; it is a free act." [38] He therefore inverts the Cartesian dictum, "I think, therefore I am," and asserts instead, "I am, therefore I think." Thought cannot exist by itself, in isolation, any more than the grin of the Cheshire cat can persist "on the vacant air," after the cat has disappeared. Thought necessarily presupposes a thinker. Reality does not exist before the perceiving subject but after it. Only the existential subject is real and free; the object is contingent and determined. Consequently, the identification of the "objective" with the "real" as made in "scientific" thinking, is an error. Scientific knowledge deals exclusively with objects, things; as such it is eminently justified within its own proper limits, and even is immensely beneficial and useful. But there are no meanings in objects; therefore, science cannot find or yield any meanings, whether positive or negative. Nor is there meaning in any mechanical contrivance, no matter how ingenious, save the function which its designer built into it. Meanings are created solely by persons, by subjects capable of a purposeful action; hence, meanings are subjective, not objective. Accordingly, apart from the reality of the spirit or of persons, there exist no meanings.

As a deduction from this radical form of his existentialist philosophy, which affirms the subject as the only real existent, Berdyaev chose the concept of objectification for his special emphasis.

> I do not believe in the solidity and durability of the so-called 'objective' world, [he writes], the world of nature and history. Objective reality does not exist, it is only an illusion of apprehension; only the objectification of reality exists which is born of a certain direction of the spirit.[39]
> In the last years I have formulated that problem [subject-object relationship] as an estrangement, by the process of objectification, of the solely real subjective world. The objective world is the product of objectification, it is a fallen, shattered, and fettered world. . . . Reality for me is not at all identical with being and even less with objectivity. The subjective and personalist world is the only genuinely real one.[40]

Stated as simply as possible, objectification means converting a subject—a spiritual entity, into an object—a thing or a commodity. The commonest and the most reprehensible of such cases is that of treating a man as a thing—an inveterate and almost instinctive practice in family,

---

[38] Nicolas Berdyaev, *Truth and Revelation* (London: Geoffrey Bles, Ltd., 1953), p. 12.

[39] *Samopoznanie*, p. 311.

[40] *Ibid.*, pp. 105-106.

social, industrial, and national relations. When one spouse regards the other as a convenience, the value of which consists primarily in the use he or she may be made of; when in society human beings are looked upon primarily as laborers or professionals or judged by the size of their bank account; when industry looks upon employees as mere "hands," a commodity to be hired for the sake of profitable production of goods; when a political ruling system uses men as means to power, as cannon fodder for the purpose of imperialistic expansion; "in short, wherever man is used as a means rather than an end, objectification takes place." [41]

Accordingly, all present-day civilization, since it represents man's creation, is thus "objectified," for in it men deal with one another not in the personal "I-Thou," but the impersonal "I-It" relationship (to use Martin Buber's phrase).

> The spirit in culture, religion, morals, science, art, and law is the objective spirit. . . . The objectified culture . . . is as indifferent and harsh toward human personality, as lacking in perception of the inward existence, as is history and all the rest of the objectified world. . . . Thus making an idol of culture is as inadmissible as is its barbaric rejection. It is necessary to accept and endure the tragic conflict. . . . It is necessary to accept history, to accept culture, to accept that fearsome, tortuous, fallen world. But the last word does not belong to this objectification. That word is spoken by another order of existence. The objective world will be extinguished in eternity—eternity enriched by the experienced tragedy.[42]

The results of objectification are destructive of human personality, dehumanizing. Any genuinely personal communion on that basis is impossible. Consequently, social relations assume a lower, impersonal level, because community is not possible without communion.

This leads to Berdyaev's concept of human personality, which he regards as of the greatest value. He asserts that he accepted Christianity because he found in it a much more firm ground for his faith in man's supreme destiny than anywhere else. Man partakes of both the body-mind organism and of the spirit. Thus he is a microcosm, the meeting point of two disparate elements, but comprising a unitary being. Since our natural and social scientists and psychologists by and large ignore or deny the spiritual nature of man, this failure of theirs constitutes the

[41] Spinka, *Nicolas Berdyaev*, p. 107.
[42] Nikolai Berdyaev, *Ya i mir obyektov* (Paris: YMCA Press, n.d., pp. 185-86. My translation. By permission. Cf. its English translation, *Solitude and Society*, which is a paraphrase.

greatest danger to our culture, which thus becomes depersonalized. But Berdyaev vehemently protests against it by insisting that man is both a body-soul organism and spirit, both an object and a subject. In so far as he is the body-soul entity, he is an object in bondage to the laws governing all matter. Within this physical realm he is determined and therefore unfree. He may, and often does, live predominantly in this realm—in the Pauline phrase, he is of the flesh. Berdyaev's term for such a man is that he is an individual, but not a person. Only as man develops his spiritual nature and makes it the dominant element in his life does he become a person. He writes:

> Personality is not the same thing as the individual. An individual belongs to the natural, biological category. Not only the animal and the plant, but also the diamond, the glass, the pencil are of this category. Personality, however, belongs to the spiritual, not the natural, category. . . . It is a break-through of the spirit into nature. Personality is not attained without an effort of the spirit over the psychical and physical nature of man. A man may have a brilliant individuality without being a person.[43]

This for Berdyaev is no mere theoretical datum. For him as an existentialist it is of immense personal concern. It is not a matter of indifference whether or not a man is a person. It is his duty; if he is a slave to anything, whether external or inward, he has failed in the supreme task of life.

But how does an individual attain the status of a person? Or in Christian terms, how is man saved from his "fallen" condition, in which he is alienated from God by his own self-assertion—the original sin (an act which Berdyaev places in the pre-existent realm)? By God's grace, man can be saved; for despite his "fall," he still possesses free will. His destiny is bound up with the freedom of choice which is within his power. For God has provided in Jesus Christ a way of redemption. The unique doctrine of Incarnation reveals the divine plan of salvation of all mankind, if mankind chooses to accept it. For Christ is not only the supreme revelation of what God is, but also of what man may and ought to be. God the Word became man, the Godman. Thus "God was in Christ, reconciling the world unto Himself." Man, too, may experience a basic transformation of his "fallen" nature into that of the son of God. Berdyaev speaks of this spiritual transformation as theanthropy, the attainment of the divine-human personality, which in his estimation is the only proper concept of personality. In this he follows the ancient Eastern Christian tradition (formulated principally

[43] *Ibid.*, p. 146.

by Irenaeus that "the Logos of God, our Lord Jesus Christ, who, on account of his great love became what we are that he might make us what he is himself" [44]), but uses the more modest and more accurate term, the "divine-human." The result of redemption is the freedom of the sons of God: "Man ought to be free, he dares not be a slave, for he ought to be man. Such is the will of God." [45]

Since man is a free spirit, capable of apprehending God's revelation of Himself, Berdyaev asserts the necessity of such a revelation. It takes many forms, but it is always a spiritual experience. The Father reveals Himself in nature, but were we to depend on this revelation alone, our knowledge of God would certainly be inadequate and even erroneous. One may see this result in the recent "naturalistic theology." It is only in the Son that the deepest spiritual levels of divine revelation are reached. But in the end, only when the human spirit meets the Divine Spirit in an existential encounter is there an immediate, intuitive apprehension of God. This is the work of the Holy Spirit. For Berdyaev, such an experience is the only adequate "proof" of the existence of God; hence, along with Kant, he rejects the traditional ontological "proofs" such as those of Thomas Aquinas. "God is not Being and the categories of being are not applicable to Him, but belong ever to thought. He exists—is the Existent—and one can think of Him only existentially and symbolically." [46] God is never an object, but a subject.

> Our knowledge of God is, therefore, basically intuitive, subjective, experiential, or, if you will not blanch at the word, mystical. It is neither exclusively intellectual, emotional, volitional, nor intuitional, but rather integral, combining all these four together with the indefinable additional element which results from this integral approach.[47]

But just because man is a free ethical agent he is capable not only of responding voluntarily to God's love, but also of repudiating it, rebelling against it and falling away from God. This results in his misery and suffering. God does not inflict it; man causes it to himself. Striving to affirm himself, to become man-god, he destroys himself, often involving others in his ruin. Hence, society is involved in destruction brought upon itself by its own choices. Modern secularism denies the spiritual

[44] Irenaeus, *Adversus haereses*, Book V, preface.

[45] Nicolas Berdyaev, *Slavery and Freedom* (London: Geoffrey Bles, Ltd., New York: Charles Scribner's Sons, 1944), p. 48. By permission.

[46] *Samopoznanie*, p. 79.

[47] My article on Berdyaev, in Carl Michalson, ed., *Christianity and the Existentialists* (New York: Charles Scribner's Sons, 1956), p. 63. By permission.

nature of man and thus depersonalizes him. Berdyaev sees in this our supreme danger; he describes the results of the process as follows:

> The living sources of creation, both human and superhuman, dry up; the aim and object of creation, which are also superhuman, disappear; and the result is man's complete disintegration. For, when man follows the path of self-affirmation, ceases to respect the higher principle and asserts his self-sufficiency, he exterminates and denies his true self according to the laws of an inexorable dialectic. . . . he becomes the slave of the baser processes, disintegrating with the elements of his own nature and becoming the victim of the artificial nature of the machine he has conjured up into life, and these de-personalize, weaken, and finally annihilate him.[48]

The Christian ethic of redemption is contrary to the worldly standards of value. For it, man as a spiritual being, and not a high standard of living and of economic well being, is of the highest value. "Man shall not live by bread alone," even though it is of concern to Christians that mankind lack not bread. The aim of the Christian ethic is the renewal of the spiritual mainsprings of human personality—the spiritual transformation of men and women. A civilization is Christian only to the degree to which it subserves this aim. For there can be no good society without good men and women. All improvements—technological, political, economic, or cultural—if they exclude this kind of basic transformation, are superficial and wholly inadequate.

This, then, is the primary and paramount task of the Christian Church—the transformation of human motivation by subjecting it to the will of God. It cannot be effected forcibly, for the life of the spirit is the life of freedom. God compels no one, forces no one; but to reject Him is to choose evil and its consequent suffering. To charge Christianity with failure to impose salvation upon society after the pattern of the "Grand Inquisitor," or of communism, is to misunderstand the Christian redemptive ethic completely. The "failure of Christianity" is chargeable only to the failure of Christians.

Because the method of Christianity is solely that of persuasion by word and life, the demand for an imminent transformation of the world is a symptom of misunderstanding of its character. Such a demand rests either on a mistaken notion of the apocalyptic hope or, more commonly, on the identification of Christianity with the secularist "progress." Thus the radical doctrine of Berdyaev that man "has a right to hell, as it were," has a direct bearing on his view of history. Berdyaev is not a historian in the accepted professional sense of the word; rather he is

---

[48] Berdyaev, *Meaning of History*, pp. 154-55.

a philosopher of history, concerned with discerning its meaning. In the first place, then, he affirms that history can have no meaning except on a religious basis; to him, history is a process wherein the human drama of redemption from sin is played, is a return of the fallen man to God. He thus recurs to Origen's conception of history even to the extent of affirming the pre-existent phase in which both Origen and Berdyaev have placed the "fall" of man. The central point of history, conceived as a redemptive process of the fallen man, is the coming of Christ. Historically, it had been the principal task of the Christian Church to witness to the fact of the Incarnation of the Word and the consequent possibility of the theandric transformation of man. But unfortunately, the Church had on the whole been unfaithful to its task and had compromised with the world; the Western Church became a papal caesarism while the Byzantine Church became caesaro-papism. In the modern era it has not sufficiently withstood the corroding influence of secularism.

Furthermore, history has meaning because it tends toward a God-appointed goal. Berdyaev thus not only rejects Nietzsche's notion of the "eternal recurrence," but even more vehemently repudiates the secularist concept of automatic and inevitable "progress." No such mechanical concept can have authentic meaning, because it lacks true teleology—an end toward which it aims. Such "progress" is not going anywhere; therefore, it is essentially meaningless. Men cannot determine the cosmic goal, since they themselves are the product of, and determined by, the cosmic forces. For all mechanical forces as conceived by the natural sciences are determined by natural laws and therefore purposeless. Only God can purpose an end and thus impart meaning to history; for this end will be the triumph of meaning. Thus the meaningfulness of history is possible only to those who believe in God and His purpose for the world.

This eschatological faith cannot be realized within human history, within time: it extends beyond time into eternity. However, a believer in God need not await it passively, as if it were an event wholly outside and beyond the possibility of his cooperation in bringing it about. In fact, he has a duty to cooperate with God in bringing it about; for although it is an event primarily determined and wrought by God, man may contribute to its accomplishment. Since "The end of history is the end of that exteriorization and objectification, a return to inwardness," [49] man has a part to play in it. For he can surely do his share; in

[49] *Samopoznanie*, p. 323.

fact, without such an effort on his part, "the Kingdom would be delayed."

And the ultimate goal is the Kingdom of God, when He will be all in all, and when all evil will be vanquished. "The final victory of God over the forces of Hades cannot be accomplished by the division into two kingdoms—divine and diabolic, the saved and those damned to eternal suffering—it can be attained only as one kingdom." [50] But how that can be done without violating man's freedom Berdyaev does not say.

[50] *Ibid.*, p. 329.

# 10

# Conclusion

We have now concluded our brief and highly selective
survey of the impact of the humanist-secularist era on
Christian thought, and I hope that we found satisfactory
and convincing evidence that the era has indeed come to
an end. If someone is still unconvinced, let him remember
that when the Roman Empire fell there were many who
were ready to swear that they did not hear it fall. In the
secularist phase, our era has turned upon itself, upon
its humanist origins and has repudiated man as the center
and criterion of its culture. But I wish to stress emphat-
ically that despite this ultimate failure to attain its objectives, the era has produced some highly valuable and
beneficial results, enlarging human freedoms. Nevertheless, like Chronos of old devouring his own children,
humanism has been destroyed by depersonalizing, dehumanizing secularism. Thus the era has gone the way of
all flesh as have all the previous cultural stages of humankind. Since the middle of last century it has been visibly
disintegrating and dying. I do not, however, wish to be
understood as asserting that all traces of humanism have
disappeared without a remnant, and that all concern about
man is altogether wanting. No culture ever passes without
leaving survivals of itself. I mean to affirm only that
humanism has ceased to be the dominant motive power of
our time.

Thus we are standing on the threshold of a new age, often referred to as the "atomic" or the "space" age. By this designation the present era is characterized as predominantly mechanistic and technological in nature. This further accentuates the passing of the former age. But since all great civilizations are born and live by some procreative idea, we may ask: Is it really a new era, possessing the necessary creative élan or dynamic centralizing idea capable of winning the enthusiastic and spontaneous cooperation of humanity? For without a new spiritual center capable of unifying the new culture, our present shattered and mutually antagonistic "ideologies" cannot create a new culture, but can at best merely continue our present hostilities and divisions. No such dynamic spiritual unity exists today. Technological attainments, no matter how great in themselves, do not and cannot transform people spiritually, do not provide the spiritual center about which the new society can arise. They are merely improved means to unimproved ends. In fact, they may be used for destructive, rather than constructive ends. It all depends on what the human beings controlling them decide to do with them. And the decision is dictated by character, not by technology.

Would it not, therefore, seem more accurate and reasonable to suppose that while as a matter of fact the old era is indeed dead, the new era has not yet been born? Are we not actually entering upon an intermediate, transitional period, a stage of cultural gestation during which the new age is taking shape in the womb of time? Is it not perhaps more realistic to regard our period as the new "dark ages" analogous to a similar era after the downfall of the Roman and the rise of the medieval civilizations? Those "Dark Ages"—although they were by no means as dark as has been thought—lasted some four centuries. But during that time the surviving elements of the Graeco-Roman culture, combined with the influence of the Christian Church, were creatively amalgamating with and assimilated by the primitive cultures of our own barbarian ancestors. They were thus molding the new culture, which eventually assumed the feudal and scholastic forms. Is it not possible that we live in a similar transitional period? It may perhaps not last as long as the "Dark Ages," for in our day all developments are incomparably swifter. Furthermore, it may in the end actually comprise the whole world instead of being confined, as before, to Western Europe alone. In fact, there exists a fair possibility that the Oriental cultural influences may very materially affect the European-American cultural matrix. At any rate, for reasons I shall later state more fully, I am inclined to accept the view that ours is a transitional, rather than a new, fully developed age.

Nevertheless, such considerations as I have just presented do not seem to be much in evidence generally. For the greatest part, the assertion that ours is a new age is usually made without any reservation. Some thinkers even now profess to discern clear outlines of the new age. The most vociferous and positive of such affirmations come from the scientists and the communists. As for the former, they invariably have in mind technological progress, which has indeed been astonishing, and promises as the time goes on to be even more so. Limited to this kind of "progress," the boast of the scientists is amply justified. The only objection to it is that as a transforming spiritual force—if indeed any such function is claimed for it—it is inadequate. But only the communists and such Western scientists as Sir Julian Huxley regard it as having such a function. Science properly understood and limited to its own field does not include any such objective among its goals. Consequently, it cannot create that dynamic spiritual force necessary for the basis of a new culture.

As for the communists, they actually claim not only that we stand on the peak of the watershed dividing two cultural ages, but that they are the pioneers of that new age. They fervently believe that their "ideology" will furnish the necessary incentive for that new age, and lead to the goal predicted by Marx—the classless society. We have already considered those claims in the section on Marx. It will suffice to point out that Marx formulated his views more than a hundred years ago, basing them on conditions then existing. These views, therefore, necessarily reflect the decadent features of the culture of the middle of the nineteenth century, and have themselves contributed to the secularizing of the then surviving humanist elements. As such, Marxism is essentially a product of the last materialistic-secularist phase of the humanist era, and not the first phase of the new. I do not mean to assert that its present form, Soviet communism, will not exert a powerful influence on that age, or that it is not now doing so. But this influence is effective principally in regions which are just emerging from primitive or pre-capitalistic conditions. For no one can deny the astonishingly rapid industrialization of the Soviet Union and China under the practically complete and forcible centralization of all power—political, economic, and cultural—in the hands of the communist regimes. The furious tempo of this colossal transforming process, imposed with ruthless disregard of liberties and even of human lives, is to be seen in China. It proves that there is a short cut to a large scale industrialization of backward countries, provided the subject peoples have not been accustomed to political freedoms and hence submit to it, since they do not feel the loss of something they have not had. It does not work in countries where the people had lived under a less restrictive regime, as those of the pre-war regimes in East Germany, Hungary and Poland. The one puzzling exception to this statement is Czechoslovakia, which under Masaryk and Beneš had been recognized as a model democracy!

Accordingly, the threat of communist conquest of large portions of Asia and perhaps even Africa is great. The peoples of the world have awakened to the realization that a low standard of living is not inevitable, and are determined to improve their lot by whatever means seem to them most effective. Moreover, they do not always control the choice. They want bread first—liberties can wait. They do not miss them. Nor should we be blind to the "corrosive acids of modernity" and their effects on Western democracies. As we have seen in the entire present study, the lack of spiritual imperative, painfully absent in these lands, has resulted to an alarming degree in moral, intellectual, and even physical flabbiness.

But an even deeper reason for regarding communism as incapable of providing the dynamic for the new culture exists exactly in the central place which materialism occupies in its ideology. Communism still fanatically identifies itself with this concept. Consequently, it denies the spiritual nature of man altogether, and therefore cannot supply the very spiritual élan needed for the future reconstruction of society. Moreover, the communist regimes have everywhere imposed themselves by force on their subjugated peoples, a feature which in itself would suffice for rejecting it in the formation of the future society. The new spiritual creative idea must be freely accepted by people, who do so because they are inspired by it, not because it is imposed on them. For these and many other reasons it is evident that Soviet communism is not capable of creating the new society.

What then is required before the conditions necessary for the new cultural era are fulfilled? I do not pretend to be able to furnish a detailed blueprint of it. As a historian, I prefer to deal with the concrete past, rather than attempt to predict the nebulous future. But surely it is possible to learn from the past certain lessons for the future! Moreover, as a believing Christian I am convinced of certain necessary spiritual foundations of any culture worthy of the name. I am aware that these are matters of faith, and I hope for their realization without asserting them as matters of knowledge. There are two such necessary prerequisites: first of all, that man as a *spiritual* being be regarded as the highest value and consequently accorded the central place in that civilization; and secondly, that in order to realize the highest development of the spiritual nature of man, faith in God be recognized as the indispensable means toward that end. Turning now to the first of these conditions, let us make plain that the suggested aim does *not* contemplate the restoration of humanism in the form it has manifested during the era just past. For since the old concept of humanism has proved disastrously disappointing and ineffective, there is no use restoring it. Moreover, there is no returning to the past, even if we wanted to do so. But we have no reason to want it. There is just one possibility—that of going forward.

The reason for the relative failure of earlier humanism was chiefly the wrong understanding put upon it: man was to be the measure of all things. But he has proved disappointingly small and inadequate for such a role. He was regarded as predominantly autonomous, and his selfishness, raised to the position of a criterion, was given a free rein until it resulted in uncontrolled license, such as is illustrated in Ivan Karamazov's dictum, "All things are permitted." This licentious autonomy of man in the end corrupted whatever was true in the humanist ideal. It was forgotten that the *highest value* in man is his *spiritual* nature, which attains its full development only in a voluntary surrender to the will of God. The old ideal of humanism is well depicted in Rabelais' Abbey of Theleme, over the gate of which was displayed the motto: "Do as you please!" In contrast to it, one is reminded of Augustine's summary of the Christian ideal of humanism: "Love God and do as you please!" Thus the transformed man alone attains the true human personality and as such is the highest value. It is this "new" humanism which must be placed at the very center of the striving of the new age, if we are to avoid the failures of the old. Essentially, it is the Christian ideal of man.

Furthermore, it is clearly evident that the exceedingly rapid technological progress of the last half-century has not been matched by a corresponding human advancement capable of coping with it. Technics have immensely outdistanced man's own ethical and spiritual growth. If Tennyson could write more than a century ago that "knowledge comes but wisdom lingers," what would he say now when knowledge comes immeasurably faster and man has spiritually regressed rather than progressed! Nevertheless, we cannot renounce technical progress and go back to the pre-atomic era. For better or worse, we can go only forward. Therefore, the supreme need today is for ethical and spiritual maturity on the part of man—the wisdom of which Tennyson wrote— to enable us to cope with the inevitable technical progress and to use it for the benefit and not the destruction of mankind. For technics as such are neutral: it depends on man how they shall be used. To place this potentially frightful instrument in the hands of ethically immature man is like placing a knife or a loaded pistol in the hands of a baby. Only spiritually transformed humanity may be trusted not to use it for self-destruction.

And for that transforming process we need more and better religion. We especially need a religion that is more vital and dynamic, more effective in producing the mature personalities needed for the living of these days. Priestley, whose convictions on this subject I quoted at the beginning of this book, concludes that religion alone can save us from the depersonalizing effects of modern secularism, and it is doubtful whether our society can endure much longer without it. For it will either destroy itself or cease to consist of persons. But the very fact that religion is either ignored, as is the case in Western civilization, or denied, as is done by communism, proves conclusively that the conditions necessary for the creation of the spiritual maturing of humankind are not clearly envisioned, or operative. But it surely is axiomatic that without good men and women there can be no good society. And until we realize that moral transformation depends upon the divine grace working on the free human spirit, no such goal can be attained.

If any further argument is needed, let us remind ourselves of Berdyaev's cogent demonstration that no true progress is possible on the purely mechanistic assumptions of the scientific point of view. For unless the evolutionary process has a goal toward which it can tend, one cannot talk of progress. For natural forces are blind and lacking in purpose, and man is unable to set up a cosmic goal, since he himself is the creature of the cosmic forces. No impersonal force, no natural law, no mechanical process, can act purposefully. Only God can set a goal for human history and for the cosmic process. Accordingly, the belief in progress—that is, in a goal and a meaning for human life as well as for the cosmos—is possible and reasonable only for those who believe in God. If God does not exist, then there is no meaning in the cosmos, and hence in human life. Only God is great enough and powerful enough to set a goal for human history and for the cosmic evolution, and to direct its progress toward that goal. And the highest good of society may be attained only if men cooperate in this divine plan. Unless and until we make this understanding basic to our common life, we cannot progress toward the creation of that new and better era envisaged for the future. Because at present that understanding is not widely enough held, I regard the present situation as transitional.

But can we realistically expect that these two conditions—the placing of spiritually transformed humanity and cooperating with the divine goal—shall be realized in the next era, since they have never been realized before? Are we not actually describing the coming of the Kingdom of God, when God's will shall be done on earth as it is in heaven? Would not that be the *eschaton*, the end of history, and are we really thinking of the next age as the last? That would indeed be comparable to the expectation of the paradise of the "classless society" fondly imagined by the communists still naive enough to entertain it seriously. I fear that to expect perfection in the new age would indeed be unrealistic, to say the least. The likelihood is that we must settle for much less. But that does not in the least make me doubt that the new age shall be better than the one just past only to the degree to which these conditions shall become normative. The higher we aim, the closer we shall come to attaining the goal.

# Selected Bibliography

## 1

Berdyaev, Nicolas, *The Meaning of History* (New York: Charles Scribner's Sons, 1936).

Bouyer, Louis, *Erasmus and his Times* (Westminster Md.: Newman Press, 1959).

Brunner, H. Emil, *Man in Revolt, a Christian Anthropology* (Philadelphia: The Westminster Press, 1947).

————, *Christianity and Civilization* (New York: Charles Scribner's Sons, 1948-49) 2 vols.

Buber, Martin, *Eclipse of God* (New York: Harper & Brothers, 1952).

Etienne, Jacques, *Spiritualism érasmien et théologiens louvanistes* (Louvain: Publications universitaires de Louvain, 1956).

Frame, Donald M., tr., *The Complete Works of Montaigne* (Stanford: Stanford University Press, 1958).

————, *Montaigne's Discovery of Man; the Humanization of a Humanist* (New York: Columbia University Press, 1955).

Hyma, A., *The Youth of Erasmus* (Ann Arbor: University of Michigan Press, 1930).

Nichols, J. H., *History of Christianity, 1650-1950: Secularization of the West* (New York: The Ronald Press, 1956).

Niebuhr, Reinhold, *Reflections on the End of an Era* (New York: Charles Scribner's Sons, 1934).

Phillips, Margaret M., *Erasmus and the Northern Renaissance* (London: Hodder & Stoughton for The English University Press, 1949).

Spinka, Matthew, ed., *Advocates of Reform* (in *Library of Christian Classics*, XIV, Philadelphia: The Westminster Press, 1953); esp. "Desiderius Erasmus."

2

Balz, Albert G. A., *Descartes and the Modern Mind* (New Haven: Yale University Press, 1952).

Feuer, L. S., *Spinoza and the Rise of Liberalism* (Boston: Beacon Press, 1952).

Haldane, E. S. and R. T. Ross, trs. *The Philosophical Works of Descartes* (New York: Cambridge University Press, 1931), 2 vols.

Keeling, S. V., *Descartes* (London: Oxford University Press, 1934).

Maritain, Jacques, *Three Reformers: Luther, Descartes, Rousseau* (New York: Charles Scribner's Sons, 1950).

Smith, Norman Kemp, *New Studies in the Philosophy of Descartes* (London: Macmillan and Co., Ltd., 1952).

Spinoza, Benedict de, *Chief Works*, R. H. M. Elwes, tr. (New York: Dover Publications, 1955).

Wolfson, Harry A., *The Philosophy of Spinoza* (Cambridge, Mass.: Harvard University Press, 1934, 2 vols.)

3

Aaron, R. I., *John Locke* (New York: Oxford University Press, Inc., 1937).

Burtt, Edwin A., ed., *The English Philosophers from Bacon to Mills* (New York: Random House, 1939).

Cranston, Maurice W., *John Locke, a Biography* (New York: The Macmillan Co., 1957).

Greig, J. Y. T., *David Hume* (New York: Oxford University Press, Inc., 1931).

Hume, David, *Dialogues concerning Natural Religion*, Norman Kemp Smith, ed. (Edinburgh: Thomas Nelson and Sons, Ltd., 1947).

Locke, John, *An Essay concerning Human Understanding* (Oxford: The Clarendon Press, 1894).

Locke, John, *The Reasonableness of Christianity*, I. T. Ramsey, ed. (Stanford: Stanford University Press, 1958).

Morris, Charles R., *Locke, Berkeley, Hume* (Oxford: The Clarendon Press, 1931).

Mossner, Ernest C., *The Life of David Hume* (Austin: University of Texas Press, 1954).

MacNabb, D. G. C., *David Hume: his Theory of Knowledge and Morality* (London and New York: Hutchinson's University Library, 1951).

4

Bishop, Morris, *Pascal, the Life of Genius* (New York: Reynal & Hitchcock, 1936).

Cailliet, Emile, *Pascal, Genius in the Light of Scripture* (Philadelphia: The Westminster Press, 1945).

Cannon, William R., *The Theology of John Wesley* (New York-Nashville: The Abingdon Press, 1956).

Fletcher, F. T. H., *Pascal and the Mystical Tradition* (New York: Philosophical Library, 1954).

Lee, Umphrey, *John Wesley and Modern Religion* (Nashville: Cokesbury Press, 1936).

Lindström, H. G. A., *Wesley and Sanctification: a Study in the Doctrine of Salvation* (London: Epworth Press, 1946).

McConnell, *John Wesley* (New York-Nashville, Abingdon-Cokesbury Press, 1939).

Mossner, Ernest C., *Bishop Butler and the Age of Reason* (New York: The Macmillan Co., 1936).

Pascal, Blaise, *Pensées and Provincial Letters* (New York: The Modern Library, 1941).

Piette, Maximin, *John Wesley in the Evolution of Protestantism* (New York: Sheed & Ward, Inc., 1937).

Spinka, Matthew, *John Amos Comenius* (Chicago: University of Chicago Press, 1943).

Stewart, H. F., *The Secret of Pascal* (New York: Cambridge University Press, 1941).

5

*The Confessions of Jean Jacques Rousseau* (New York: Random House, 1945).

Schleiermacher, F. D. E., *The Christian Faith*, H. R. Mackintosh and J. S. Stewart, trs. (Edinburgh: T. & T. Clark, 1928).

———, *On Religion: Speeches to its Cultured Despisers*, John Oman, tr. (New York: Harper & Brothers, 1958).

Selbie, W. B., *Schleiermacher, a Critical and Historical Study* (New York: E. P. Dutton & Co., 1913).

Wendland, Johannes, *Die religiöse Entwicklung Schleiermachers* (Tübingen: J. C. B. Mohr, 1915).

6

Adickes, Erich, *Kants opus postumum* (Berlin: Reuther & Reichard, 1920).

Findlay, John N., *Hegel, a Re-examination* (London: Allen & Unwin, 1958).

Frank, S. L., *A Solovyov Anthology* (New York: Charles Scribner's Sons, 1950).

Hegel, G. W. F., *Early Theological Writings*, T. M. Knox and Richard Kroner, trs. (Chicago: The University of Chicago Press, 1948).

———, *Lectures on the Philosophy of History*, J. Sibree, tr. (London: George Bell and Sons, 1905).

Jones, William T., *Morality and Freedom in the Philosophy of Immanuel Kant* (London: Oxford University Press, 1940).

Kant, *Critique of Pure Reason*, Norman Kempt Smith, tr. (London: Macmillan & Co., Ltd., 1929).

———, *Religion within the Limits of Reason Alone*, Theodore M. Greene, tr. (La Salle, Ill.: The Open Court Publishing Company, 1934).

Löwith, Karl, *Von Hegel bis Nietzsche* (Zürich, 1941).

Mackintosh, Hugh Ross, *Types of Modern Theology, Schleiermacher to Barth* (New York: Charles Scribner's Sons, 1937).

Paton, Herbert J., *The Categorical Imperative; a Study in Kant's Moral Philosophy* (Chicago: The University of Chicago Press, 1948).

Solovev, Vladimir, *Lectures on Godmanhood*, Peter P. Zouboff, tr. (New York: International Universities Press, Inc., 1944).


7


Dru, Alexander, tr., and ed., *The Journal of Søren Kierkegaard* (London: Oxford University Press, 1938).

Kierkegaard, S., *Either/Or*, (Princeton: Princeton University Press, 1944, 2 vols.)

———, *Concluding Unscientific Postscript* (Princeton: Princeton University Press, 1944).

Ritschl, Albrecht, *The Christian Doctrine of Justification and Reconciliation*, H. R. Mackintosh and A. B. Macaulay, trs. (Edinburgh: T. & T. Clark, 1902).

Swenson, David F., *Something about Kierkegaard* (Minneapolis: Augsburg Publishing House, 1945).

Swing, A. T., *The Theology of Albrecht Ritschl* (New York: Longmans, Green & Co., 1911).

Thomte, Reidar, *Kierkegaard's Philosophy of Religion* (Princeton: Princeton University Press, 1948).


8


Brinton, Clarence Crane, *Nietzsche* (Cambridge, Mass.: Harvard University Press, 1941).

Carr, E. H., *Karl Marx* (London: J. M. Dent and Sons, Ltd., 1938).

Comte, Auguste, *A General View of Positivism*, J. H. Bridges, tr. (Stanford: Academic Reprints, n.d.).

Feuerbach, Ludwig, *The Essence of Christianity*, George Eliot, tr. (New York: Harper & Brothers, 1957).

Hubben, William, *Four Prophets of Destiny: Kierkegaard, Dostoevsky, Nietzsche, Kafka* (New York: The Macmillan Co., 1952).

Jaspers, Karl, *Existentialism and Humanism: three Essays*, E. B. Ashton, tr. (New York: R. F. Moore Co., 1952).

Kaufmann, Walter A., *Nietzsche: Philosopher, Psychologist, Antichrist* (Princeton: Princeton University Press, 1950).

Lubac, Henri de, S.J., *The Drama of Atheist Humanism* (New York: Sheed & Ward, Inc., 1950).

Marx, Karl, and Friedrich Engels, *The Communist Manifesto* (The International Publishers Co., Inc., 1948).

Morgan, G. A., *What Nietzsche Means* (Cambridge, Mass.: Harvard University Press, 1941).

*The Philosophy of Nietzsche* (comprising Thus Spake Zarathustra; Beyond Good and Evil; The Genealogy of Morals; Peoples and Countries; Ecce Homo; The Birth of Tragedy. (New York: The Modern Library, 1937.)

9

Berdyaev, Nicolas, *Dostoevsky*, Donald Attwater, tr. (New York; Meridian Books, 1957).

Gorodetzky, N., *The Humiliated Christ in Modern Russian Thought* (London: SPCK, 1938).

Guardini, Romano, *L'univers religieux de Dostoievsky* (Paris: Editions du Seuil, 1947).

Lowrie, Donald A., *Rebellious Prophet, A Life of Nicolai Berdyaev* (New York, Harper & Brothers, 1960).

Spinka, Matthew, *Nicolas Berdyaev, Captive of Freedom* (Philadelphia: The Westminster Press, 1950).

Zander, L. A., *Dostoevsky* (London: SCM Press, 1948).

Zernov, Nicolas, *Three Russian Prophets, Khomiakov, Dostoevsky, Soloviev* (London: SCM Press, 1944).

# Index

Feuerbach, Ludwig A. (*Cont.*)
basic contradiction in humanism of, 165
career of, 163
education of, 163
influences on, 163
principal works of, 163
the influence of, 167
view on:
baptism of, 166-167
God of, 164-165
man of, 163

# G

God:
as noblest work of man, 164
as supreme reality, 38
as trinitarian, 131
in the new cultural era, 229-231
prominent place in Cartesian system of, 29
the essential nature of, 131
view of:
Berdyaev on, 220-222
Berkeley on, 55-56
Comte on, 182-183
Descartes on, 28-30
Dostoevsky on, 201-204
Feuerbach on, 164-165
Hegel on, 129-131
Hume on, 62-64
Kant on, 117-118
Kierkegaard on, 153-154
Locke on, 45
Nietzsche on, 187-188
Pascal on, 70-72
Ritschl on, 158-159
Schleiermacher on, 102, 105-106
Solovev on, 140-141
Spinoza on, 36

# H

Hartlib, Samuel, 74
Hegel, Georg W. Friedrich:
aims of, 129
as influenced by Romantic movement, 128
as monist, 127
denial of pantheism by, 130
earliest education of, 128
greatest discovery of, 128
influence on subsequent period of, 135
later education of, 128

Hegel, Georg W. Friedrich (*Cont.*)
reality according to, 128-129
view on:
divine Providence of, 133-134
God of, 129-131
man of, 132
reason of, 129
sin of, 133
universe of, 130
Hegelianism:
influence on Karl Marx of, 168
the revolt against, 146-161
History:
as tends toward a God-appointed goal, 223
Berdyaev's view on, 223
Hobbes, Thomas, theory of social contract of, 41-42
Holiness, as aim of Christian life, 110
Humanism:
and modern economics, 12-13
and politics, 11-12
and science, 13
as undermined by mechanistic rationalism, 33
atheistic, of Feuerbach, 163-167
beginning of, 1
change in central characteristic of, 4
Christian, the prophets of, 194-224
cultural decay of, 2-3
Erasmus as representative of, 14-16
modern philosophy and, 11
Montaigne as representative of, 16-22
the age of, 1-22
the dying of, 1-2
the Protestant Reformation and, 9-11
two early representatives of, 14-22
Humanist age, secularism as phase of, 3
Human nature, as dynamic, 41
Hume, David:
analysis of philosophical doctrines of, 61-62
and Lockean empiricism, 56-65
education of, 56
mental perceptions and, 57-58
skeptical conclusions of, 60-61
system of, as applied to modern art, 60
view on:
God of, 58
human reason of, 59-60
ideas of, 58-59
miracles of, 62
proof of existence of God, 63-64
religion of, 61-62
Huxley, Sir Julian, 227